D1617179

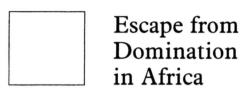

Escape from Domination in Africa

Political Disengagement & its Consequences

Escape from Domination in Africa

Political Disengagement
& its Consequences

Bruce Baker
Research Fellow, Coventry University

JAMES CURREY
OXFORD

AFRICA WORLD PRESS
TRENTON, NJ

James Currey Ltd
73 Botley Road
Oxford
OX2 0BS

Africa World Press, Inc
PO Box 1892
Trenton
NJ 08607, USA

First published 2000

1 2 3 4 5 04 03 02 01 00

British Library Cataloguing in Publication Data

Baker, Bruce L.
Escape from domination in Africa : political disengagement
& its consequences
1. Political participation – Africa 2. Conformity 3. Africa –
Politics and government
I.Title
320.9'6

ISBN 0-85255-838-4 (Paper)
0-85255-837-6 (Cloth)

Chapter numbers hand drawn by Michael Harvey
Typeset in 10/11 pt Plantin
by Saxon Graphics Ltd, Derby

Printed and bound in the United States

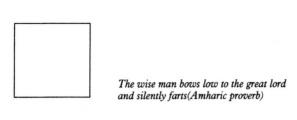

The wise man bows low to the great lord and silently farts(Amharic proverb)

Contents

List of Figures, Maps & Tables

Foreword

All political systems have in place structures that promise, or actually deliver, sanctions in order to gain the compliance of individuals or groups. Likewise, all political systems have their quota of rebels and dissidents who, rather than trying to change the structures of domination, opt to evade or withdraw from them. The phenomena associated with such political withdrawal are considerable. Writers have listed migration, anti-establishment activity, localised autonomy, counter-culture movements, economic separation, selective evasion of control, abandonment of civic culture and non-participation in formal and informal politics. Can a single unifying concept embrace this apparently disparate collection? 'Disengagement' boldly claims this ground and it is with this specific mode of response that this book is concerned. It aims to examine the nature of the escape that African people seek from oppressive domination and the general social conditions in which specific strategies of disengagement are attractive.

At its centre the study seeks to differentiate a bounded pattern of action from other similar but different patterns and to examine the internal structure and dynamics of this pattern. Put in concrete terms, the research question asks whether there is any similarity between a second-hand clothes smuggler, a secessionist fighter, a political migrant, a member of a theocratic exclusive community and one who abandons voting in parliamentary elections. Is there a similarity in what they want and what they think they need to do to get it (Stinchcombe 1978: 120)? The book sets out to establish that there *is* an analogy, and that it lies in a shared outlook on domination and shared consequences of their responses for the political system. The shared outlook is that the political authority is unacceptable, but that the resources to remove or change it are insufficient and hence disengagement is the preferred response. The shared consequences lie in the contribution to delegitimation and destabilisation of that authority through human and material resource loss. The more deeply this analogy can be established, the more convincing the concept of disengagement will be.

The methodology of this book is not so much to bring forth fresh data as to make sense of previously published material, seeking to develop new explanatory generalisations about the essential characteristics and potential consequences of a particular response to unacceptable domination: one that I regard as a distinct configuration. To establish the reality of such a configuration and to generate a useful political model necessitate a broad survey across sub-Saharan Africa over a long time period in search of concrete historical examples. An obvious problem, however, is that the clandestine nature of disengagement phenomena conceals them from accurate recording. Inevitably much of that classified as disengagement is unknown and unrecorded. And, where it is recorded, it is often by officials with less than objective standards, bearing in mind that disengagement is invariably seen by them in a negative light or that they themselves may be in collusion with it. Or the problem may be that the political nature of the phenomena encourages the public authorities, who are the object of the disengagement, to manipulate the data to their own advantage – for example, to underplay the scale of popular support for secessionists or mask the lack of support for the elections. In addition, the statistics commonly available have frequently been designed for ends other than quantifying disengagement. As a result they often conflate disengagement with other processes, such as non-engagement. Quantitative indicators of disengagement, therefore, can only be obtained by the removal of extraneous material from the data by subjective interpretation. In the body of the study, I raise issues such as the confounding of engagers with disengagers, when, for instance, election boycotters are included with disengagers in figures for the percentage of the population not voting, or when surveys of unrecorded economic activities do not distinguish between those that are legal and do not attempt to avoid the state and those that are illegal.

Inevitably, the emphasis of this book is on qualitative rather than quantitative material. Since my aim is to establish analogies, not only between events bearing a single description, such as secession, but between events as distinct as political migration and the illegal second economy, the narratives have had to be contained and selective, whilst hopefully being sufficiently varied and detailed to make a single concept convincing for apparently dissimilar events. The historical dimension is also crucial, since it demonstrates that the research question is one of explaining, not so much change over time, but persistence – the persistence of a phenomenon even throughout the social and cultural upheaval wrought by contact with the West. This raises the concept of disengagement to a level more profound than being the product of the exigencies of particular times, social conditions and types of regimes. There is nothing specifically Zimbabwean, Nigerian or Angolan about disengagement. As Marc Bloch puts it: 'The unity of place is merely disorderly. Only a unified problem constitutes a central focus' (quoted in Skocpol 1984:383).

Much of the current debate on sub-Saharan Africa has focused on improving the performance of the economy and the activity of the state (its governance and economic management). What must not be overlooked, however, is that disengagement constitutes an erosive and delegitimising force working against the best laid plans of rulers for improving their authority and support. Without understanding the scale and effect of disengagement in society, programmes for introducing democracy and for establishing good governance and economic growth are likely to be seriously flawed.

Acknowledgements

This book began during my graduate studies at the University of Coventry, especially through reading the writings of Professor Victor Azarya and Naomi Chazan on African politics. When I first considered examining the concept of disengagement for a PhD thesis, Professor Azarya was kind enough to read some initial theoretical thoughts and to encourage me to pursue the project.

I am indebted to Roy May and Angela Browne at Coventry University, who were the chief cause of my interest in African politics even before the research for this book began. As the work progressed, they, along with David Podmore, have made valuable criticisms and offered positive suggestions. To Roy I owe the regular provocation to expose my ideas to the critical peer review of conferences and journals and an irrepressible ability to encourage more pessimistic souls like myself.

I am very grateful to the African Studies Centre at Coventry for providing financial support throughout my research and a travel grant for a field trip to Zimbabwe in 1997.

Introduction

The evasion of power ... has proved to be the most
devastating answer that Africa's poor could give to the
irresponsibility of their rulers. (Lonsdale, 'Political
Accountability in African History')

Defining disengagement

Against multiple and variable power that is unacceptable, the inhabitants of sub-Saharan Africa have devised a range of strategies so as to survive, avoid or at least soften its grip. Confrontation is the material that makes the headlines in the popular and academic press, but, as history has shown, it is not always a wise and successful strategy, even when it is feasible. Alternative strategies that are within reach and low in resource demands and that entail minimal risk may not offer the ideal of total freedom from those that dominate, but for many they are an improvement on doing nothing. Just as what is not said is often overlooked, though vital, in textual analysis, so what is not done – the non-voting, the non-rebellion, the non-membership, the non-conformity, the non-payment of taxes, and the non-formal employment – is often overlooked and yet vital in political analysis. Individuals are not controlled by dominant elites in the way those elites intended or imagined. Between the source of power and the individual there are, as it were, voltage loss, cable breakage, short-circuiting and domestic disconnection reducing or interfering with the supply. This escape from domination is known as disengagement.

This book aims to examine the concept of disengagement. It is a concept which has surfaced periodically in the fields of political science, political sociology and political economy for nearly thirty years. One of the first to introduce the concept of disengagement, though in a limited physical sense, was Hirschman (1970; 1978–9). Under the terminology

1

of 'exit/voice', he argued that, in all deteriorating social organisations, protest as public voice and protest by private exit to an alternative organisation (in the case of the state, political migration) are the options open to the dissatisfied. It was subsequently developed by Azarya, Chazan and others, as disengagement from the state without outmigration, namely social, cultural, religious, political and economic withdrawal from or evasion of the state's administrative and judicial control (Azarya and Chazan 1987; Azarya 1988; Chazan 1988a).[1]

Yet, despite its long history, the concept has never been systematically explored for its social breadth, historical depth and current political significance for sub-Saharan Africa (or any other region of the Third World). This neglect is to be regretted since, in my view, disengagement provides a profitable lens with which to examine and interpret a large array of socio-political data that are not usually correlated. As a working definition, disengagement can be said to occur when individuals or groups attempt to detach themselves from the unacceptable dominance of individual rulers and authoritarian systems, whether state or non-state. Those disengaging will seek to ignore, evade, mitigate or ward off (but not change or destroy) what ceases to have legitimacy in their eyes. The phenomena within its scope include political migration, discontinuance in formal and informal politics, secessionism, cultural withdrawal, such as localised autonomy and self-sufficient communities, and second economy activity that wilfully avoids the law.

All the evidence is that disengagement is a universal phenomenon, crossing social categories, such as age, class, gender, religion and ethnicity, and that it spans historical periods. Of the nineteenth century peasant, Figes wrote:

> He lived outside the realm of the state's laws – and that is where he chose to stay ... the peasant had a profound mistrust of all authority outside of his own village. What he wanted was ... freedom and autonomy without restraints from the powers that be ... As the state attempted to extend its bureaucratic control into the countryside the peasants sought to defend their autonomy by developing ever more subtle forms of passive resistance to it ... The village elders ... selected to serve in the organs of state administration in the villages ... were, in the words of one frustrated official, 'highly unreliable and unsatisfactory', many of them having been chosen for their incompetence in order to sabotage government work. There were even cases where

---

[1] Hirschman believes that the voice option would be a more likely response to such basic social organisations as the family, the church, and the state in which the exit outlet is less available, whereas exit would be a more likely response to corporations and voluntary organisations. Our focus on disengagement from the state attempts to show that the reverse might also be true, that is that exit may be the residual option when voice is unavailable or ineffective and that it can be a very likely option even in relation to the state. (Azarya and Chazan 1987:108, fn.7).

the peasants elected the village idiot as their elder. Meanwhile, the real centre of power remained in ... the old village assembly. (Figes 1996:101–2)

But Figes was writing of rural Russia. The dominated of Africa have no monopoly of devious methods to escape outside power. Though it may vary in scale, sometimes an individual response, sometimes a spontaneous mass movement and sometimes an organised collective movement, this responsive strategy is ubiquitous. Where there is a strong repressive authority, those too ill-resourced to oppose domination confidently (or to negotiate some accommodation) will resort to 'defensive disengagement'; and, where there is a weak/collapsing authority, those left without provision by that authority will, in 'opportunist disengagement', take advantage of the lack of social control.

Its relationship to other responses to domination

Life's hardships and sufferings may be put down to personal shortcomings or to fate, but the translation of inequalities to inequities and the projection of resentments on to the ruling authorities are common. Not without justification, political decisions outside their control are blamed by the dominated for undermining the means of subsistence, the transfer of resources by force and the unfulfilled promise of better things to come. Identifying the cause of inequity, however, does not ensure that action will be taken against the dominant elite. Rather, it is commonly shrugged off as being the nature of things and/or seen as inescapable and borne stoically. Thus the serfs who worked for Fulbe masters claimed: 'whoever says a Fulbe and a serf are equal, it's true for the blood, but for the law, that which Allah has made, they are not equal' (Derman 1973:247). Only when inequity is perceived as reaching intolerable levels and doors of opportunity for change stand ajar are people inclined to take action to alter their relationship with those who dominate them. Political party propaganda can still make legal opposition attractive at election times, or when crises provoke rising excitement which takes the protest outside the chambers of the legislature and on to the streets in mass demonstrations, strikes and boycotts.

An alternative to opposition is an interactive strategy with those in a position to give and receive commodities, money, employment, prebends and contracts. Though the networks of contact, exchange and complicity are in modern times often with state personnel, the latter are not in this instance acting in their official capacity. De Boeck calls the process of adaptation accommodation and collaboration 'l'arrangement', quoting the popular Zairean phrase 'tout finit par s'arranger' (De Boeck 1996:95–9).

For those who have particular difficulty in breaking into such survival-sustaining networks and whose every path to overcoming suffering seems blocked, violence can appear attractive – if not to seize the desired ends through the use/threat of a cheaply purchased gun or a downtown looting spree, at least to get revenge in what is often mistaken for mindless violence. Serious collective violence, or rebellion, triggered perhaps by the authorities' intransigence or severe repression, requires quite specific conditions that only come together very occasionally. For instance, it needs charismatic and skilful leadership, motivating ideology, resource mobilisation, possibly military organisation and manifest weakness on the part of the authorities.

These responses of opposition, accommodation or violence are ones of engagement. A very different response and one equally common, although receiving much less attention, is disengagement. This offers an escape from, or at least mitigation of, unacceptable domination, largely without recourse to violence and often without the need for organising collective action. Those who disengage do not have within their sights the change of the system or the overthrow of the oppressors; rather, they seek a readily available alleviation, or at least a means of protest that is invisible enough to avoid the wrath of the authorities. The two tendencies can divide even the smallest of groups. Take, for instance, the twenty-eight hotel workers at the Flor de Volga hotel, Chimoio, Mozambique. In February 1992 they held a meeting to discuss their poor wages and working conditions and resolved to seek redress. But when it came to the confrontation with the management only twelve of the workers turned up, and these only met with the threat of dismissal. Meanwhile the others had chosen a more invisible, but more effective, protest. They helped themselves generously to the kitchen food to take back home to their families and did laundry for the clients for a payment. One even went so far as to let rooms at discount and, offering no receipts, was able to pocket the money (Chingono 1996:154). Thus was domination avoided without raising a voice or risking losing their job. Within a spectrum of increasingly active and organised resistance, namely resignation, mitigation, evasion, accommodation, formal opposition, rebellion and revolution, disengagement spans the lower bands of mitigation and evasion. The relationship between engagement and disengagement is shown in Figure 1.1.

Its scope

Elsewhere I have discussed the range of analytical perspectives that have taken up disengagement and have offered a critical assessment of each (Baker 1997a). My own analysis of disengagement in sub-Saharan

Africa has convinced me that its breadth, history and ambiguities are best accommodated within the social power perspective, where disengagement is conceived of in terms of withdrawal from social power wherever it is exercised without consent and against another's best interests. It seems to me that this alone does justice to the breadth of the social and political expressions of disengagement. The thrust of disengagement in this view is escape from the grasp of all unacceptable power and does not restrict itself to that confined to evasion of an ill-defined (and undefinable) 'state'. After all, as Chazan says, the state is not:

> the sole magnet of social, economic and political exchange. It constitutes merely one of the many foci of social action. The dynamic combination of social confrontations with constantly changing circumstances may help to account for the heterogeneity of African political processes and the multitude of directions they are taking ... politics, power and control are not necessarily coterminous with the state. (Chazan 1988a:123)

It is a very artificial division that restricts the study of disengagement solely to the state. Were the oppressed Ganda, Toro and Lozi seeking to withdraw from British colonial control or from African sub-imperialism (Padmore says of the Nigerian chiefs appointed by the British: 'no oriental despot ever had greater power than these black tyrants'; quoted in Mamdani 1996:53)? Were the single women of rural Kenya, Southern Rhodesia and Belgian Congo in the colonial era evading a patriarchal state that forbade migration to the towns, or evading an indigenous patriarchy that sought and found official help to keep its workforce? Were the 'internally displaced' of Sierra Leone fleeing Revolutionary United Front (RUF) rebels to seek sanctuary with the state or fleeing Sankoh's de facto state? Are the Hutu of Burundi trying to evade the state in the form of its Tutsi-dominated army or to evade Tutsi racial and class hegemony? And are the diamond smugglers of northern Angola evading the União Nacional por Independência Total de Angola (UNITA), or the Angolan authorities, or the Democratic Republic of Congo (Zaire) authorities (where the gems are sold), or the powerful racketeers of Kinshasa, made up of politicians, dealers and top military personnel? All certainly get very upset if a proportion of the value evades their treasuries. The social power perspective is better suited to this variety of cross-cutting authorities, where the state only occupies one of the several public spaces and where other authorities, such as rural and kinship/ethnic associations, frequently occupy others (Osaghae 1995:194).

In Africa's segmented political spaces, what Migdal calls 'dispersed domination' prevails:

> Here neither the state nor any other social force has established an

overarching hegemony; domination by any other social force takes place within an arena or even across a limited number of arenas but does not encompass the society as a whole. (Migdal 1994:27)

From the viewpoint of those contemplating disengagement, unacceptable power might include a whole variety of social forces. To list some examples: legal determination of the limits of social and private conduct by the state or elders; institutional practices that create or reinforce barriers to the public airing of policy conflicts; cultural constraints maintained by patriarchal, religious or senior figures; predation and exploitation by those holding superior economic power; violence by coercive forces – whether state, rebel groups or local 'lords'; impediments to production and self-betterment by local, state or domestic 'rulers'; and inadequate or failed patronage. Foucault is surely right when he says:

one impoverishes the question of power if one poses it solely in terms of legislation and constitution, in terms solely of the state and the state apparatus. Power is quite different from and more complicated dense and pervasive than a set of laws or state apparatus. (Quoted in Lemarchand 1992a:180)

Within the social power perspective, disengagement can be seen as the attempt within society's multiple arenas to avoid, prevent or resist the processes of domination. By focusing on the processes by which values are authoritatively allocated and resisted, disengagement is delinked from its institutional state association. The farmer threatened by the crop-purchasing arm of the state (or parastatal marketing board) and its pricing policy withdraws into subsistence farming; but so would s/he if it were 'market forces' (and the dominant class manipulating those 'forces') that offered insufficient remuneration. Internal migration may represent fear of the state, but it might equally represent fear or failure of a regional patron, armed landlords, rebel groups, religious leaders or even male household heads. Political detachment might be a reflection of disillusionment with the entire institution of the state, but it could be a statement about how the prebendal system exploits them locally or how the patriarchal system marginalises them. Those who retreat into religion/magic are rejecting not only the values disseminated by the state, but also those promoted by the dominant class, or local traditional majority, or by whoever controls the media, public opinion and behavioural codes.

Disengagement predates modern concepts of country, institutional state, class, civil society and elections. To confine discussion within these concepts would be anachronistic and artificial. Instead, the social power perspective gives us the opportunity to use all of the other focal points of power, as best suits the historical, social and political circumstances. The single intention of avoiding political domination that is harsh and neglectful is a consistent motive that runs like a single thread through history's textile.

Different arenas but common strategies

Disengagement becomes a political activity, as opposed to plain lawlessness, when there is an explicit rejection of the authority's right to command and/or when that authority's interpretation is that this is the significance of the action. The political domination which is being rejected can be disaggregated into five arenas: (i) territorial politics or domination of the population of a location – discussed in Chapter 2; (ii) institutional politics or domination of the agencies and institutions of the authority – discussed in Chapter 3; (iii) constitutional politics or domination of the rules governing ruler/ruled relationships – discussed in Chapter 4; (iv) cultural politics or domination of ideology, values and morality – discussed in Chapter 5; and (v) economic politics or domination of production and distribution – discussed in Chapter 6. Disengagement seeks to escape domination within these arenas by withdrawing persons from the land (for example, political migration) or withdrawing the land itself (for example, secessionism); withdrawing participation in governance and competition for control and influence over the political system (for example, electoral discontinuance and disaffiliation from political/civic organisations); withdrawing ideological/behavioural conformity (for example, autonomous communities and counter-culture networks); and withdrawing production and revenue (for example, illegal second-economy activities). I have sought to capture the relationship of disengagement and engagement to the power centre diagramatically in Figure 1.1. The figure also enables one to see the relationship between disengagement and engagement within each political arena. My conception of the relationship between centre and periphery and within the periphery underlies the remainder of the book.

Though these five arenas where disengagement operates are distinct, they share similar withdrawal strategies (Table 1.1). Firstly, there are those that can be characterised as indifferent, where the individual or group acts as if the authority of the dominant group were not there. For example, there are those who abandon participation in elections or voluntary associations. More controversially, one might include some forms of begging as a type of disengagement from economic control and also that nomadism which is more motivated by political than cultural considerations or which, under pressure from centralised states, is politicised. Secondly, there are those withdrawal strategies that can be

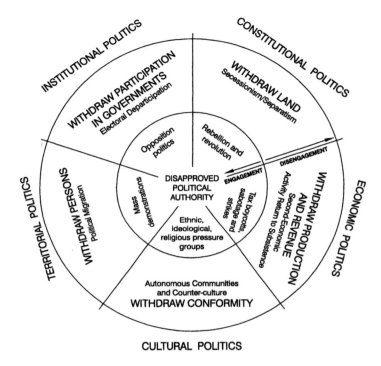

Figure 1.1 Disengagement and engagement within political arenas

characterised as avoidance, where the aim is to escape the unacceptable forces of domination by movement or deception. This would include border-hopping to escape coercive forces, going 'underground', economic activities supposedly controlled by the state but evading it, opportunism (foot-dragging, dissimulation, false compliance, feigned ignorance) and non-registration on electoral rolls. Thirdly, there are those withdrawal strategies that can be characterised as the attempt to exercise autonomy and non-cooperation. This attempts to establish a realm, physically, mentally or in the market, where the rejected authority cannot penetrate. It might include permanent exile, internal safe havens, maroonage, criminal economic activities that ignore the state and operate beyond its reach, urban no-go areas, secessionist regions and theocratic communities. The strategy of rebellion, from sabotage and tax revolts to armed conflict, has been excluded as being engagement with authorities so as to bring about change.

Table 1.1 A typology of disengagement

Withdrawal strategy	Arenas of domination				
	Territoral politics	Institutional politics	Constitutional politics	Cultural politics	Economic politics
Autonomy	Permanent exile	Passive resistance to law	Open declaration of secession	Counter-culture communities	Smuggling and other criminal economic activity
	Internal exile to safe haven				Self-encapsulated mining communities
	Maroonage				
Avoidance and deception	Border-hopping	Non-registration		Underground and secret communities	Unrevealed production and trade
	Hiding 'in the bush'				Opportunism
					Labour evasion
Indifference	Political nomadism	Discontinuance with elections, lobbying, campaigning	Disregard of central edicts	Disaffiliation from voluntary associations	? Begging

Its scale

The hidden nature of much disengagement makes it hard to arrive at accurate measurement; nevertheless, it is beyond doubt that very large numbers are involved in each of the political arenas. The details are discussed in each chapter but some general points about the overall scale of disengagement can be made here.

Political migrants declare with their feet that they find it intolerable to live under or to be influenced by those authorities over them. In the period since independence alone, millions of Africans have fled within or beyond state borders to escape dictatorship, war, persecution and the consequences of political mismanagement. They include many of the 5.8 million who were defined by the United Nations (Bascom 1995:197) as 'refugees', that is those who have known or who are threatened with violence and have crossed international boundaries. But, in addition to those who have crossed international boundaries, there are the uncounted millions who, to escape armed force and persecution, have fled within their own countries to isolated forests, rebel-held territory or official safe havens or have gone 'underground'.

Discontinuance from formal politics, whether the withdrawal be from consulting political figures, from political campaigning, from joining/contributing to a political organisation or from participating in elections, can only be measured by surveys. The most readily available published data are voter turnouts. Unfortunately, these figures are subject to widespread manipulation and too often are based on inadequate electoral rolls. In addition, they confound those disengaging with those who have never participated or those who are withdrawing as part of a deliberate political boycott; and they overlook those who failed to vote through organisational failure, intimidation, official exclusion or their own inadequacy. Yet, even making allowance for the imprecise nature of the data, the turnout figures indicate, at the very least, that large numbers of African citizens are not engaging in the most elementary of political acts and, of these, there must be many that are actively disengaging from competition for social power and influence over it. For example, in many elections since redemocratisation – presidential, parliamentary and municipal/regional – less than half the eligible voters have actually voted.

Secession is the withdrawal from membership of a polity by a section of that community. Whether attempted or achieved, secessionism involves political amputation. In the present era, at least twenty-three significant secessionist movements have troubled African states since the Second World War. Currently, Somaliland acts as an independent state in northern Somalia, and has done so since 1991. Groups of varying strength calling for self-government have had largely unimpeded movement through much of Ethiopia since 1990 and within large sections of southern Sudan for nearly forty years. On a smaller scale, discontented peoples seeking to detach themselves from state control are engaged either in contentious negotiations – for example, Anjouan, Comoros Islands – or in military and terrorist operations. The latter are found, or have been until very recently, in anglophone Cameroon; Kivu Province, Democratic Republic of Congo; the Cabinda enclave, Angola; the Bakongo area in Republic of Congo; the Touareg areas of northern Niger and Mali; northern Chad; the Afar areas of Djibouti, Eritrea and Ethiopia; Ethiopia; Bioko Island, Equatorial Guinea; and the Casamance region of Senegal. Taken as a whole, hundreds of thousands have undertaken this risky and usually unsuccessful strategy of escape.

The hegemonic goal of the political elite is to bring the diverse outlooks and beliefs found across their domain into subjection to their own, not by using force, but through persuasion, integration and cooptation. Such a project, however, does not go unchallenged. A whole array of social organisations maintain distinct popular political cultures or, in reference to the surrounding dominant culture, develop 'contra-cultures'. In particular, ideological movements, both secular and religious, play a vital role in redefining norms and beliefs (and their appropriate expressions) in relation to authority. For many organisations, the response to cultural domination is no more than self-enclosure, evasion, impassivity and indifference. Others will engage in a more active promotion of an explicit counter-culture or will adopt an ideology as a basis for resisting the state. Those most opposed to the promotion of a single cohesive cultural framework are those groups that seek to monopolise the provision of members' needs and consequently demand total allegiance. Fundamentalist groups, ethnic associations and ideological movements can try to replace the state and squeeze out alternative views and interests. Such organisations of cultural withdrawal, whether communalist or separatist, are widespread.

Economic disengagement is the most problematic of all the forms of political disengagement. Though commonly applied to the second economy, it is hotly debated as to what exactly the second economy includes and whether any part is truly political. In my view, since elements of the second economy quite deliberately seek to avoid the eyes of rulers and states, it implies a rejection of political authority, though admittedly much of it straddles the legal–illegal, state–society, economic–political boundaries. I confine economic disengagement to illegal second-economy activity, namely what I call the criminal, the unlawful and the venal. Criminal refers to the production and distribution of goods and services that are illegal in and of themselves, such as poaching and drug trafficking. Unlawful refers to the production and distribution of goods which, though legal in and of themselves, are traded in such a way as to evade taxes and customs dues, such as smuggled consumer goods. Venal refers to the illegal use of state position where the boundaries between state and society, public and private are regularly breached. Newspaper reports and published surveys indicate that that part of the second economy that fits this definition of economic disengagement is very large across Africa.

Some difficulties with disengagement

Broad explanatory models are always only one way of perceiving phenomena and of organising data, and thus are never without their limitations. Some of the data under their purview inevitably escape clear conceptual boundaries. As a result, disengagement has been criticised on several fronts.

First, it is argued that it is unsatisfactory that the same phenomenon is capable of being classified in one instance as disengagement and in another as engagement – a situation that even a proponent of disengagement admits is a 'vexing' problem that creates a 'methodological quandary' (Azarya 1988:10–11). For example, take armed opposition to the state. Armed opposition aimed at replacing the rulers and/or changing the rulers' policies is 'engagement', whereas that which is aimed at secession or regional autonomy is 'disengagement'. The logic of the distinction is not as confused as some would make out. The state as an institution needs to be seen as distinct from those that control and manage it – that is, the government. The secessionists are anti-system and therefore disengagers; the coup faction may be anti-incumbent but they are pro-system and therefore engagers. The same resolution can be applied to differentiating those in the illegal second economy who are involved in it with reluctance and are 'knocking at the door' of the state to be legalised from those who have no desire to be incorporated. The logic once more is that, though both are anti-law and anti-government (the lawmakers), the former are still pro-system and essentially engagers, whilst the latter are anti-system and essentially disengagers.

Secondly, there is the ambiguity that the same individuals/groups can appear to be disengaging and engaging simultaneously. For example, actors may be withdrawing from participation in state elections, whilst welcoming loans from state development agencies. As a general point, it should be recognised that disengagement is properly ascribed to actions not persons. Individuals are not 'disengagers' as if this described the totality of their outlook. (Mamdani (1996) argues that the free African peasants have in fact never known total autonomy, for force from local and state power has always impinged on their existence.) This may appear too easy an answer, in which case attention should be given to the composite nature of a political institution like the state. The perceived difficulty of locating 'straddlers' arises from a failure to disaggregate the concept of the state. Comprising so many agencies, it is virtually impossible for it to act as a whole, in a rational and coherent fashion, strategically following a defined set of interests. Nor do individuals perceive it as a whole, but as a set of agencies in their local setting, some of which offer resources and some of which demand resources. Their 'straddling', therefore, is not because they are inconsistent in their view of the state as a sole institution (assuming they even have a view), but because they are consistent in their desire to maximise their own benefits. Straddling is the recognition that some powers are beneficial and to be engaged with, and some powers are detrimental and to be disengaged from, and that these powers themselves vary over time and place and within their different agencies. Bratton can thus describe the relationship between society and the state as an 'ebb and flow as state and social actors each exercise a range of engagement as well as disengagement' (Bratton 1989a:415).

Thirdly, there are the difficulties associated with conceptually differentiating between disengagement and the closely related concepts non-engagement, expulsion and apparent disengagement. It is possible that the phenomena normally associated with disengagement may be the evasion of engagement in the first place. A long history of negative experiences that people have had with authority has made many wary of powerful outsiders (Migdal 1974). They know that the poor and weak are vulnerable to unfair treatment. Tropical farmers, records Hill, have 'a proper and controlled contempt for external authority – a contempt which they often delight in concealing under a veneer of acquiescence' (Hill 1986:1). Many of the peasantry according to Hyden, even in the late 1970s, remained 'uncaptured' in subsistence economies. 'The extent to which peasants' autonomy has been reduced obviously differs from one African country to another. Still, evidence suggests that the peasants by and large remain uncaptured by other social classes' (Hyden 1980:30–1). Though some have subsequently argued that peasants are in fact far more engaged in and responsive to the state than Hyden was prepared to admit (Hansen 1992; Mamdani 1996), the possibility of non-engagement remains, even if not on the scale or to the degree first anticipated. In the arena of formal politics, African farmers may not be indifferent to central government policies, but it is striking, as Widner has observed, that, in the wave of political liberalisation that swept over sub-Saharan Africa in 1989–91, farmers were rarely evident as important actors in the many new opposition parties and unions contending for authority (Widner 1994:193).

Besides the problem of non-engagement, there is that of expulsion.

In other words, not all disengagement is voluntary. Take, for example, state-sponsored disengagement (Kasfir 1974; Bratton 1989a). The state may dissolve voluntary associations, such as trade unions and parties, abandon peripheral parts of the country in terms of control and services and keep at arm's length sections of the illegal second economy pressing for incorporation. More drastically, it may exile or expel political 'agitators', disenfranchise long settled immigrant groups or abolish political participation. Likewise, other authorities may banish, excommunicate or cut off patronage. Determining whether the 'push' preceded or confirmed the withdrawal is not always straightforward.

A number of commentators have questioned the extent and reality of much that is termed disengagement. They have argued, for instance, that the illegal second economy is not the large area free from government control it is often portrayed as. On the contrary, the state may in numerous ways be active outside the institutional channels, in informal markets.

> Africans who do manage to survive within the informal sector cannot escape the state ... Surveys of the informal sector repeatedly stress the need for favourable government policies in areas such as training, credit, infrastructure and technology if the informal sector is going to play a significant role in the economy ... [nor can the informal sector] protect the vast majority of the population from the ramifications of government decisions [such as price increases and an undervalued currency]. (Herbst 1990:196, cf. Mamdani 1987, quoted in Bratton 1989a:419)

In a similar vein Reno argues that 'oppositional state–society logics downplay the extent to which economic and political advantages in each sphere are connected, require accommodations and provoke conflicts that are distant from any notion of disengagement' (Reno 1995a:16). Neither is migration to the cities the disengagement from rural authority it might seem. Very often migrants retain their attachment with their rural background:

> The urban Bamileke participates in the life of his chiefdom with all that that implies in terms of his physical presence at meetings and in financial expenditure. His social success is not complete if it is not accompanied by holding a title in one of the societies of notables. He contributes to the development work in his area, which he frequently initiates ... In the south of Cameroon, the habit of returning to the villages on retirement suggests the move towards city dwelling is not irreversible. (Bayart 1989:12; cf. Sangmpam 1994:120)

With the increasing phenomenon of state collapse and warlordism in Africa, there is considerable difficulty in determining which protagonist is the predatory state and which the agent of societal resistance.

Concerning Liberia during the civil war, for instance, Reno asks where the state/society distinction is to be found when domination of societal networks, accumulation and power are all connected and where many armed groups claim to represent state power while resisting other claimants (Reno 1995b).

There is no easy answer to these difficulties of conceptual differentiation, beyond the insistence that analysts take great care and, where judgements are made in ambiguous areas, that there is a transparency concerning both the reasons behind them and their tentative nature.

Propositions

As indicated above, the intention is to interpret the material within the social power perspective, with its focus on dispersed domination and with an emphasis on the mutual interplay between social actors and social structures. The goal is a set of generalisations that will constitute a model to account for the social structure and processes under review, and which will be helpful to others in understanding and explaining other empirical cases that can be classified as disengagement. I offer below ten propositions concerning political disengagement which will be examined closely throughout the book as to their applicability. There is clearly something tautologous about my method. The configuration that has been called disengagement has been identified in terms of actions selected as patterned, and hence the actions subsequently examined necessarily support the identification. The problem of this interpenetration of the theory of the form of the pattern and the form of the patterns themselves is probably impossible to circumvent in configurational analysis. It does not, however, in my opinion, invalidate the overall model building process. The ten propositions are as follows.

1. The nature of disengagement.
    (a) Disengagement is a universal phenomenon.
        (i) It will cross social categories such as age, class, gender, religion and ethnicity.
        (ii) It will span historical periods.
    (b) Disengagement is a multi-scale phenomenon. It will occur as an individual response, as a spontaneous mass movement and as an organised collective movement.
    (c) Disengagement is a responsive strategy, a reflection of the relationship between rulers and ruled.
        (i) Where there is a strong repressive authority, those too ill-resourced to oppose domination confidently (or to

negotiate some accommodation) will resort to 'defensive disengagement.'

    (ii) Where there is a weak/collapsing authority, those left without provision by that authority will, in 'opportunist disengagement', take advantage of the lack of social control.

2. The pattern of disengagement.

    (a) The specific form of disengagement in a particular context will depend upon macro-scale and micro-scale factors.

        The macro-scale factors include the availability of the strategy, the pattern of domination and the cultural norms, with their corresponding sanctions. The micro-scale factors include personal efficacy, assessment of utility, available resources and personal norms (for example, concerning the legitimacy of using violence or submitting to 'worldly' authority). The macro-scale and micro-scale factors are linked by networks of influence and domination. The action plans and norms promoted, reinforced and sustained by the interpersonal network will both shape the individual's choices and be a unique interpretation of the society-wide norms to them.

    (b) Different disengagement phenomena are related, in that they all arise from a common rejection of domination.

        Phenomena, therefore, will occur concurrently, as different expressions of the same rejectionism, or consecutively, as strategies fail and/or circumstances change.

    (c) Discriminatory domination will promote spatial and social clustering of disengagement.

        Persistent hostile domination and networked histories will ensure that there will be particular concentrations of activity over time or cultures of disengagement in distinct geographical areas or among distinct social groups.

3. The significance of disengagement.

    (a) The nature and extent of disengagement at any given time will provide a measure of the nature of political authorities, their legitimacy, power, penetration and conformity to societal values.

    (b) Disengagement will threaten the power balance of political systems.

        The scale of withdrawal will vary, as will the responses of the non-disengaging population, the dominant classes and the external powers to the disengagers and to one another. According to the particular combination, systems may adjust or undergo widespread reform, on the one hand, or become unstable or even collapse, on the other.

(c) The scale of disengagement will determine if and when there is democratic consolidation.

This is because disengagement is, by definition, a non-democratic method of protest, sidestepping the democratic process and claiming a veto on the action of democratically elected decision-makers.

(d) Disengagement, where it is known to the authorities, will usually be resisted by force as the first resort.

Only when it is apparent that the numbers and/or arms of the disengagers make the imposition of a solution by force impracticable are more peaceful measures resorted to.

At the end of each chapter, I shall return to these propositions to compare how closely the empirical data have or have not confirmed them.

Political Migration

Of all the types of avoidance protest, denial through exit requires the greatest preparation, the strongest commitment, and the most pronounced break with the peasant's past life. (Adas, 'From Avoidance to Confrontation')

Towards a framework for the study of political migration

'Throughout the centuries one of the common man's most frequent and effective responses to oppression [has been] flight,' writes Barrington Moore (1978:125). Widespread and regular as it may be, it nevertheless contains many distinct strands. Newitt calls it the 'complex kaleidoscopic rearrangement of peoples seeking the maximum freedom for themselves and new economic roles' (Newitt 1981:120). Simply taking the motives behind it alone, the range is enormous. In Bayart's words, people leave home because of:

> The search for a little bit of money – enough to enable one 'to stand up straight' and particularly to take a wife – the attraction of the town and all its riches, the curiosity of travel and boredom with life in the bush, drought or, if one is to believe the theoreticians of the articulation of modes of production, the structural necessity of a capitalist economy … [or because of] the domination of elders and fear of their witchcraft, the underpayment of agricultural labour and the brutality of territorial administrations and the armed bands who patrol the countryside. (Bayart 1989:258)

Despite the variety both of cause and in effect, scale and permanency, it is clear that amidst the movements in every era are to be found what may be called political migrations. In these cases, migrants declare explicitly or implicitly that they find it intolerable to live under or be influenced by certain authorities and, by their change of location, seek to alleviate or escape that domination. This is not to say that migration is ever undertaken lightly. There is considerable cost in the abandonment of kin, homes, villages, grave sites and fields which might represent generations of toil. Further, migration entails physical risk, and the acceptance by a new patron or community is by no means automatic.

From the evidence of archaeology, linguistic research and oral tradition, J. Vansina (personal communication, 27/3/95) concludes that during the precolonial period it was a common practice for 'big men' to leave with their followers and for villagers to move from one chief to another. Similarly, Colson says of the kingdoms of that period:

> Given provocation subjects could migrate beyond the borders as well as within the boundaries of a kingdom. Malcontents either joined some pre-existing polity or they rallied behind a leader of their own, a junior member of the royal line or a commoner who established a new dynasty by founding a new state. (Colson 1970, vol. 2:44)

In the colonial period, too, it is clear that people fled the physical violence, forced labour and heavy taxes which threatened their physical safety and food security. Of the period 1900–30, Isaacman concludes:

> Flight seems to have been most commonly used by peasants to maintain control over their own labour ... Porous colonial boundaries and the availability of large unoccupied tracts of arable land facilitated the flight of millions of disgruntled peasants. Many fled to neighbouring colonies. Others ... to sparsely populated areas ... beyond the effective control of the colonial regime. (Isaacman 1990:34)

In the period since independence, millions more Africans have been displaced within their states or migrated beyond the state borders to escape from dictatorship, war, persecution and the consequences of political mismanagement. The proportion strictly categorised as 'refugees' by the United Nations (UN) Convention numbered as many as 5.8 million in Africa in 1993 (Bascom 1995:197).[1] There can be no doubt, therefore, that, as Bayart puts it, 'Escape – the action of escap-

---

[1] The United Nations High Commission for Refugees (UNHCR) definition of a refugee is a person

> who owing to well-founded fear of being persecuted for reasons of race, religion, nationality, membership of a particular social group or political opinion, is outside the country of his nationality and is unable to or, owing to such fear, is unwilling to avail himself of the protection of that country. (Article 1 of the 1951 Convention and Protocol relating to the status of refugees, as amended by Article 1 (2) of the 1967 Protocol).

ing from a place – is still one of the consistent strategies of the production of politics and social relations' (Bayart 1989:259).

Though the phenomenon of political migration is widely acknowledged, its analysis has faltered for several reasons.

First, initial efforts to divide migration into two mutually exclusive categories of 'political' (involuntary, spontaneous flight from violence and persecution) and 'economic' (planned, peaceful, voluntary movement) have been discredited by evidence that both elements can be present in migration flows, or even combined in a single individual when political conditions cause deteriorating economic problems that lead to migration. In reality, there is a continuum between those decisions to move made after due consideration of all relevant information and those decisions made in a state of panic facing a crisis situation which appears to leave few alternatives but to flee.

Secondly, it suits would-be receiving states to insist that refugee status (that is, political migrants) be granted only to those who have known or who are threatened with violence. This insistence on violence and forced flight excludes the movement of political dissenters who, though their movement is free and not necessarily in reaction to specific events, yet find the conduct, ideology and/or legitimacy of their rulers intolerable. Victims of what Zolberg calls 'nefarious political routine' are not regarded as refugees in the same way as 'those singled out as targets of extraordinary malevolence by some agent' (Zolberg *et al.* 1989:25).[2]

Thirdly, for reasons of history and the politics of the 'international community', much analysis has been state-centred. Yet, as the social power perspective of disengagement predicts, it is not always the state that people are fleeing, but often oppressive and intolerable forces that are quite distinct from and not under the control of the state.

Fourthly, the traditional definition of 'refugee' requiring that migrants cross an international border to be so classified has meant that internal political migration has often been unjustifiably separated from external migration, if not overlooked altogether. These displaced persons, numbering at least 16.9 million in Africa in 1993 (Bascom 1995:200), are often indistinguishable from 'refugees' in terms of the

---

[2] The Organisation of African Unity (OAU) in its convention on refugees in 1969 faced this problem and added a further definition of refugee to that of the UN, namely:

every person who owing to external aggression, occupation, foreign domination or events seriously disturbing public order in either part or the whole of his country of origin or nationality, is compelled to leave his place of habitual residence in order to seek refuge in another place outside his country of origin or nationality. (quoted in UNHCR 1993:164).

In addition to these definitions, the Central American nations, in the Cartegena Declaration of 1984, added those subject to 'massive violation of human rights'.

causes, social composition and experiences, and may even share the same refugee camps. For instance, the Hartisheik refugee camp, Ethiopia, in 1993 was reported to contain:

> Somalis who have fled the violence and disorder at home in Somalia; Ethiopians (some of Somali stock) who had been refugees in Somalia from the fighting in Ethiopia and who were then driven back when the conflict in Somalia intensified; local people who were seriously affected by both the drought and the conflict nearby; and soldiers demobilised from the Ethiopian army after the defeat of the Mengistu regime. (UNHCR 1993:25)

Such interpenetration on the ground strongly argues for analysing the whole range of political migration, internal and external, together.

Finally, political migration, like other areas of resistance studies, suffers from a concentration of research on the large-scale movements that are the prime interest of international aid agencies. As a result, local internal movements, like maroonage and internal 'boundary-hopping', receive little attention.

For the purposes of this study, political migration is defined as population movement, within or across state boundaries, where political determinants are involved in either a primary or secondary role. Following Richmond, major determinants are designated as precipitating events and enabling circumstances and secondary determinants as those factors that reinforce the breakdown of supportive institutions – that is, predisposing factors (Richmond 1993). Those migrating are explicitly or implicitly rejecting the authorities they are leaving behind – they no longer desire to live under or be influenced by them.

The migrants' rejection may be based on quite different aspects of the powers' values and practices. It may be the powers' inefficacy – namely, their failure to protect migrants personally (or their cultural groups or their community) from armed conflict and violence (or the threat of it), from environmental hazards and from major human rights abuses. And inefficacy can extend to failure to provide the means or opportunity for economic sustenance. Or the rejection may concern the powers' policy and practice – where migration is brought about by the authorities acting directly against migrants' (or their social group's) interests, persons and human rights, or following policies that reproduce these adverse consequences as side-effects. Then again, it may be the powers' ideology that is the cause of the rejection. The religious, moral and political values of the authorities may deeply contradict those of the migrants and be an abhorrence to them. Finally, rejection may be based on the powers' illegitimacy – where migrants do not acknowledge the right of the authorities to hold power because of the absence or abuse of the recognised legitimating processes, such as elections or consultation.

The statist approach is, in my opinion, insufficiently discriminating as a framework. Instead, I have followed a framework based on social movement, with attention being given to distinctions within the authorities being deserted and within the communities being chosen. Hence my typology is according to the migrants' chosen community of refuge. This is central to my concern with withdrawal, is measurable and, in my view, marks significant discrete groups. Five distinct 'destination' communities can be identified outside the effective (if not legal) control of the authority that has been rejected: a foreign community; a foreign refuge; an isolated ('maroon') community; a safe haven; and a hidden/secret community. Each is now considered in turn.

Migration to a foreign community

This is the chosen community of those migrants that intend to settle permanently in a 'foreign' village, ethnic/regional group or state, with or without conquest. In precolonial times, migration beyond the jurisdiction of the political community was a common expression of discontent. It might be 'big men' leaving with their followers on a small scale or villagers moving from one chief to another. Either way, no authority was strong enough to stop it, since land was freely available to maintain food production similar to what had been previously enjoyed. In addition, strangers were invariably accepted by recipient societies where status belonged to those who could attract extra labour, whether they be heads of households or kinship heads (Mamdani 1996:140). Indeed, the Kongo royal title 'Ntotila' means 'the assembler' of people (J. Vansina, personal communication, 27/3/95). 'There is good reason to believe', writes Herbst, 'that in large parts of Africa circumstances have overwhelmingly favoured exit in the form of migration as the appropriate response for people faced with deteriorating economic and/or political fortunes' (Herbst 1990:184).

Though most migration in the precolonial period was on a small (and unrecorded) scale, it could at times be on a grand scale. For instance, the Bornu nation (an important power on the west of Lake Chad during the fifteenth and sixteenth centuries) was born of clan disputes within the Kanem state in the thirteenth century. When one lineage lost its dominance, it migrated *en masse* and, with the people it subjugated, plus captured slaves, formed a new nation (Cohen and Brenner, in Ajayi and Crowder 1974, vol. 2:94). In the mid-fifteenth century the reign of Oba Ewuare (Benin) 'was said to be so unpopular that it generated waves of protest migrations which ostensibly led to the foundation of many communities' (Asiwaju 1976b:578, fn.6). Or again, throughout the seventeenth century, massive migrations took place in the Akan lineages (of present-day Ghana) following political conflict, civil wars and secessions (Person, in Ajayi and Crowder 1974, vol. 2:262–301). And the Bemba chiefs left the Lunda of modern eastern Democratic Republic of Congo (Zaire) for modern north-east Zambia in the seventeenth century because, as non-Lunda followers, they 'felt neglected or humiliated' (Vansina 1966:88–91).

But perhaps the most massive upheaval was the 'Mfecane', which shook east-central Africa in 1820–1850. (The following summary is based on Omer-Cooper 1966). The Zulus' defeat of the oppressive Ndwandwe, the principal regional power of south-east Africa, set off, directly or indirectly, mass flights. Whole kingdoms embarked on wandering conquests, gathering numbers as they went from their defeated foes. They fought their way in a zigzag movement northwards, driving out or assimilating the peoples of their final destination (Map 2.1). One great movement started as two bands of the ousted Ndwandwe themselves, or Ngoni as they were to be called. They wandered for over thirty years before they settled in modern eastern Zambia and Malawi. In Omer-Cooper's words, their invasions brought:

> a long era of peaceful existence to a violent end ... villages [were] destroyed ... thousands were massacred and others dragged away to join Ngoni ranks. The terror of the Ngoni raids prevented normal cultivation and famine was widespread. Great displacement of population was another result ... [yet] more than any other group they perfected a system for uniting peoples of different cultures in enduring units. (Omer-Cooper 1966:84)

From two bands they became six substantial kingdoms, including those of the Maseko, Tuta, Gwangara, Mapenzi, Mombera and Ciwere. Another movement, stemming from the same instability, was that of the Kololo. Initially, seven villages fled an invasion of those who were themselves under pressure from the Zulus. Their flight led them, twenty years later, to found the Rotse kingdom in modern western Zambia. A third great migrant horde was the Ndebele. Beginning as a small secession from the Zulus, it fled before the latter's retaliatory attack and fought its way north until it settled in modern Zimbabwe.

In the colonial period, state borders were introduced, but these were very permeable, due to their isolation from the centre of power and the difficulty of patrolling such distances over hostile terrain. The most significant universal feature of this new era was the greatly heightened incentive to migrate. Initially this was the result of the colonial invasion. Some groups fled rather than attempt futile military resistance, such as the 'preacher-prophet' Marabouts and their followers in Senegal (Coulon 1985:356). Others only left after defeat. In some cases, the conquests created large numbers of war refugees (Curtin *et al.* 1978:521). But migration continued throughout the colonial occupation. The scale

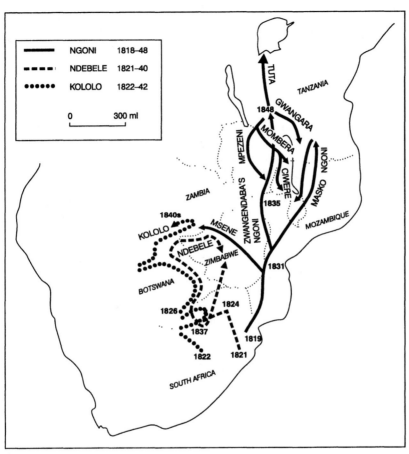

Map 2.1 The Mfecane

of it and the extent to which people went to escape are a measure of the oppression from which they were suffering. In the first third of the twentieth century, thousands of Africans in British, Belgian and particularly French and Portuguese colonies left 'individually and in groups ... their historic homelands and the protection of local and territorial cults of ancestor spirits to avoid the excesses' of colonial rule (Isaacman 1976:98; see also Crowder 1973:94–5; Asiwaju 1976b:578).

From Mozambique they fled to the neighbouring British colonies of Southern Rhodesia and Nyasaland, sometimes as entire chieftaincies led by their chiefs. It is estimated that, between 1895 and 1907, more than 50,000 Africans left Zambesia for these British territories (Isaacman 1976:107–8) and that, between 1900 and 1920, 300,000 Makua left for Nyasaland (Newitt 1981:119). The reasons given to officials by the migrants for their flight are enlightening: excessive poll tax; rigorous collection; enforced labour on plantations for tax defaulters; payment for work in (worthless) Portuguese paper currency; arrest and detention of women when the man was not found; and the violation of women by police at their houses (Alpers 1984). In other words, the Portuguese not only had no entry legitimacy, but had failed to establish performance legitimacy. Racially, economically, socially and morally, they were an illegitimate authority in the eyes of the migrant.

The same was true of the French. Equally large numbers fled their territories of Senegal, Guinea, Upper Volta, Niger, Ivory Coast and Dahomey, largely to British territories. At times, such was the scale of the protest migrations that whole villages and townships were abandoned and extensive areas severely depopulated. Two early examples were the Fulbe and the Mossi. In the 1850s, 200,000 Fulbe of the Senegal Valley and, between 1862 and 1890, a further 16,000–30,000 left in response to the Islamic call to separate from the 'corrupt' French, to settle in Karla and to wage a holy war (Hanson 1994:37–60). The Mossi of Upper Volta, appalled at the death rate of the labour migrants and their low wages, which were not enough to cover the taxes demanded, turned in their thousands to the Gold Coast – some as annual migrants (perhaps up to 180,000), but as many on a permanent basis (Skinner 1965:60–84).

The period of forced conscription during the two world wars only aggravated the movement and between 1914 and 1945 at least 62,000 fled French West Africa (Crowder 1968:338–9, 439; Suret-Canale 1971:246; Asiwaju 1976a:141–5; Boahen 1985:301). The French authorities at the time tried to make out that the migrations were for socio-economic reasons. The fleeing migrants, however, gave British officials very different reasons, namely: stringent fiscal charges; forced labour conscription; requisitions; removal of chiefs; relocation of existing settlements; abuse of women; arbitrary arrest; and summary punishment.

Though economic factors were not absent, for the British did offer cheaper goods and higher-paid jobs, the weight of the evidence must surely point to the political element being strong in these migrations.

Though the colonial authorities' first response was usually to seek physically to prevent migration, there was one important exception, namely, the case of slaves wanting to return to their homeland following colonial emancipation. Though French enforcement of the law against slavery was not wholehearted, given that they also wanted to avoid antagonising traditional allies, neither did they respond with anything but half-hearted measures to prevent or return the runaways. (The British followed a similar line (Cooper 1980:47–51)). What was normally a slow leakage, however, could at times be a mass exodus. Thus, between 1905 and 1908 in the middle Niger valley, something like 200,000 (or one in three of the slaves) left the plantations of the Maraka and returned to their homelands in Senegal, despite the use of intimidation and force by their masters, so as to seize the new economic opportunities in groundnut cultivation (Roberts and Klein 1980).

In the period since independence, political migration across borders has been severely restricted by host state authorities. They have preferred to give migrants only temporary settlement prior to repatriation or expulsion. Exceptions have been rare and not without strong contestation. Usually they have involved cases where there was a close racial identity between the migrant community and the receiving community – for example, Somalis from Ethiopia to Somalia, 1987 (Zolberg *et al.* 1989:119); Swazis from South Africa, 1974–8 (McGregor 1994:555–6); and Ethiopian Jews (Beta Israel) to Israel 1979–84 (*Economist* 28/9/85). A more complex case was that of Rwandans in Uganda. Hutu-Tutsi violent rivalry was widespread in the period 1959–63. By 1966, there were 185,000 Tutsi outside Rwanda, 50,000 of whom went to Uganda, where there were already one million long-time Rwandan settlers (including late nineteenth-century Tutsi invaders with their Hutu clients and, in the 1920s, labour migrants). The Banyrwanda (as they are called in Uganda) constituted 40 per cent of the population of Buganda (southern Uganda). Though strangers from the local community's point of view, at Uganda's independence they had acquired Ugandan citizenship. The new arrivals in 1960, however, were seen as a political threat by President Obote, since the Banyrwanda had generally sided with his opponents. He therefore confined the refugees to camps and:

> in 1969 attempted to exclude even the established Banyrwanda from the political process, on the grounds they were not true Ugandans. The target group therefore welcomed Idi Amin, who in turn allowed many refugees to leave their camps and settle on available land. The Banyrwanda went on to play an important role in the tyrant's secret police ... Having become

identified with Amin, after Obote's return they were disenfranchised and therefore began supporting their kinsmen Museveni [and his NRA]. (Zolberg *et al.* 1989:67–8)

Forced out of their homes by the ruling party's youth wing, 20,000 chose to return to the camps and 44,000 to leave the country, until Rwanda itself closed its borders, on the grounds that the migrants were 'Ugandan'. In a final twist, most of the emigrants returned to Uganda after the coup there in 1985.

Migration to a foreign refuge

This is the 'destination' community of those wanting the temporary protection of a foreign authority, whilst remaining part of their own social and ethnic group. The choice of separation, rather than assimilation, in a foreign land is not always a voluntary one. With the closing of the borders, begun under colonial rule and completed with independence, the concept of migrants being routinely allowed to settle in their chosen location died (Herbst 1990:190). It was replaced with the concept of a refugee, a migrant unable to settle permanently where s/he has been forced to live and who must therefore be held in detention or in a border camp. Having said that, most contemporary refugees have been found to regard their flight as temporary and look forward to repatriation as soon as circumstances permit. When offered settlement programmes, they have been unenthusiastic, or even bitter at the suggestion that the migration should be seen as anything more than temporary. For example, the Eritrean Liberation Front, commenting on Sudan's decision to settle the refugees, said:

> We consider the resettlement project as a conspiracy against our revolutionary situation and an injustice to the Sudanese people and their total sovereignty over their land ... we reject the plan to take the Sudanese people's land as a substitute for ours, for the liberation of which we fight. (quoted in Kibreab 1985:52–3)

The reliability of migration statistics, especially those of refugees, remains highly suspect. Inadequacy of data collection, the inflation of figures to dramatise the problem and the overlooking of those who have entered the country without reporting to the camps have all added to the uncertainty. What is not beyond doubt is that there are very large numbers. Millions of Africans have chosen to withdraw to foreign refuges in the post-Second World War period. The collective fear, resentment and alienation this represents as regards the authorities they left is hard to imagine or quantify.

In the period prior to independence, the intolerable conditions that provoked migration were the results of being caught in the crossfire between guerrillas fighting for independence and colonial counter-insurgency measures. With no authority able to protect them, people had little choice but to cross state borders and await the outcome. They included 400,000 Bakongo from northern Angola (that is, 66 per cent of the local population) in 1961; 50,000 from Mozambique in the late 1960s; 75,000 from northern Namibia in the 1980s; and 216,000 from Southern Rhodesia in the later struggle of the 1980s.

Following independence, the subsequent state consolidation often involved violent regional, ethnic and class conflict, which prompted further migration (for refugee figures see Table 2.1). The withdrawal was from both warring and persecuting groups and from the state authorities, which, if not directly involved, were either unwilling or unable to protect their citizens. Conflicts in Chad, Sudan, Ethiopia, Somalia, Angola, Mozambique, Burundi and Rwanda stand out. In Rwanda alone, the crisis of 1994–5 saw 2.2 million Hutu flee for their lives.

Where consolidation of rule following independence did avoid armed conflict, it was often at the cost of tyranny by personal rulers. Tens of thousands fled Bokassa's Central African Republic (CAR), Mobutu's Zaire, Macia Nguema's Equatorial Guinea (more than 33 per cent of the total population) and Sekou Touré's Guinea (more than 25 per cent of the total population).

If state consolidation was a painful process, state disintegration was even more so. In the Democratic Republic of Congo (Zaire), self-sufficiency, the second economy and the vast distances to the borders seem to have kept most of the population within the borders, but in other countries, such as Uganda, Somalia, Mozambique, Chad, Angola, Liberia and Sierra Leone, civil war degenerated into squabbling criminal warlords terrorising the population and causing hundreds of thousands to flee.

A special case of a 'foreign community' providing temporary refuge is that of a rebel group. Based within the nation, it nevertheless acts as a pseudo-state. Their own political strategy might be to engage with the authorities to bring about social and political change, but many travel to live among them for no other reason than that they provide protection from state violence. Thus, when Liberian state troops 'directed violence against civilian communities in Nimba county [following the National Patriotic Front of Liberia (NPFL) incursion 1989] without discrimination or restraint [burning villages and massacring their populations] ... youngsters who escaped quickly rallied to the NPFL' (Richards 1995:138). Similarly, the Dinka of southern Sudan, when faced with civil war and famine, fled to areas of the south

Table 2.1 Origin of African International Refugees (to nearest 10,000)

Country of Origin	1966	1972	1975	1981	1982	1985	1992	1995
Angola	25	42	50	14	24	28	30	31
Burundi	0	6	10	40	3	?	18	18
Chad	0	0	193	15	4	7	6	0
Eq Guinea	0	8	6	5	0	0	0	0
Ethiopia	5	5	7	5	113	140	78	?
Guinea Bissau	6	8	9	0	0	0	0	0
Liberia	0	0	0	0	0	0	67	?
Mali and Niger	0	0	0	0	0	0	5	12
Mauritania	0	0	0	0	0	0	8	7
Mozambique	2	6	7	?	?	?	134	18
Namibia	0	10	?	?	?	?	0	0
Rwanda	16	15	15	3	34	?	43	220
Sierra Leone	0	0	0	0	0	0	10	5
Somalia	0	0	0	0	0	0	72	100
South Africa	0	0	0	1	2	3	0	0
Sudan	12	13	0	0	1	12	27	?
Togo	0	0	0	0	0	0	0	15
Uganda	0	?	?	14	23	28	3	0
Western Sahara	0	0	0	5	15	15	17	?
Zaire/DRC	7	4	5	7	6	6	7	?
Zimbabwe	0	0	0	22	0	0	0	0
Total (all Africa)	67	102	?	362	304	?	539	732

internal conflict |||||||||||| external conflict ≡≡≡≡

(Figures based on United Nations High Commission for Refugees (UNHCR) data and *Africa Research Bulletin, Political Series* (ARB) reports)

under the control of the Sudan People's Liberation Movement (Salih 1994:190).

Migration to an isolated ('maroon') community

The word maroon was coined in the seventeenth century to describe 'a class of Blacks originally fugitive slaves, living in the mountains and forests of Surinam and the West Indies' (*Oxford English Dictionary*). As a more general term for isolation it was introduced into Africanist literature by Isaacman in the 1970s. It describes the chosen community of those who want to live in a peripheral area beyond the reach of the authorities, even though legally/formally within their territorial jurisdiction. Normally these fugitive societies are located in inhospitable and inaccessible terrain.[3] Apart from raids necessitated by the difficulty of food production, most maroon communities attempt to avoid confrontations and only use arms to defend their new homelands.

This was one of the common exit options of precolonial African societies. A ruler almost always had difficulty exerting control over outlying provinces, given the limited means he had to support a loyal standing army of any size and the fact that the weapons of the people were as good as those wielded by his own men. Under provocation, subjects could migrate to the margins of a kingdom, as for example, in the kingdom of Merina, Madagascar, where, 'in reaction to the harsh labour and tax requirements, an estimated 100,000 peasants and slaves fled to peripheral areas outside the control of the kingdom during the nineteenth century' (Isaacman 1990:26), or, faced with persistent slave and cattle raiding, other subjects withdrew to the natural rock escarpments and caves hidden in the forests of northern Angola or away from the centre of conflict in central Chad (Miller 1983:123–6; Cordell 1983:69).

During the colonial period instances of maroon communities avoiding the authorities are fairly common. Among the rugged mountains along Mozambique's border with Rhodesia, groups successfully eluded colonial rule in 1900–20, rejecting all European promises to redress grievances in return for submission (Isaacman 1976:109; Isaacman *et al.* 1980:595, 598, 607). But the largest and longest in duration in Mozambique was near the coast in the Qua Qua river basin. Known as Mucombeze, it attracted large numbers of those faced with high taxes, enslavement, land appropriation or land shortage. From the late 1870s until its elimination by Portuguese troops in 1891, it attracted not only local people, but people from as far afield as Malawi, Zambia and Angola (Ishemo 1995:170).

In the contemporary period, maroonage has been recorded in Democratic Republic of Congo (Zaire) and the CAR:

> In 1970 it was estimated that some 15,000 Kitawalists of the Zairian province of Equateur had retreated into the forest and lived an independent existence based upon farming and hunting. According to the very rare

---

[3] Only one true maroon community of ex-slaves has been reported, namely the Island of Annobon, São Tomé. A slave uprising in the sixteenth century caused the evacuation of the Portuguese planters (Vansina 1983:102). Cooper, however, does describe viable local communities of runaway slaves in Zanzibar from the 1870s (Cooper 1980:49).

accounts available, they refused to use Zairian money except the 20-makuta note which bore a portrait of Lumumba, and they used coins from the First Republic. Their primary motive seems to have been rejection of taxes, a principle for which they declared themselves ready to fight. (Bayart 1989:257)

It was police and military harassment in the CAR in 1972–3 that was the prime cause of large groups of people there abandoning villages and creating new settlements in remote forest areas:

One such group has established itself in the forest … about 200 km north of Bangui. Here they have planted cassava and hunt wild game … They live in an enclosed subsistence economy out of reach of the administration. (*Africa Contemporary Record* 1972/3; vol. 5:B510)

Migration to safe havens

These are chosen as areas protected from the local authorities, whilst lying within the effective jurisdiction of these authorities. They normally have the explicit or implicit support of an outside and stronger power.

The 1860s saw the ruling class of the southern flood plains of Angola beginning to adopt 'feudal' relationships with the peasantry. Chiefs, faced with the exhaustion of ivory supplies and deep debt to traders, turned to cattle and slavery to maintain their living standards. The raiding parties for these slaves and cattle were mounted and armed with rifles, such that defence was near impossible for the peasantry. Some migrated to other tribal areas or took temporary employment in the mines of South West Africa, but many more sought the protection of safe havens. 'In early 1896 there were an estimated 2,000 Kwanyama settled around the [Portuguese] fort at Humbe … flight to mission stations provided another alternative' (Clarence-Smith 1979:79).

Mission stations also came to the rescue of those Tswana faced with armed frontiersmen from the Cape Colony, who in the 1820s looted their herds and threatened their lives. The mission station at Kuruman was said to be an 'asylum of the destitute and forlorn' (Iliffe 1987:77). Similarly, they were active in East Africa, harbouring runaway slaves (Cooper 1980:49), but probably their most important refuge role was that offered to rural women wishing to escape the patriarchal system of their villages. Not that patriarchy was absent from mission Christianity, but the mission stations did allow them to escape wife-beating, forced marriages and the near slave status of some junior wives. Schmidt writes that the mission stations of Zimbabwe in the 1920s and 1930s 'vehemently opposed to child pledging and forced marriages ... encouraged young girls to seek refuge at the missions where they were able to work and go to school. Many even built hostels to accommodate the numerous runaways' (Schmidt 1992:116). Even after pressure from traditional authorities brought a change in the law so that mission stations could no longer give refuge to a woman or girl who did not have her guardian's permission to be there, the missionaries flouted the law, particularly giving sanctuary to women fleeing forced or polygamous marriages (Schmidt 1992:117).

Between 1887 and 1910, the French West African state itself provided refuges, or 'villages de liberté', for those slaves who needed sanctuary despite their legal emancipation. They particularly attracted the old, sick or very young (Iliffe 1987:144), although on arrival they found that they were still forced to provide all the administration's requirements for labour gangs and porterage (Mamdani 1996:149). State provision has continued to the present day, largely associated with attempts by the international community to provide some form of protection for refugees fleeing war zones when their own governments were unable to help. The following are two examples of French provision. When Libyan and rebel forces invaded the north of Chad in 1974–86, the French created a protection zone south of the sixteenth parallel. Because of the rebels' exaction of food, already short because of the war, 30,000–50,000 crossed into it. There was a similar French intervention in 1994 when Hutus fleeing the Tutsi rebel army were offered temporary refuge in the south-west of Rwanda.[4] The most localised refuges in recent years have been embassy compounds. These have housed not only individual dissidents – for example, Burundi in 1996 (*Africa Research Bulletin, Political Series* – subsequently referred to as the *ARB* – 1996 vol. 33, 8:12372) – but also, as in the case of the compound of the US embassy in Liberia in 1996, thousands of migrants.

Migration to a hidden community

This is often an individual response to move beyond detection by the authorities of the area. When the investigative branches of the authority are weak, hiding requires little sophistication, but, when authorities commit fuller resources to detection, it may require logistical support, regular movement and the techniques of subterfuge and disguise. Examples of both may be given.

---

[4] On a smaller scale, the UN established camps within south-west Uganda in 1985 to shelter 120,000 from civil war belligerents, and Economic Community of West African States' Monitoring Group (ECOMOG) forces created several safe areas in Liberia to encourage those who had fled the warring factions to return.

To avoid French tax and labour demands, the people of Upper Volta, particularly young males, adopted the tactic in 1914–39 of moving a short distance away from their usual place of residence:

> Merely by finding a new location for a household or indeed an entire village, people could avoid colonial exaction for a few months a year or longer. Crossing the boundary into another cercle frequently increased the chances of remaining unlocated for a longer period ... we can deduce that sometimes hundreds and often thousands of people left Koudougou for other cercles on an annual basis to avoid the requirements of the colonial administration. (Cordell and Gregory 1982:220)

Likewise, in 1911–12, Anglican teacher-evangelists in Makoni, Southern Rhodesia, saw their schools empty as their pupils took to the hills to avoid the overenthusiastic Native Commissioner's attempts to recruit young men from the Reserves for work on white farms (Ranger 1984:329). Even as late the 1970s and 1980s, villagers in Shaba, Zaire, were fleeing at the approach of the agricultural 'moniteur', whose task included the enforcement of the forced labour cropping (Mamdani 1996:164).

Where the force of domination was economic, such as oppressive landlords, refuge was sought on estates whose operations were reputed to be less demanding. Known as 'jumping the fence' in South Africa, it also occurred with great regularity during the 1910s and 1920s in Mozambique (Isaacman 1976:109) and in the highland regions of Kenya, where 'peasants fled from those estates whose owners opposed squatters owning livestock, to those who tolerated it' (Isaacman 1990:34–5).

Another way of going underground is to flee from the rural areas to the big, anonymous cities, where a new identity can easily be assumed. In the city, writes Wallerstein, 'deviants had a place to go', a place that was not under the authority of the traditional tribal hierarchy (Wallerstein 1965). Schmidt (1992) and Mbilinyi (1988) argue that African women followed this strategy in growing numbers from the 1930s, so as to escape oppressive male-controlled economies with their increasing demands on female labour and oppressive marriages or intended forced marriages. Nevertheless, with residence in the colonial towns often being forbidden to single women and having no access to capital to pay desertion penalties or to repay the bridewealth, many 'runaways' had to take with them or find new male patrons to be informal husbands or temporary liaisons. This exit-from-patriarchy interpretation has not gone unchallenged. Jochelson (1995) questions why women would flee patriarchal control as daughters and wives only to re-enter it in the form of lovers or prostitutes. Nor is she happy with its portrayal of these migrants as victims. She prefers to see them as

women deliberately choosing to migrate so as to support their families •
economically or because it is a mark of adulthood. Even so, they would
still be escaping traditional control, backed by colonial authority, in
their pursuit of social improvement, and the testimony of many of the
women is that there are degrees of patriarchal oppression.

In recent years, the going into hiding of individual political leaders
or their supporters has been a more organised affair. For instance, thousands of black youths joined the African National Congress (ANC)'s
underground military wing within South Africa after the Soweto rebellion. Their movement, however, is problematic to a study of disengagement, since their primary aim was not to avoid the authorities but
to engage in terrorist activities against them.

Historical patterns in political migration

The specific strategies of political migration that have been considered
so far have not been equally popular, nor has their usage remained constant in time. Rather, the significant macro-scale changes through
Africa's history have been paralleled by changes in the migration patterns. This historical relationship will now be explored.

In the precolonial period, the salient structural factors facing would-
be migrants were the non-existence of clearly defined and defended
boundaries of an authority's rule; the availability of large tracts of arable
land to provide food security outside the area of influence of the present
authority; the prospect of likely acceptance by another society should
the move be made; the knowledge that any weapons that might be used
by the authorities to resist dissidents could be equally matched; and a
socially condoned tradition of political migration. In the circumstances,
migration to a foreign or maroon community, though entailing loss, was
both relatively straightforward and therefore common. More evasive
techniques or ones requiring force for protection were largely unneces-
sary. The only dissenting voice to this account is Wallerstein. He has
argued, somewhat unconvincingly, that linguistic differences, roads
obstructed by hostile forces and, above all, the difficulty of securing status in a new society equal with what had been enjoyed before would
have severely restrained precolonial movements. 'Under such conditions the natural inertia of loyalty to one's own birth community would
largely outweigh the various pressures to leave' (Wallerstein 1965:149).

From the dissident's perspective, the colonial period reduced the
availability of certain strategies. It brought the novel experience of distinct boundaries, decreasing available land and weapon inferiority. True,
the boundaries, especially in the early days, were porous, but, given the
great size of domains such as the state, they were often physically too far

away to reach. This was especially so before the colonial networks of rail and road were established. The unavailability of land was not simply due to population increases, but to the privatisation of land ownership. The migrant was now faced with being an illegal squatter on land that traditionally had been communal or free. The widening gap between the weapons available to the general population and those in the hands of the authorities had a twofold effect. On the one hand, it restricted local wars and thus the need to flee their violence. On the other hand, migration could be opposed by the superior force and therefore more evasive techniques or illicit access to arms were required to facilitate it. The overall effect of these structural changes meant that crossing state boundaries to foreign communities, though still physically possible, was far less attractive. It therefore became restricted to those nearest the border in those less inhabited areas where the border was not patrolled. As for internal movements, maroonage began to be replaced by living with political rebels or social bandits holding out against the authorities through matching their fire-power. For those with no access to state borders or weapons, alleviation, if not a solution to their discontent, could be found in internal boundary-hopping or migration to the fast-growing colonial cities. The different strategies were different manifestations of the same fundamental rejection of colonial rule and the determination to evade it.

The coming of independence closed the borders (even using fences electrified to lethal levels, as on the South Africa/Mozambique border) and strangers became foreigners, who at best were refugees that most governments had neither the will nor resources to accept on anything other than a temporary basis prior to their repatriation or expulsion. Even where state rhetoric concerning migrants was positive, the experience in those regions penetrated by migrants was at best ambivalent. Cultural norms among the hosts were changing, bringing previously unknown social barriers to the migrants. True, social integration of many transborder communities has still played a part in receiving refugees. Bascom records that the affinity between the inhabitants of Senegal and Guinea-Bissau was so strong that the local population shared lodging, tools, seeds and food stocks with the refugees in the 1960s. Likewise the Luuali-speaking people of Zambia gladly provided for their kin fleeing the fighting in Angola in the 1980s (Bascom 1995:204–5). Nevertheless, there are signs that such kinship support is under increasing strain. The commercialisation of farming has reduced the possibility of refugees simply stepping into shifting cultivation and pastoralism in uninhabited land at the periphery of the host country. McGregor found in eastern Swaziland that, though kinship and lineage networks were important and could create opportunities for economic well-being, 'they may at the same time provide only limited protection, and sometimes provide none at all' (McGregor 1994:557–8). Ethnic connections or not, hospitality is still a function of resource availability, and those resources, especially land, are much more restricted than in previous periods. Within the states, the shortage of unowned and/or unoccupied land reduced the possibility of internal migration. At every turn, the would-be migrant was faced with tight administrative control on movement, habitation and productive activity, backed up by coercive forces that held and used overwhelming fire-power. Nevertheless, for all these structural changes, internal movement and the crossing of state borders have never been on such a large scale. This anomaly is a measure of the steep decline in the standard of state conduct and of the lack of security offered by the state. In particular, it was prompted by the numerous regional military conflicts fuelled by the Cold War. However, though the numbers moving are vast, few now see external migration as a permanent solution. From a strategy of permanent relocation, it has become a strategy of temporary respite. For those who still seek permanent relief from unacceptable political domination, organisations that are democratic/reformist, secessionist or revolutionary offer more attractive options.

The impact of political migration on social power

The evidence shows that political migration has a significant impact on the socio-political systems deserted. Whereas non-disengagers show a remarkable passivity in the face of the upheaval thrust upon them by the social and economic loss of migrants, the authorities have demonstrated a range of reactions. They have been relieved to be losing 'troublemakers'; embarrassed at the bad publicity; jealous of the neighbouring power's superior pull; infuriated by the interference of outsiders in support of the rights of dissidents; anxious over the loss of key personnel or social groups; fearful of opposition movements organised by émigrés, possibly with rival power assistance; or angry at those who defied their authority and escaped their control. Taking the political systems as a whole, however, the main consequences may be summarised as resource shrinkage, preventive measures, reform or policy changes and, in extreme cases, power collapse.

RESOURCE SHRINKAGE

Migration can unsettle a political system because of the loss of key personnel or groups. By the late 1980s, the UN estimated that Africa had lost no less than one-third of its total high-level manpower to migration. Of Guinea in the 1980s, Azarya and Chazan write:

Escape is prevalent among the better educated elements and causes a serious brain drain. In Guinea the exodus of trained persons is endemic and has nullified government attempts to form a corps of well educated officials. Those sent for study overseas have chosen not to return to the precarious environment of Conakry. Members of the diplomatic staff have left their posts or have chosen to defect at the end of their terms of service ... the Polytechnique of Conakry was in a state of suspended animation because it lacked qualified teaching personnel. (Azarya and Chazan 1987:118)

This migration robs developing nations of their opportunity to secure legitimacy based on economic success, which, in view of the absence of legitimacy based on democratic choice or even single nationhood, is crucial.

PREVENTIVE MEASURES

Seeing migration as a threat, authorities in all periods have at times undertaken extensive authoritarian measures to prevent it. Zolberg *et al.* regard prohibitions against exit as a hallmark of the twentieth century. They believe it may be 'a normal concomitant of state directed economic autarchy', where, for instance, a large internal supply of labour is needed to keep wage costs down (Zolberg *et al.* 1989:16–18), though this argument ignores state fear of a large, restless mass of the unemployed turning to crime and/or violent demonstrations. It is true also that the harsh attitude towards emigration has been shaped in part by the widespread use of cross-border camps by insurgents or the use of refugee camps for recruitment to the insurgents' cause. In this situation, it is feared that leaving the country will swell the ranks of the guerrilla forces. For totalitarian regimes, prohibition has also served the more pragmatic role of reducing publicity about the regime's unpopularity.

POLICY CHANGES

In the colonial period, migration played a role in bringing successful pressure to bear on authorities to dilute or change their policies. 'Bloody and costly as the anti-French armed risings were, they did not worry the French as much as the problem of migrations. For migrations meant a loss both of labour and taxable population' (Asiwaju 1976b:144). Both the French and Portuguese colonial powers found that there was a limit as to how far they could go, beyond which coercion was counter-productive and provoked mass emigration. Consequently, they revised their harsh labour policies, though not with any enthusiasm.

In South Africa, the very threat of migration to landowners who operated less repressive regimes was an effective weapon in the hands of the peasants to ensure that the relative leniency of some continued. By 1910, the owners of the farms were reluctant to impose new and more stringent terms upon their tenants because they were aware that they needed their subsistence plots to survive. Further demands would only have risked driving them to leave (Trapido 1978:28–9). The peasants, aware of this, acted accordingly and, as a result, few landlords had labour agreements, and those that did had ones that were widely regarded as 'derisory'.

POWER COLLAPSE

Where the scale of the haemorrhaging through political migration is extensive, it is a sign of a political authority on the verge of collapse. Indeed, it may even precipitate its final demise. Examples of such extensive disengagement can be given from the nineteenth and the twentieth centuries.

The Old Oyo Kingdom (northern Nigeria) contained some of the most densely populated parts of Yorubaland before 1800. After factional division and Fulani pressure had provoked half a million into moving south between 1800 and 1830, the kingdom disintegrated, with famous towns destroyed or evacuated. By 1830, two-thirds of the kingdom had become the least populated area of the region (Ajayi and Crowder 1974, vol. 2:144).

In recent times, there have been three occasions when between 25 and 33 per cent of the total population of a state has fled. In the cases of Guinea (25 per cent) and Equatorial Guinea (33 per cent), the tyrannies survived, thanks to external assistance from political allies. In Rwanda (30 per cent) the situation continues to be very fragile. The legitimacy of the government, dominated by the minority Tutsis and installed by force in 1994, was clearly challenged by the fact that, though many of the 2.2 million migrants who remained loyal to a former Hutu government returned, the instigators of the genocide remained outside and in control of significant weaponry. These migrants, however, have subsequently been decimated by the Zairean rebel movement (aided by Rwanda, Uganda and Angola). This has temporarily secured the Rwandan government's position, but leaves unresolved their long-term requirement of securing the support of the majority of the nation's population. The stability of the state, therefore, remains uncertain.

The impact of political migration on democratisation

One particular reform has been the preoccupation of much opposition politics in Africa in the 1990s, namely, democratisation. Does political migration promote or hinder its appearance and consolidation? Hirschman's central thesis (1970, 1978–9, 1993), maintained over thirty

years, is that, because protest (voice) and departure (exit) are antagonistic, the one can gain only at the expense of the other. It follows, in
his view, that large-scale migration undermines the development of
voice. As an example, he gives eastern Europe. In the early years after
the Second World War, when exit, or the hope of it, was extensive, the
dissident movement was very weak. Following the erection of the 'Iron
Curtain' and extremely tight controls on emigration, resistance began
to grow. For contemporary Africa, the evidence is less conclusive, but
it is true that none of the countries that saw political protest calling for
reform and democratisation in the early 1990s experienced widespread
migration prior to or during the demonstrations – for example, Benin,
Burkina Faso, Cameroon, CAR, Comoros Islands, Côte d'Ivoire,
Gabon, Kenya, Niger, Mali, Sierra Leone, Togo, Zambia and
Zimbabwe. The only exception was Zaire.

Hirschman recognises two important exceptions when exit promotes
internal reform. The first is when exit itself acts as voice. He cites as an
example the events of 1989 in East Germany. The large-scale flight via
Hungary to the West, instead of undermining protest as its alternative,
was so public as to be a protest in its own right and had the effect of
stimulating public voice back in East Germany. Thus, in certain
'momentous constellations,' he concedes, 'exit can cooperate with
voice, voice can emerge from exit and exit can reinforce voice'
(Hirschman 1993:202). The closest African parallel is Rwanda, where
exit in 1994 was voice that could be heard worldwide. The reform it has
provoked, however, has been minimal, since the regime is more
confident about the loyalty of its security forces than the East German
leadership.

The other important case of exit promoting reform, in his view, is
where a weakened opposition provides a window of opportunity for a
nervous regime. Though dissidents may regard the loss of radicals as
simply providing the regime the opportunity to continue its oppression
with still less resistance, from the regime's point of view it can lessen
the risks of introducing change. Hirschman has suggested that, following the loss from European countries of so many dissidents to America
in the early twentieth century: 'it became comparatively safe to open up
the system to a larger number of those who stayed on ... [and] for
democratisation and liberalisation to proceed in several European
countries prior to World War One without political stability being seriously imperilled' (Hirschman 1978–9:103).

The closest African example is possibly Ghana in the early 1980s
when the state's educated class was decimated by flight. Chazan writes:

> The PNDC [Provisional National Defence Council] came to power on a
> wave of popular protest that ... favoured the pursuit of radical alternatives

... [it carried out] a campaign against what it considered to be enemies of the revolution. These included former government officials as well as traders, professionals and entrepreneurs. The techniques employed in this connection were particularly repressive: killings, incarcerations, public beatings, and summary trials were commonplace ... Professionals, religious leaders, university lecturers, lawyers, market women, senior civil servants, army officers and ex-politicians were either persecuted or ridiculed. (Chazan 1992a:126–8)

In addition, the government compressed the wage and salary structure to a ratio of only 1.8:1.0 between the top and the bottom. The subsequent emigration of the educated class was enormous. Overall, between 1960 and 1986, Ghana may have lost between 50 and 66 per cent of its experienced top-level professional manpower, numbering more than one million (Rado 1986:563). Yet, though the loss entailed the removal of many leaders and supporters of democratisation, from the viewpoint of those who sought the 'Rawlings' Revolution', it was indispensable. How could the priorities of the regime fail to be, as Chazan puts it, 'expedited by the extent of the shredding of the fabric of political life ... facilitated by the separation of the regime from political social groups, [and] by the weakness of its opponents' (Chazan 1992a:131)? It should be noted, of course, that it was not so much the scale of the migration that was the determining factor, but the nature. Large numbers of relatively apolitical peasants do not constitute the same window of opportunity as a small number of the politically active professional class.

Others have repeated the 'safety valve' theory concerning Third World regimes that could not absorb and accommodate the expectations of migrants for improved socio-economic and political conditions (for example, Heisler and Heisler 1986:21). There are doubts, however, as to just how cut off from state affairs modern émigré groups are, given the ease of communication, which keeps them well informed and enables them to communicate and organise campaigns from any distance. If states in the past could say 'good riddance' to emigrating opponents, today they are on record as following them to their safe havens to eliminate what is seen as a continuing threat.

The link, therefore, between migration and political/democratic reform is complex. Most contemporary migration is related to war, just as most return movements are related to renewed peace. In conflict circumstances, migration is unlikely to have a reformist effect, nor will it cease simply because democratic institutions have been introduced. If the variable of war is removed, then migration ceases when democratisation is introduced. For example, in 1986, there were 35,000 South Africans living as refugees in other parts of Africa. By 1992, the number had dropped to 8,700. Likewise, those countries enjoying peace and a measure of democracy, such as Tanzania, Zambia,

Botswana and Malawi, have minimal migration despite severe economic difficulties.

How does political migration relate to the propositions?

At the end of Chapter 1, ten propositions were put forward concerning all forms of disengagement. How far do those generalisations apply specifically to political migration?

First, concerning the nature of disengagement, it was hypothesised that disengagement is a universal phenomenon, a multi-scale phenomenon and a responsive strategy.

The chapter has demonstrated that political migration is a phenomenon universal in time and place. It embraces every social category and is as ancient as socio-political power in Africa. Further, it has been shown that political migration is a multi-scale phenomenon. In every age, there are records of political migration at both the individual and the mass scale. Finally, both the defensive and the opportunist responsive strategies have been in evidence in the account. Millions have fled wars, discrimination, ethnic cleansing initiated by those in power or hostilities from other groups from which no protection was offered by the central authorities. Slightly fewer, but still large numbers, have taken advantage of the weak or non-existent socio-political control, frequently brought about by armed conflict, to seek out places offering greater security and prosperity.

Secondly, concerning the pattern of this form of disengagement, it was hypothesised that disengagement depends on macro-scale and micro-scale factors. (The common roots of disengagement phenomena and their occurrence in concentrations as spatial and social clusters and as cultures of disengagement will be considered in the concluding chapter, which compares all the phenomena together.)

The chapter has given ample evidence of the interplay of macro-scale and micro-scale factors. Macro-scale factors have proved crucial, though, as has been seen, they have varied over time. The pattern of domination became much more restrictive on movement during the colonial and independence periods, nor were the uninhabited or communally owned spaces so available. There is little evidence that the cultural norms of the 'sending' societies towards migration changed, but economic constraints do appear to be making 'receiving' societies less amenable to welcoming incomers, even when they are ethnically related. Micro-scale factors, such as utility, have always been significant, but are rarely taken alone. The individual's choice of migration is shaped by the encouragement and discouragement of personal networks, whether relatives/kin across the borders or in the cities; of others intent on the same course of action in the individual's/family's village; or of respected religious, guerrilla and political leaders.

Thirdly, concerning the significance of disengagement, it was hypothesised that it provides a measure of the nature of political authorities, threatens the power balance of political systems, delays democratic consolidation and usually initially provokes resistance by force.

Political migration does provide a measure of the nature and strength of systems of rule, for it is a measure of the lack of legitimacy of political authorities in situations where they lack the power to stop dissidents withdrawing. In addition, maroon and hidden communities are a measure of the limits of the authorities' penetration. Further, where political migration is on a massive scale, it is an indicator of the imminent collapse of power.

The power balance within ruling systems has indeed been unsettled by political migration. Examples have been given of powers adjusting their policies so as to survive the delegitimising process of political migration or enhancing their coercive forces so as to maintain their domination.

Democratic reform and consolidation are, according to the argument of the chapter section above, delayed by political migration, in that the development of a vibrant opposition is undermined by loss of personnel. This generalisation needs to be qualified, however, to take into account 'vocal' exit and active opposition groups working from abroad.

The use of coercion to prevent political migration has a long history. Most major flights take place while an internal war is in progress. At such a time, coercive forces are stretched or even excluded from the refugee zone, making restriction difficult. It may also make military sense to allow non-combatants in a conflict zone to evacuate, especially if they have been lending logistical support to the rebels, or if rebels are using them as a human shield, like the Hutu militias in the refugee camps of the Democratic Republic of Congo (Zaire). Ordinarily, however, where practicable, authorities have resorted to coercion as their first response to political migration, whether it is the Zulu leaders' hot pursuits outside their own domains or the tight border controls and emigration permits operated in nineteenth-century French West Africa and in the twentieth-century totalitarian regimes, such as Angola, Ethiopia, Mozambique and Nigeria. They regarded all emigration as disloyal (and therefore as political), as a rejection of their regimes and as likely to publicise their failings. Their response was to force dissidents to come to terms with the prevailing political and social order and to refuse passports. Tight restrictions have also been applied in Namibia, South Africa, Rwanda, Tanzania, Cameroon, Togo, Somalia and Sudan (Weiner 1995:34). Though economic reasons, such as maintaining human resources for production, are often given as justifications for these oppressive measures, there can be no doubt that political considerations have weighed heavily as well. An obvious consideration in the authorities' response is the widespread use by rebels of cross-border facilities. In these circumstances, migration is likely to boost their strength (Zolberg *et al.* 1989:16–18). Only on the much rarer occasions when migration coincides with the interests of the authorities and is readily permitted, or even promoted (such as to relieve unemployment and increase remittances from abroad), is coercion ruled out.

In all its forms, whether mass or individual, temporary or permanent, long-distance or short, political migration is about the withdrawal of persons from territory controlled by authorities who are regarded as unacceptable. It is the escape to territory outside the control of those authorities. For the Hutu in 1996, the strategy was a failure. But, having marched back to their homeland, they are unlikely to return to the high level of participation in formal politics that characterised them in the 1988 elections. Even if such participation were offered them, their bitter experience of the frailty of power won democratically in the face of force will ensure discontinuance in formal politics. The next chapter echoes this alternative strategy of moving from territorial disengagement to institutional disengagement, that is, to withdrawal of participation in the exercise or choice of governance, though still remaining within the territorial control of a hostile or discredited authority.

Discontinuance from Formal Politics

Things will be the same if you vote or if you don't vote, so I won't. (Harare market woman, prior to Zimbabwe's presidential elections in 1996)

Establishing definitions and meanings

POLITICAL PARTICIPATION AND DISCONTINUANCE DEFINED

Participation is used here to describe actions by citizens intended to influence, or to facilitate influencing, the choice of political decision makers and/or their political decisions (of policy formulation and policy implementation). This need not be restricted to government officials and political representatives. As Bienen has pointed out:

> Groups try also to directly influence each other or to eliminate others from an arena ... We can go so far as to say that much of politics in developing countries takes place as groups deal with each other without government as an intermediary. (Bienen 1974:15–16)

He defines political participation as activities 'used by various groups and individuals as they try to influence each other and government on public and potentially public issues' (Bienen 1974:17). Participation may be differentiated according to its activists, scope, modes, intensity and quality. Thus, it may be large-scale or small-scale regarding the numbers involved; it may be restricted or universal in the scope of the issues it promotes; it may be institutionalised or informal, symbolic or substantive, legal or illegal in the modes it involves; it may be frequent or infrequent in its intensity; it may be effective or ineffective, willing or coerced in its quality (see Kasfir 1976:9–14).

Those participatory activities that people might withdraw from can therefore include: keeping informed about politics through the media and talking about it (strictly speaking, this does not meet the definition of influencing and so is excluded by Almond and Verba (1963) from participation, though, as Bienen (1974) points out, such symbolic acts may be translated into influence at some later date); persuading others to a point of view or consulting a political representative/party official/ government officer about a problem; joining an organisation that has (or is developing) a secondary role in politics; voting for political representatives in elections and on specific issues in referendums; joining an explicit political organisation; contributing time or money to a political campaign; taking a job in a political organisation; demonstrations and protests to advocate a policy review; entering government through election or acceptance of an appointment; entering government through a *coup d'état* or revolution (adapted from Kasfir 1976:7).

Though the act of voting is one of the least active forms of political participation, only requiring a minimal commitment every few years that may last no longer than the casting of a vote, it is the one that has attracted the most attention of researchers and thus, reluctantly, much of the discussion of this chapter will concern electoral discontinuance alone.

POLITICAL ALIENATION DISTINGUISHED FROM DISENGAGEMENT

Alienation, anomie and apathy concern feelings – alienation emphasising hostility, anomie bewilderment and apathy lack of interest. Disengagement, on the other hand, concerns activity. Political alienation has been defined as 'a deep seated and relatively enduring feeling of estrangement, rejection, negativism and unhappiness with the political system or its salient parts' (Milbrath and Goel 1977:62). Similarly, Lane has defined it as, 'a person's sense of estrangement from the politics and government of his society ... [and] the tendency to think of the government and politics of the nation as run *by* others *for* others according to an unfair set of rules' (Lane 1959). It is commonly subdivided into normlessness, cynicism and inefficacy. Normlessness is alienation with respect to the regime/system – a dissatisfaction or rejection of what it is, of its principles, values and standards. Inkeles calls it, 'The feeling that politicians are not complying with the rules' (Inkeles 1969:1125). Such alienation will tend to be profound and not readily altered. Cynicism, or lack of trust, is alienation with respect to the individuals that lead and manage the system; it is a feeling that the government is not delivering the results desired. Rush and Althoff describe its manifestation as: 'the feeling that politics is "a dirty business", that politicians are not to be trusted, that the individual is at the mercy of manipulating groups, that the "real" power is exercised by "faceless men" and so on' (Rush and Althoff 1971:92). Arguably it will be less durable than normlessness, seeing that it is closely associated with performance.

Though normlessness and cynicism are related, they are not always concurrent. For instance, individuals may accord legitimacy to the regime, but distrust its current leaders. As Easton reasons, 'There is likely to be a wide abyss between feeling distrustful or cynical about authorities in general and refusing to accept outputs as binding' (Easton 1975:453). The point being, as he says, that system support (what he calls 'diffuse support') consists of a 'reservoir of favourable attitudes of goodwill that helps members to accept or tolerate outputs to which they are opposed or the effects of which they see as damaging to their wants' (Easton 1965:273). Insensitivity to outputs has an obverse side, namely, where regime support is negative it represents a reserve of ill will that is not easily shifted, whatever the government's achievements.

Though support for the government usually varies with perceived benefits or satisfactions, the effect on political participation is variable. According to a study by Inkeles, those who scored highly on participant citizenship in Nigeria were often more hostile and dissatisfied with the government's performance than non-participants (Inkeles 1969). On the other hand, in East Pakistan (Bangladesh), the most active citizens were also consistently satisfied with the government's performance. Cynicism is associated with participation in Nigeria, but with non-participation in Bangladesh. Citrin's explanation is that whether a political cynic is active or non-active depends on the interactions among factors such as the support levels of networks of influence for 'alienated behaviour, the availability of an "alienated" response option in the concrete situation, and the individual's social status and personality' (Citrin 1974:979). In conceptual terms, the decision of a cynic to participate or not is usually attributed to efficacy – that is, the feeling that an individual can and does influence political decisions and that their involvement individually or in a group does make a difference. Where efficacy is low and combines with cynicism, significant disengagement is likely, as appears to be the case in Bangladesh. Where efficacy is high, the presence of cynicism will not produce significant disengagement, as Nigeria appears to illustrate.

Milbrath and Goel have shown the relationship between efficacy and trust (the opposite of cynicism) diagramatically as shown in Table 3.1 (adapting an earlier model of Gamson 1975). It will be seen that disengagement is associated with low efficacy and low trust. (Normlessness will determine how total and permanent the disengagement is.)

Though the relationship between efficacy and participation is widely acknowledged, the sequence may not always be efficacy followed by

Table 3.1 Modes of political participation related to efficacy and alienation

	High trust	Low trust
High efficacy	Active, loyal and conventional participation	Radical action or unconventional participation
Low efficacy	Supportive, patriotic and ritualistic participation	Withdrawal from politics

(Adapted from Milbrath and Goel 1977:70)

participation. In other parts of the Third World, peasants that were incorporated into peasant unions, for whatever reasons, grew in efficacy as they took part in discussion and action and saw the tangible benefits. Participation clearly created and sustained efficacy (see Mathiason and Powell 1972). In addition to the crucial factor of efficacy, other secondary factors may play a part. For instance, it has been suggested that abstention may be significant where an individual is faced with controversy or cross-pressures, and where spurs to action are absent so that the event seems irrelevant to personal and material needs (Rosenberg 1954, quoted in Rush and Althoff 1971:90–2).

INTERPRETING VOTER PARTICIPATION FIGURES
The figures most widely used for comparison are for actual voters as a percentage of registered voters. Provided political systems are not in crisis, a low turnout figure can be interpreted as a measure of citizen disaffection with the electoral process and its principal actors. It should be remembered, however, that the total number of registered voters may differ considerably from the actual number of people of voting age. Samoff gives a striking example of such discrepancy for postcolonial Tanzania (Table 3.2).

Table 3.2 Voter registration in Tanzania (in millions)

	1965	1970	1975	1980	1985
Eligible voters	5.1	6.6	7	8.2	9.6
Registered voters	3.2	4.9	5.6	5.6	6.9
Difference	1.9	1.7	1.4	1.2	2.7

(Adapted from Samoff 1987:162–163)

Table 3.3. Voter registration in selected countries

Country	Year		Vote as % registered voters	Vote as % estimated eligible voters
Ghana	1960	Referendum	78	47
Ghana	1969	Parliamentary	63	47
Upper Volta	1978	National Assembly	40	29
Kenya	1979	Parliamentary	75	60
Niger	1992	Referendum	55	38
Zambia	1996	Parliamemtary/ Presidential	46	21

(Figures from Hayward 1987 and the *Africa Research Bulletin, Political Series*)

Similar discrepancies have been recorded elsewhere (Table 3.3).

What causes the discrepancies between those of voting age and those on the electoral roll? Often it has nothing to do with disengagement and more to do with the desires of the political elite to promote enrolment. The latter may use the legal system, party organisation and plain corruption to extend or decrease the electoral rolls according to their perceived political advantage (Powell 1980). The legal system will discourage enrolment when it makes it voluntary as opposed to compulsory or when registration is not automatically granted to those eligible, but rather requires an application. Participation, of course, will not be assisted where the legal requirements are not readily understood (as was alleged in Mauritania in 1991) or where there are no penalties for non-registration.

The effect of party organisation depends on how strong the linkages are between parties and demographic groups and the degree of political advantage to be gained by calling on those loyalties to be translated into registration. One of the most successful party campaigns to promote registration was undertaken in Botswana. The Botswana Democratic Party, faced with a falling turnout, which dropped as low as 31 per cent in 1974, set about extending its legitimacy by devoting a very considerable effort to voter registration campaigns. Before the 1979 and 1984 elections, it 'mounted a massive propaganda campaign through the media using slogans, jingles and cartoons to urge people to vote' (Wiseman 1990:45). The voting turnout improvement from 58 per cent in 1979 to 76 per cent in 1984 is attributed to this effort. By 1994, however, those registered for the polls had dropped to 74 per cent. More recently, in Senegal, the party competition in the 1993 elections was intense enough to promote efforts to mobilise supporters to register, but only in the rural areas was the party–client relationship strong enough to translate that desire into significant response. Ironically, therefore, it was the more educated and unionised urban constituents, who are said to be far more committed to social change and democratisation, that the political parties failed to mobilise (Diouf 1994:10–12).

Few governing parties can be so confident of their majority that they feel no pressure to exceed lawful methods. Some are sustained only by the most fragile of coalitions with equally self-seeking leaders; many face widespread unpopularity for their failure to deliver the promised benefits of rule; some have lost the charismatic leader that won independence; and still others are afterthoughts when those who have seized power want an organisation to mobilise support for their illegal rule. For all these less than secure governing parties, the appeal of electoral corruption is very great. Their methods certainly have not lacked ingenuity: phantom persons have been added to the electoral rolls, whilst those who have died have not been deleted; or people have been simply removed from electoral rolls in known opposition areas. The results have sometimes been as bizarre as they have been blatant. In 1970 Radio Kinshasa announced that the votes cast in the Zairean (Congo) Referendum had been 10,131,828 and that the registered voters numbered 10,101,330. In seeking to explain this unusual phenomenon, the radio said it was the result of the movement of people from one centre to another in pursuit of their daily occupations (*Africa Research Bulletin, Political Series*) (*ARB*), 1970 vol. 7 (11) 1928). In 1988, Cameroon increased the number of deputies in the National Assembly from 170 to 180, ostensibly because of the increase in the general population. Yet the registered voters in 1984–8 fell by 334,105 (*ARB* 1988, vol. 22 (5):8881)! The scale of the manipulation in Nigeria was revealed when the 1991 National Census (the first accurate one) disclosed 20 million fewer than the number that had been assumed and that had been used for apportioning federal monies! Before the census, the National Electoral Commission had had 70 million registered. This was reduced to 50 million by the removal of ghost voters. Even this reduction, however, still gave 54 per cent of the population a vote, whereas most population experts said that no more than 40 per cent of the population were above voting age (*ARB* 1992, vol. 29 (3):10500). Even under so-called democratic elections, serious violations occurred. For instance, in Ghana in the 1992 elections, the overall voter turnout was larger than the statistically possible number of voters by 1.4 million (according to the International Foundation for Electoral Systems, quoted in Oquaye 1995:267). Or, again, there was clear evidence of interference by the National Provisional Ruling

Council (NPRC) government of Sierra Leone in the 1996 election. Riley writes:

> They did this in relation to the registration of displaced persons outside the country, and by changing, and delaying publication of, the electoral registration rules until the last moment before the scheduled elections. Voter registration was poorly funded, rushed, and took place under difficult conditions as a consequence of the 'rebel war.' ... As a result, INEC [Interim National Election Commission] were only given permission by the NPRC to register voters outside the country at an impossibly late date, and also had to produce a 'Supplementary Voters List' at the last minute. (S. Riley, personal communication, 28/9/96)

If the 'percentage of registered voters' is a questionable figure due to irregularities in the electoral roll, it is equally dubious because of the manipulation of the absolute figures for voters. Though in the nature of things such malpractice by governments is hard to prove, few will put much trust in the large number of elections that claim virtually 100 per cent voter turnout. Such ill-disguised interference with the electoral process at the registration or counting level might be thought to be a pointless, if not counter-productive, exercise. Why entertain elections which one can only win through cheating? This is to misunderstand the unelected ruler's dilemma. Rulers crave legitimacy not only because it flatters their ego, but because it reduces their need to rely on costly and never totally effective coercion. Rulers that have no entry legitimacy are therefore invariably drawn, sooner or later, to attempt to secure legitimacy at a later date. But it is an exercise they dare not lose, hence the irresistible temptation to load the dice. Consequently, turnout figures should be used with care when assessing the degree of non-participation in electoral politics.

Electoral non-participation: the record

THE DATA

Full details of the published voter participation figures for African states since 1957 are given in the Appendix at the end of the book.

Figure 3.1 summarises low turnout figures, since these may indicate significant disengagement and are less likely to be grossly exaggerated than the very high figures. It will be noted that, even under competitive democratic rules and assuming that there is a high registration and accurate recording, in many countries less than half of those on the electoral roll actually voted. Are these to be seen as millions of disengagers? To answer that, we must distinguish between political non-participation and political disengagement.

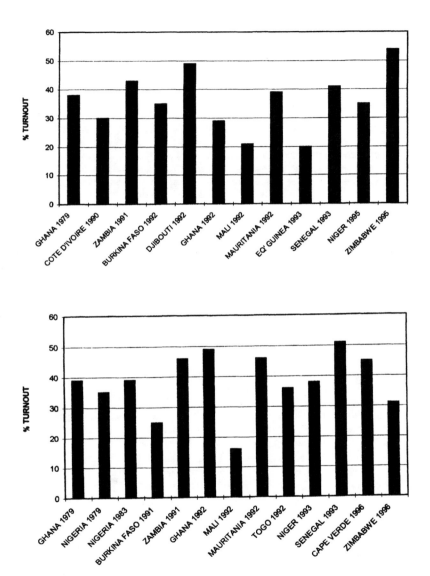

Figure 3.1 Competitive elections with high rates of non-participation for registered voters. (Top) Parliamentary National Assembly elections (Bottom) Presidential elections

NON-PARTICIPATION DISTINGUISHED FROM DISENGAGEMENT

Not every occasion when a citizen ceases to vote can be called disengagement. A number of other factors may be present.

Individual limitations

Commenting on turnout figures of 20 per cent in the Ivorian general election of 1980, the *ARB* (1980, vol. 17 (11):5857) argued:

> For the man in the street who has not voted, democracy is not easy. In fact, many ill prepared voters were seen to hesitate before the complex machinery of the voting procedures. Choosing between candidates is not easy in the face of illiteracy, neither is the selection of the right ballot paper. Not even the provision of different coloured paper for different candidates helped in this matter. Therefore, many of those entitled to do so, did not vote.

Or, again, difficulties were experienced in the Mauritanian referendum of 1991 concerning the distribution of voting cards. Most voters were illiterate and yet were required to find their names and numbers on very long lists put up in the prefectures in order to obtain their voting cards, which were then drawn up on the spot (*ARB* 1991, vol. 28 (7):10194–5).

Organisational failure

All manner of problems have beset elections through inadequate electoral administration, wilful or otherwise, or through weak/non-existent mobilisation by political groups. There have been low turnout figures as a result of an inadequate number of polling stations in vast areas (for example, Kenya in 1969) and names poorly transcribed on electoral lists (for example, Cape Verde in 1985) (*ARB* 1986, vol. 22 (12):7894). Nor has the matter been removed by democratisation. There have been insufficient ballot papers and these with printing errors (for example, Senegal in 1996) and the accidental destruction of the electoral lists (for example, Mali in 1992) (*ARB* 1992, vol. 29 (1):10414; 1996, vol. 33 (11):12463). Nor is it surprising that 'confusion was paramount' when an election was held in the midst of a civil war, as in Sierra Leone in 1996. Apart from the intimidation of soldiers attacking civilians as they went to vote and missing voter lists, only 1.5 million of an estimated 2.6 million voters were able to register, due to being cut off by warring factions or being refugees in neighbouring countries (*ARB* 1996, vol. 33 (2):12144), and of these only 750,764 actually voted – that is, 29 per cent.

As regards political parties, poor organisation and lacklustre campaigns (often, of course, because poorly funded) have frequently been said to explain, at least in part, low turnouts. Even in Tanzania's first independence elections in 1965, perhaps one-third did not register, often because they knew very little about the forthcoming election or the implications of not registering (Hyden 1967:63). Certainly very few will vote who have not been subject to party or government official persuasion. Surveying two regions in Kenya in 1960, researchers found that voters came to register 'without any persuasion' (14 per cent and 34 per cent); 'as a result of persuasion by government officials' (69 per cent and 60 per cent); and 'as a result of persuasion by a political leader' (4 per cent and 2 per cent) (Bennett and Rosberg 1961:68).

Intimidation
The threat of violence or personal loss has frequently prevented people from participating either at all or with opposition groups in particular. The threats may be very general, as in the 1967 local government elections in The Gambia. Here the local MP and governing party propagandists toured villages warning people that, if they did not support the ruling party candidate, the government would 'punish them'. However vague, the threat certainly kept most women from voting and men only dared vote for the opposition by wearing many jujus (Weil 1971:116). The abandonment of secrecy at the polling booth for novel, open methods, such as 'measuring' the level of hand-clapping (Zaire in 1975) or the length of the queue for each candidate (Kenya in 1988), likewise frightened off support for opposition candidates. Few were prepared to be so public about their rejection of the government party before the very officials that would very probably determine their enjoyment or otherwise of government benefits in the coming years. More recently, the 1995 Guinean election was marred by armed military personnel scrutinising those at the polling stations (*ARB* 1995, vol. 32 (6):11882).

State exclusion
By this is meant the closing down of opportunities for popular involvement. State departicipation strategies have included the reversal of federal structures to centralised ones; the harassment or banning of opposition political parties and press; the closing of polling stations; decreasing regard for legislatures; state take-overs of voluntary organisations; the running down of single-party machinery at local level; the transfer of many local government functions to central government; a change from elected to appointed political representation at regional level (see Kasfir 1974, 1976; for Kenya in the 1960s, see Gertzel 1970). Even multi-party constitutions have not removed all problems. In Mali's 1992 election, only two minutes' air time was granted to the twenty-one parties on the state media each day. As a result, parties confined themselves to simply repeating their slogans (*ARB* 1992, vol. 29 (1):10414).

Deliberate political strategy

Boycotts, whether organised or spontaneous and individual, are engagement, not disengagement, and reflect political awareness, not apathy. In Uganda, the kingdom of Buganda feared that an independent unitary state would be led by non-Bagandans, who were often, after years of domination by and privilege for the Bagandans, anti-Bagandan. Having failed to secure promises of independence or federalism in negotiations, they boycotted the Legislative Council election of 1961. Only 35,000 of the estimated one million eligible voters enrolled – that is, 3.5 per cent (Low 1971, ch. 6). In Benin (Dahomey), the opposition campaign was so effective in the 1968 presidential election that only 25 per cent voted overall and in the northern departments of Borgou it was down to 3 per cent. Such was the scale of abstentions that even the military rulers had to accept that the election had no legitimacy and they annulled the results. Perhaps surprisingly, with the nomination of their own candidate as president shortly afterwards, they secured a 73 per cent participation rate, despite a renewed opposition call for a boycott. A spontaneous boycott occurred at the Ghanaian 1987 'Unigov' referendum, where the turnout was only 42 per cent. As Chazan says, the high rates of abstention can hardly be due to apathy, given the 'almost inhuman effort to ensure voter turnout'. In her view, the figures reflected:

> a large, but tacit rejection of the Union Government proposals. They also mirrored a more fundamental dissatisfaction with Unigov opponents as viable alternatives to the military regime. The sub-surface process of detachment, of the desire to disavow association either with the political community or the state, was given expression by the voters' inclination to forego participation in state–centre power conflicts. (Chazan, in Hayward 1987:78)

Organised boycotts have continued to be used under the new democratic regimes. Let us take two examples. In the 1993 Togo presidential election, the overall turnout was 36 per cent, with less than 13 per cent in the thirteen southern prefectures where the main opposition leaders came from, and about 17.5 per cent in Lomé the capital (*ARB* 193, vol. 30 (8):11109); and the 1995 presidential election in Côte d'Ivoire saw a boycott in protest against an electoral code that aimed to eliminate from the race the only serious candidate. It secured abstention rates of 80–100 per cent in opposition party strongholds (*ARB* 1995, vol. 32 (10):12003).

But, if non-participation is not always, or entirely, disengagement, there are occasions when low turnout can be linked with political disengagement. In the parliamentary elections of Upper Volta (Burkina Faso) in 1978, only 40 per cent voted. Some put this high abstention rate down to the coming of the first of the season's rains on the polling day, with the peasants, who formed 90 per cent of the population, preferring to work in the fields. More convincing, however, is the argument that the abstention, despite the urgent appeal to vote by the president, 'may be attributed to disillusionment with a range of politicians which had hardly changed since Independence and which is divided by personal quarrels, some of long standing' (*Le Monde*, quoted in *ARB* 1978, vol. 15 (5):487). The observer also noted 'the hostile reserve of the trade unions' and 'the scepticism of much of the civil service'. That it was disillusionment with the candidates, and not field duties, seems confirmed by the equally low turnout of 43 per cent later in the month for the presidential run-off election. Large numbers of the Mossi, who make up 66 per cent of the population, were unwilling to vote for Lamizana, who did not speak their language. Yet the traditional chiefs urged them not to vote for the alternative candidate, Yameogo, since he had abolished some of their traditional privileges. Faced with this cross-pressure, many did not vote at all.

The repeated themes raised by those no longer voting are: lack of, or diminishing, affiliation to the state; preoccupation with survival, for which elections seem an irrelevant sideshow; a sense of the results being a foregone conclusion; the lack of appeal to self-interest; and the minimal differentiation between the candidates. Reflecting many of the 69 per cent who did not vote in Zimbabwe's presidential elections in 1996, one Harare market woman said, 'things will be the same if you vote or if you don't vote, so I won't' (*Economist* 16/3/96), whilst a consultant working for the Ministry of Local Government told me: 'What's the point of voting? It won't affect the result. Only one party can win' (interview, 1997).

Electoral non-participation over time

NON-PARTICIPATION AND POLITICAL SYSTEMS

Do electoral participation and non-participation vary over time and according to political systems? This section will examine the main periods in African electoral history. Though they are not always synchronised across Africa, five periods can be distinguished. They are (i) traditional (precolonial); (ii) imperial (the colonial period prior to universal suffrage); (iii) early democratic (from self-rule under colonial authority through to the dismantling of democratic structures shortly after independence); (iv) authoritarian (the days of single-party or no-party rule); and (v) late democratic (the reintroduction of multi-party elections in the 1990s). Most, but not all African countries, went through these five periods in sequence, each with its distinctive patterns of participation and non-participation in formal politics.

The traditional period

For many African societies, leadership was hereditary within the dynasty's lineage (though not always uncontested) upon the death of the leader, or transferred in his later years (Coissoro 1966; Beach 1980). Yet there is also an extensive, although by no means universal, tradition of leaders being 'elected' upon the predecessor's death. There were six salient characteristics of these traditional 'elections'. First, candidates were usually chosen from the elite (normally the royals) by the elite. Secondly, the selection or confirmation process was informal, seeking consensus through debate, possibly institutionalised within a council (Kimambo 1969:54–7). The Ashanti actually granted commoners a veto in this process (Busia 1968:9–11). Thirdly, with a few exceptions, men dominated the procedure. Exceptions include some of the Oyo rulers of Nigeria (Smith 1969) and the matriarchal communities that arose in Malawi in 1900–30 (White 1987:101).[1] Fourthly, there was face-to-face contact between those desiring leadership and those adults who by custom selected and/or approved them. Fifthly, the process was parochial, in that only small numbers from small areas were involved. Sixthly, the emphasis was on the personable and ascriptive qualities of the candidates, rather than on their programme. For instance, the Ashanti looked for those who had intelligence, humility, generosity, manliness and physical fitness (Busia 1968:9–11; Davidson 1992:61). The kingmakers of Oyo not only sought a ruler 'who would respect and conform to the constitutional conventions of the kingdom ... [but] deliberately avoided a candidate whose presence or personality seemed too commanding' (Smith 1969:112).

In other words, for the vast majority of the people, there was no opportunity given for participation in the formal selection of the leaders and little expectation of such. According to Santos, the sixteenth-century Catholic priest and trader, if there was political dissent, it took the form either of the alignment of the people behind one or another member of the ruling dynasty or of emigration (Beach 1980). The picture portrayed by some of a near universal system of participation based on a suspicion of executive power (e.g. Davidson 1992) is rightly taken to task by Mamdani as a presentation of uniformity that flies in the face of the administrative chiefs of conquest states and the widespread 'unfreedom of Africans in the time of turmoil that was the nineteenth century' (Mamdani 1996:40).

---

[1] For an example of the extraordinary power of the wives of a former seventeenth century Shona king to veto the appointed successor, see Beach 1980:97–8.

The election of traditional chiefs was not necessarily abolished by colonial and independence rulers, but where it has survived it has been marginalised, since chiefs have less and less land to distribute and other resources invariably lie within the hands of the state. With marginalisation has come a diminution in the contestation of chieftaincies and an increasing move towards automatic selection through the eldest male heir.

The imperial period
The colonial powers assumed the right to appoint local and regional leaders. For those loyal to the new authorities, it could mean the reward of confirmation. Others saw their chieftaincies simply abolished under amalgamations and reorganisations that suited colonial social control. Still others were replaced by more 'suitable' appointments, according to colonial moral standards and requirements of pliability (Mamdani (1996) gives a masterly account of the nature of indirect rule). Whether these appointments were invented/reconstituted African hierarchies, for example the Nigerian emirs, or were elevated outsiders, for example France's 'canton chiefs', what Lan says of Rhodesia could be extended to a much wider area: 'in exchange for their political security and economic advancement [they] were obliged to relinquish the greater part of the authority that their predecessors held'. Thus they lost the rights to try criminal cases and to redistribute land. The only function they did have was the authority to collect taxes.

> All in all the chiefs had become minor civil servants with powers of constables. As such they were subject to the wishes of their masters, the Native Commissioners, and no longer to those of their ancestors ... or of their people. (Lan 1985:137–8)

Participation, therefore, was removed from the people at the level of their daily experience. In addition, a new structure was superimposed over the local level, and this drew each village into a common destiny with a multitude of others, even though they were far removed from them in geography, history and culture. This structure was the nation-state (Davidson 1992). Like the local level, this too had largely unelected officials making decisions that profoundly affected daily life. Yet in this case the officials could not even claim a measure of legitimacy based on cultural and linguistic familiarity. The small fraction of colonial power that was open to election by a few Africans was little more than tokenism. Collier summarises the data for territorial elections as follows:

> Before 1945 very few elections had been held in any African colony at the territorial level and those that did occur involved in important measure a franchise restricted to European residents. Among the British colonies the

vote was extended to European settlers in Kenya in 1920 and in Zambia in 1924 and to a small number of Africans residing in the capital city or a few other municipalities in British West Africa also in the mid-1920s [namely Ghana, Nigeria and Sierra Leone, where some Africans were elected to the Legislative Councils]. In French Africa the vote [for the French National Assembly] was granted in 1848 in Senegal to French citizens, the category which included natives of France and of the four overseas communes established in Senegal. In addition, a very limited franchise was introduced in 1925 in Dahomey, Ivory Coast, Guinea and Mali and in 1936 in the four colonies of French Equatorial Africa. (Collier 1982:34–5)

Details have not been preserved about local area elections, although some local councils, with at least some elected members, are known to have been established. There is information, however, about the municipal councils set up in African cities. Unlike most local area elections, these predate the territory-wide elections. In fact, Freetown, Sierra Leone, had one as early as 1787:

> In French Africa, before World War II, five municipal councils were set up in the four colonies of French Equatorial Africa, but membership on these was by appointment. In French West Africa, twenty three municipal councils were set up before World War II, fourteen of which were in Senegal and only nine in the seven other colonies of the Federation. Some of these ... had councils elected by a restricted suffrage; the others ... had appointed councils. (Collier 1982:34, fn. 2).

The imperial period, despite its democratic rhetoric, was one of departicipation and exclusion by the state of African people from formal politics (Mamdani 1996). The redrawing of the constituencies at the local and national level only further removed the possibility of Africans identifying with the electoral institutions. Parallel to the nonparticipation by exclusion, however, was a society-initiated and 'spiritual' disengagement from foreign occupying powers.

The early democratic period
After the Second World War, the British and French colonial authorities expanded the franchise and gave the opportunity to those Africans eligible to contest and vote in the territory-wide parliamentary/assembly elections. Not that the breakthrough was due to colonial generosity and democratic benevolence. Rather the continual expansion of the franchise was more the result of African (largely the elite) and external (for example, the United Nations (UN) and the USA) pressure for participation, self-determination and independence. Elections marking the first steps in state-wide democratic participation took place in the 1950s in Tanzania (Tanganyika), The Gambia, Ghana (Gold Coast), Senegal, Sierra Leone and Guinea.

For these new elections, larger and more formal political structures were required than had previously been known. The traditional face-to-face contact with and intimate knowledge of the candidates were not restored. As for the 'national' issues that the campaigns were fought on, only self-rule and independence gripped the whole populace. In addition, voters were introduced to a new world of electoral conduct, from ballot and secret voting to supervised counting, detailed public announcements and gallant defeat. Nevertheless, despite the confusion, after so many years of state denial of participation, one is not surprised at the mixture of dignity and exuberance that was reported at the very first elections with universal suffrage, especially those that formed the first independence governments.[2]

Though there is little information at the micro level regarding participation/non-participation, figures between colonies can be compared. Interestingly, the participation levels in the French and British colonies are not identical but are higher among the French. Collier's explanation is that the French held more elections and a bandwagon effect provided additional opportunity for the highly dominant party of each territory to extend its organisation and to mobilise the electorate. In her view, new participants readily responded to and identified with the dominant party, since primary group ties were not so readily politicised in a regime of direct rule and list voting (Collier 1982:92–4).

The British preference for decentralisation and indirect rule, on the other hand, reduced considerably the opportunity for one party to dominate. Instead, local and traditional rulers had a much greater opportunity to enter the political arena and seek support from those with ties of affinity. The disadvantage from the point of view of electoral participation, however, was that the multitude of parties kept them small and too limited financially to mount widespread mobilisation. In addition, they had less 'practice' at contesting elections compared with their French counterparts, owing largely to the British policy of not holding ballots in uncontested single-member constituencies.

In summary, Collier's argument is that, despite similar participation rates in the colonies, very different factors were at work. In the British colonies, with the fractionalised elite, it was competition among parties that stimulated voter participation. In the French colonies, with their single cohesive elite, it was mobilisation by a single dominant party that was crucial.

---

[2] Caute's account of Harare's main polling station on 27 February 1980 describes a line a quarter of a mile long, which was quiet and sober in the immediate vicinity, but around the corner he met 'wave after wave of crowing "cocks", young men prancing and strutting like roosters'. Or, again, in Kambazuma township he was surrounded by young men speaking 'passionately of land, liberation and land again' (Caute 1983:41).

The evidence of these first nationwide elections based on universal suffrage is that high participation by those on the electoral roll was the norm. Thus, the figures for parliamentary elections in Uganda (excluding Buganda) in 1958 were 85 per cent; for Mauritius in 1959 91 per cent; for Zaire in 1960 80 per cent; for Zambia in 1962 90 per cent; and for Cameroon in 1964 91 per cent.

The authoritarian period
Mobilisation at the time of independence was relatively easy. The anti-colonial message was universally popular and the promises of a bright future were readily believed. Once in government, however, ruling parties had to reconstitute themselves from nationalist protest organisations into development agencies working within limited budgets. It was a transition that most were to find extremely difficult. The gulf between the electorate's expectations and the harsh reality of resources available, encouraged both foolhardy expenditure and over-sensitivity to criticism about broken promises. Disillusionment quickly followed. Said one villager in Kwilu Province, Congo, in 1962:

> Before Independence, we dreamed that it would bring us masses of marvellous things. All of that was to descend upon us from the sky ... Deliverance and salvation [would come] ... But here it is more than two years that we have been waiting, and nothing has come ... On the contrary life is more difficult, we are more poor than before. (Quoted in Fox *et al.* 1965–6:91)

In this situation, most governments saw that the only way to secure their position and to drive through the economic changes was to take away popular participation. Chazan argues that notions of democracy were held only superficially by most nationalist leaders anyway. At best, its content was little more than the demand for freedom from colonisation (Chazan 1994b:67–70). In the name, therefore, of national unity, management efficiency and development acceleration, opposition parties were eliminated, local government was emaciated, voluntary associations that could be a political platform for interest groups were taken over and the media were gagged. Even if the elected governments did not do this, the military, who invariably intervened at a later date, certainly did.

What impact did government-initiated departicipation have? In Tanzania, for example, where the government party dominated political life, the take-over of government functions was almost total. Local administration, welfare activity, police investigation and criminal adjudication (along with social criticism) became roles of the multifaceted single party. In practice, it introduced party patronage (and its corresponding corruption) into service provision formerly carried out by non-partisan government agencies and contracts. As a response to faltering support and participation the policy only exacerbated matters. Miller (1970:556) observes that, in the period 1964–9, rural people, faced with financial irresponsibility and embezzlement, coercion to join in party activities and abuse of office for personal gain, chose to withdraw still further from any form of political participation. They simply offered lip service to the party aims, but little tangible support. In Hyden's words, the Tanzanian peasants:

> soon learned ways of inducing the officials to believe that they were enjoying widespread support [for the development projects they were promoting] ... Many politicians did not realise that the peasant orientation to outside intrusions into their local affairs did not really change with independence. Peasants retained an instrumental view of the politician ... Politics remained a superstructural phenomenon with little or no relationship to rural production. (Hyden 1980:86–8)

Denying the people participation did not bring the hoped-for unity and, seeing that non-accountability worsened performance, it did not bring performance legitimacy either. What it did produce was an entrenchment of disengagement. The reality of that disengagement was not lost on President Nyerere, whose frustration was evident in a broadcast on 6 November 1973 on Radio Tanzania. Having reminded the people of all the benefits that his government had brought to them, he then asked what the peasants had done in return. Answering his own question, he claimed they had done virtually nothing, but had remained idle and evaded their responsibilities (Hyden 1980:130). Yet the disengagement was not as total as he imagined. As in other African countries, election subjects were officially delimited, but the forbidden subjects of the substantive problems facing the government and the nature of the polity inevitably arose in covert debates (Chazan 1979:147). What appeared as non-participation was participation that had been re-routed out of sight.

Variation in electoral non-participation within social groups

Discontinuance may be universal, but it is not uniform. It is necessary to look, therefore, behind the quantitative totals of voter turnout figures to the qualitative differences between social groups.

RELIGIOUS GROUPS
Religious groups cover the entire spectrum of political responses, from accommodation and quietism to radical opposition and rebellion.

Vinger categorises them as 'aggressive sects' and 'avoidance sects' (Vinger 1971). Many have highlighted the role religious leaders have played in encouraging or discouraging their followers as regards their participation in politics generally and elections in particular. Sometimes the withdrawal doctrine has been temporary and partial, reflecting particular circumstances, such as colonial rule. But, with other groups, the position of steadfast refusal to take part in elections is part of an anti-state, anti-politics stand, based on principle, and all members are required to follow it, whatever their participation may have been before their conversion. A more extended discussion of separatist religious groups is given in Chapter 5, but it may be noted here that those who viewed the state as the propagator of force and/or evil values wanted nothing to do with choosing its representatives or giving it legitimacy. This has been rare among Christian mainstream denominations. Even fundamentalist Christians, despite their commonly avowed political neutrality, have increasingly shown interest in social issues with political overtones, such as Islamicisation and public corruption (Marshall 1991:36; Haynes 1996a, b). The one section that does stand out as largely indifferent, if not hostile, to formal politics and participation is made up of the separatist and independent Christian movements. Among them may be numbered the Jehovah's Witnesses, South African Zionist Churches and the Apostolic Churches. Their stand, not surprisingly, has attracted government party resentment, harassment and, in the case of Malawian Jehovah's Witnesses in 1967–83, a persecution amounting to little less than a pogrom, driving up to 35,000 out of the country (Hodges 1985). Despite the persecution of separatist groups, their members have steadfastly refused to engage in formal politics any more. They wish to withdraw from power rather than to capture it.

CLASSES

Inasmuch as turnout figures are available for individual constituencies, it appears that the urban proletariat, in particular, shows least interest in voting. Following the Zimbabwean election of 1995, union leaders spoke of workers not bothering to vote and the lowest national turnout figures appeared to be in the industrial sections of the three largest urban areas of Harare, Bulawayo and Mutare, each recording something like 30–40 per cent. Elsewhere, too, it is the largest cities that stand out as having the lowest figures in recent elections; for example, Libreville, Nouakchott and Abidjan have all drawn comment.

The social class most extensively examined for its distinctive political behaviour has been the peasants. Migdal (1974) has characterised the precapitalist era as one marked by inwardly orientated peasant communities. That is, peasants minimised contact beyond the family and the immediate area. It was a disengagement based on bitter experiences of exploitation at the hands of traders, merchants, moneylenders, bandits and the state (in the persons of tax collectors and police). Yet it was a policy that only heightened their political powerlessness, for it cut them off from forming a political alliance with other peasants, which could have given them a more effective influence on the ruling classes.

A number of phenomena compelled the peasant village to one of outward orientation and engagement. There was the rising population, with its associated land shortage and falling incomes; the cash economy, including state tax demands; and external employment opportunities, whether seasonal work on the plantations, or long-term contracts in the distant urban markets. With the new phenomena, the peasant political world changed shape. The exclusive importance of the local village was diminished by political units determined by the state and often larger than any peasant had ever travelled. Further, the key role of the village chief, which the peasants had often had a role in selecting/confirming, was now replaced by a constituency representative, which the peasants voted for but whom they may never have seen before the election and who had been selected by a political party run by and in the interests of the urban elite.

Though most peasant households faced increasing economic hardship as a result of the socio-economic changes, they perceived that new resources were to be had from the state, provided they had a sympathetic representative. Typical of a rural party was the Parti Solidaire Africain of the Congo (Democratic Republic of the Congo). It offered on its 1960 campaign posters: 'Total reduction of unemployment and work for all; ... free primary and secondary education; rises in salaries for all; improvement of housing; ... free medical care for all non-salaried people' (quoted in Fox *et al.* 1965–6:87). In its campaigning, it also promised that every village would have a petrol station dispensing free petrol; an abundance of vehicles for transportation; a mill to grind manioc; and a pump to draw water. On these promises, it won thirteen seats in the National Chamber of Deputies and joined the coalition government of Lumumba. In circumstances like these, which were reproduced all over Africa, it is hardly surprising that:

> the notion that the representative is elected to look after national rather than constituency interests has very little currency in contemporary Africa. Elections are not perceived as a means of choosing the rulers most able to rule the nation as a whole, but of choosing those who will best promote and protect the interests of the community. (Chabal 1992:208)

Lacking the resources, organisation and leadership (lost through social mobility) to form their own independent parties, peasants have opted for patron–client relationships with other parties. They have bargained with the only resource they have, that is, numbers: numbers that can secure the individual constituency and enough constituencies to secure the government; numbers that can swell rallies and demonstrations to something newsworthy; numbers that can threaten opposing groups if mobilised. For these services, they expect occasional benefits.

Given this instrumental view of the politician, it is not surprising that peasant electorates actually show quite low levels of non-participation in voting and party membership. As long as there is something tangible to be had, then, whatever the overall party programme or ideology, there is little gain in disengagement. Rothchild, for instance, depicts Rawlings as having, by and large, won the support of the rural areas of Ghana in 1992 through cocoa price rises, electrification and the like (Rothchild 1995). The figure he quotes of 60 per cent support may not be so overwhelming in view of the fact that the turnout figure was only 49 per cent (and that based on a weak and outdated enrolment); nevertheless he was impressed by the extent of backing for Rawlings that he saw in the rural areas. Interviewees made clear to him 'that the rise in civil service salaries, increased job prospects, rises in cocoa prices, and the prospects of additional services all figured in Rawlings's support in the rural areas' (D. Rothchild, personal communication, 29/8/95). Hyden goes further and argues that, in the case of at least the 1965 parliamentary election in Tanzania, the depth of the peasants' evaluation of an incumbent's political performance was beyond that of western electorates (Hyden 1980:89). It may have been made on a utilitarian basis, but it was not biased by such institutional factors as party and religious loyalty. A similar sophistication is reported by Barkan and Okumu (1978) from Kenya in the 1970s.

Where, therefore, there is peasant non-participation in elections, it is unlikely to be political apathy, but more a cool, if selfish, calculation about benefits and costs. Certainly, as improvements in lifestyle have faltered during the 1980s and 1990s, many peasants have become convinced that the state has no solutions to their needs. (For Tanzania, see Miller 1970:564–5).

GENDER

Overall, there is a pronounced tendency for women's political participation to be less than men's, even when government parties have actively sought to recruit them, as Touré's Parti Démocratique de Guinée (PDG) did in Guinea and Nkrumah's Convention People's Party (CPP) in Ghana. But this generalisation masks some important variations. Amadiume speaks, for instance, of anti-power movements, such as indigenous women's movements, which have their own autonomous organisations. They do not want to be part of a state system, but only wish to defend and maintain that autonomy (Amadiume 1995:35). For those who do want to be involved, they are much more likely to be involved in politics informally, such as participating in short-lived campaigns and makeshift direct-action organisations or, in the case of intellectuals, activity in non-governmental organisations (NGOs). Again, they are more likely to participate indirectly in a male-dominated political world, either through their menfolk or through taking part in women's associations (Randall 1987:52–66). The Women's League of the Zimbabwe African National Union – Patriotic Front (ZANU-PF) in Zimbabwe, for instance, is 'huge and extremely effective in mobilising votes', male as well as female, for the male-dominated party (J. Kazembe, personal interview, 26/3/97). Then a distinction must be made about the level at which they participate in formal politics. Hirschmann (1991) argues that African women are most active where politics fuses with economics and community. This often means that the local, rather than the national, arena is the centre of their interest, for it is at this level that their concerns about schools, child care and social services are decided. It is also this level that is most acceptable and at which they may feel they can hold public office without the same degree of male prejudice.[3]

Parpart, on the other hand, argues that female non-participation at the national level is not so much due to the agenda as to male dominance:

> Despite women's active and important role in the nationalist struggles, decolonization was essentially a transfer of power from one group of men to another. Consequently, African women have been under-represented in the state and have reaped few of the benefits which the state provides. Many women have reacted to this inequity by pulling away from the state, concentrating on economic survival instead. For the most part these women see the state as an obstacle to be avoided, rather than as a benefactor to be milked. To that end they have employed a wide variety of strategies to ensure their survival in the face of an often hostile, male-dominated state. (Parpart, in Rothchild and Chazan 1988:235)

Where political interest among women has been found to flourish, it has often been when most of the men have been removed by labour migration or war. For example, between 1900 and 1930 in southern Malawi, there arose matriarchal communities as a result of the male absence on plantations for three to eight months of the year, combined

---

[3] The claim that women's participation will vary according to the level of government is, apparently, not just an African phenomenon. Hayes and Bean found it to be so amongst Western nations (Hayes and Bean 1993:681).

with traditional matrilineal inheritance laws. Whilst the villages 'belonged to the women', even in the selection of chiefs the women had the principal voice. The successor, though usually a man, had to be a maternal brother or nephew of the deceased. However, when men abandoned the plantations to live permanently in the villages once again, the balance of power shifted back to them and the women resumed their focus on 'domestic' politics (White 1987:101).

A second example may be taken from Kenya in the 1960s, where there was a strikingly high proportion of women among the registered voters:

> This was said to be as high as 80 per cent in one part of Kiambu district. Such a figure is to be explained in part by the high Kikuyu labour migration, particularly from the southern area to Nairobi and in part also by the high male death roll of the Emergency. Moreover, the Emergency has made women a highly conscious political group among both the Kikuyu and their associated tribes, particularly the Embu. The high registration of women in the Central Province and in some districts elsewhere provided a marked contrast to the African election of 1957 in Kenya when, through the then existing qualitative franchise, less than 1 per cent of the registered electorate was women. (Bennett and Rosberg 1961:65)

Even the temporary removal of men turned to the advantage of women in Tanzania. Attempts were made by men in the 1960s to avoid tax payment in a situation where the tax collecting personnel were also the electoral registration officials. 'This fear might explain the fact that in several constituencies more women [who are not eligible for this tax] were registered' (Harris 1967:29).

Yet, despite these exceptions, African women generally feel at a disadvantage compared with men when it comes to engaging in politics. This is especially true in Muslim societies, where women are sometimes kept at home, segregated from outside contact. But ideologies that prescribe the private domestic sphere as the female domain and the public and political as the male prerogative predominate throughout Africa. So, even where women have actively entered the male-dominated urban economic world, many have shunned the politics that regulate it after an initial interest. They have found the terms set by the male elite too restrictive. Their allocated role has too often been to be cheer-leaders for the men, from the ranks of the party's women's wing. When they have overcome the blocking tactics and penetrated the policy-making arenas, they have been accused of abandoning their proper female role, ridiculed, vilified or, worse, sidelined and ignored (Geisler 1995). Manzvanzvike's analysis of educated feminists in Zimbabwe was that they fell into two camps: either those who had sought to penetrate the ruling party at the cell level and, finding themselves blocked, left politics disillusioned; or those who had never attempted to enter formal politics on the grounds that the whole political system was irrelevant to the issues that concerned them, preferring feminist organisations as pressure groups (T. Manzvanzvike, personal interview, 20/3/97). Examples abound of women ignoring conventional politics and concentrating on their own economic associations (such as the Ghanaian and Nigerian market women) or (especially those professionals with a social agenda) withdrawing into the NGO sector. Such autonomy, however, magnifies gender participation gaps in formal politics and confirms women's marginality there (Staudt 1987:207).

AGE GROUPS

In many African countries, there appears to be a clear pattern of non-participation according to age, with the youngest being least involved. In 1965 (according the Radio Addis Ababa 24/6/65, quoted in *ARB* 1965, vol. 2 (6):316), the Chairman of the Ethiopian Election Board complained of the unimpressive number of registered voters for the parliamentary elections. In particular, he was critical of the 'so-called educated young people' in Addis Ababa, 'who have shown no interest in registering themselves either as candidates or as voters.' Other concerns mentioned by the Election Board were that the electorate in the past, instead of electing candidates for their personal ability and sense of responsibility, had 'returned the persons they hated so as to get rid of them for their area, or on certain corrupt grounds'! Peil gives a more substantiated account of the same phenomenon in Nigeria. While her survey showed that 30 per cent of men over forty-nine had contacted the local government in the survey period, only 8 per cent of men under twenty-five had done so. For women the proportion was stable at about 10 per cent for those aged twenty-five to forty-eight and for those over forty-nine, but only 2 per cent for those under twenty-five. Her conclusion was that it appeared that age gave men 'increased influence or feeling of efficacy' and these increased their willingness to participate. On the other hand, 'personality and economic success are probably more important than age for women' in determining efficacy and participation (Peil 1974:308). More specific factors have been suggested in Zimbabwe for young people's indifference, including consumerism, the absence of the politicisation through civil conflict that their parents experienced, the diminishing influence of party coercion to vote and a general disillusionment with politicians, who, after sixteen years of independence, have failed to make any significant improvement in their standard of living (S. Nkiwane, personal interview, 26/3/97).

The relative significance of macro-scale and micro-scale factors

The difficulty with considering variation in patterns of political discontinuance by social group is that the latter are concepts rather than real entities. Those classified a member may not necessarily have an awareness of their membership and are unlikely to have anything but a passing acquaintance even with a very limited number of their category. In practice, collective activity falls to much smaller groups or personal networks. Though these may have a high proportion of members from a single category, there is no inevitability about homogeneity. Generalisations about groups that are no more than statistical aggregates have their place (through them the likely outlook of a person can be predicted) but they explain little about the process by which the opinions are formed: these are a product of both macro-scale and micro-scale factors.

The balance between the two in determining the form of political discontinuance has been the subject of much debate. Four principal perspectives attempt to conceptualise the relative significance of macro and micro factors in accounting for the majority of decisions to participate or not. The first focuses on the individual's perception (psychological); the second on the individual's status or resources (resources); the third on the party system (mobilisation); and the fourth on government achievements (performance legitimacy).

PSYCHOLOGICAL PERSPECTIVES
Many of the electoral reviews of the 1960s and 1970s concentrated their attention on attitudinal studies, as they sought to measure political alienation, political anomie and legitimacy. Subjective evaluations of political interest, political ideals, personal trust/cynicism, government responsiveness, system performance, and civic pride and duty were undertaken (Gamson 1975; Inkeles 1969; Miller 1970; Verba 1972; Verba *et al.* 1978; Miller 1974; Easton 1975; Muller and Jukam 1977; Muller and Williams 1980; Hart 1978; and Kaase 1988). In essence, the studies claimed that negative evaluations about the political system and/or its leaders were associated with low levels of political participation. Although the emphasis was on independent variables, such as personality characteristics and reactions to political decisions, policies and events, objective categories, such as race and social background, were also accorded a place.

Though there was much debate at the time, and has been since, about the reliability of the indicators used in measuring the variables, an important and lasting outcome of the research was the disaggregation of the concept of support. As Hart puts it:

There is little in common between those who reject the norms of democratic politics and ground their discontent upon some alternative philosophy and those who judge their polity in the name of democracy and reject only its violation in practice. If alienation is estrangement, then it is the former group who are alienated, for their rejection of democratic politics is permanent and profound; the rejection of the distrustful is temporary and remedial. (Hart 1978:30)

As Citrin has noted, not every cynic is an 'alienated cynic' who sees no viable alternative to the incumbent authorities and rejects the current constitutional order. There is also the 'partisan cynic' – that is, the partisan of the 'outs', who can see no good with the 'ins' – and the 'ritualistic cynic', who shouts 'shoot the ref'' and calls all politics rubbish as a matter of course, but still wants the game to continue (Citrin 1974:978). To use Easton's succinct conceptual summary, there is diffuse support and specific support (Easton 1965, 1975). Unfortunately, much of African governance in the past thirty years has caused a profound distaste both for individual rulers and for the system that brings them to power and keeps them there. Establishing a distinction, therefore, may prove largely academic.

Clearly, this is a perspective of participation where the individual is content to have achieved only some of their objectives. People will disengage when they perceive no rewards for having participated in the past and when they have no expectations of any rewards for doing so in the future. What each individual regards as an unsatisfactory reward and an unattractive prospect will be determined by their own values, which in turn reflect the prevailing values and customs of their surroundings. The individualism of personality characteristics, however, is a weak base for theory building, for it abstracts the individual from his/her social context and is therefore excessively voluntaristic. Further, research must rely on subjective self-assessment rather than objective measurements and makes difficult, or even denies the validity of, the social categorisation that facilitates the prediction of disengagement in given situations.

RESOURCE PERSPECTIVES

The shift from individual to structural factors was observable in the 1980s. Initially, the prime concern was socio-economic status, especially how income and education affected participation. At the international level, turnout figures were shown to be related to gross national product (GNP) per capita, whilst, at the national level, lower participation was shown to be a feature of those with lower education and income levels. Economic development and social class were seen, then, to have a role in political mobilisation.

Certainly, some of the resources needed for political participation, such as money and civic skills, are closely related to educational and work performance/opportunities. But that is not the whole story. Some civic skills are less stratified; for example, communication and organisational skills may be learnt in 'congregational' churches and associations, irrespective of status. These anomalies have led to Brady *et al.*'s refinement of the socio-economic status perspective. Brady and his colleagues argue that the key element for political participation is a broader definition of resources. Where there is inadequate time to take part in activities, insufficient money to make a contribution or under-developed civic skills, effective participation is unlikely (Brady *et al.* 1995). Although particular political activities require particular resources to be effective, such resources in fact vary in their association with socio-economic status. Money is obviously highly related to socio-economic status, but civic skills are less so and time hardly at all. Therefore, the degree of class basis behind political participation or non-participation differs according to the nature of the political activity. In the case of elections, it is evident that the key resource is not money or civic skills, but time, though political interest is stimulated by the level of educational experience. This would be largely true of campaigning as well, again with education assisting in the ability to express oneself. Resources, therefore, are not distributed between, or even within, different classes. Different activities require different configurations of resources, and thus groups that choose not to engage may not be clearly distinguished by their class alone. For instance, it has already been noted that the gender factor in African politics cuts across class divisions.

The third focus of participation perspectives moves away from the individual's psychology or status/resource to the political system or, more particularly, the party system.

PARTY SYSTEM PERSPECTIVES

It could be said that people do not participate in politics because they do not want to (the psychological emphasis); because they cannot (the resource emphasis); because they are not allowed to (the human rights emphasis); or because nobody asked them. The latter implies isolation from the recruitment networks through which people are mobilised into politics.

For some, the key is the relationship between party systems and national cleavage structures. Where national parties correspond with these, whether they be religion, occupation, income, language/ethnicity or land-holding, identification and therefore participation are increased, since the outcome of the election takes on an easily identifiable significance. Powell claims that:

> Where these linkages are relatively stable, they provide cues to even poorly informed and less interested voters as to the interpretation of issues and candidate choices in given elections ... The presence of strong, continuing expectation about parties and cleavage alignments, not only creates easily identifiable choice for citizens, but also makes it easier for parties to seek out supporters and mobilize them at election time. (Powell 1980:13–14)

Certainly one recognises this identification in Africa's many ethnic-based parties, which command near-total support from their regional strongholds. Powell's argument would suggest that increased levels of party competitiveness will raise the voting turnout. Or, to put it in terms of Hayward's typology of elections as being competitive, semi-competitive and non-competitive (Hayward 1987), competitive elections that offer a chance to change office-holders and even regimes will engage the highest proportion of the voters.

This framework, however, works best where national parties compete for the support of those who have a strong loyalty to and interest in the state as a whole. In reality, in Africa, neither of these assumptions must be taken for granted. Where politics has been 'tribalised', a national competitive election may be a one-horse race within the ethnically homogeneous region/constituency. Even given a national consciousness, minority groups that support their ethnic party are faced with the disincentive of the dictatorship of the majority. Powell anticipates lower turnouts in situations where the election outcome is a foregone conclusion and yet, as Collier observes in colonial French West Africa, an overwhelmingly dominant party will have such a control on available resources that it should be able to organise an extensive and effective mobilisation. The conflicting currents are seen at work in Zimbabwe. In the 1996 election, such was the dominance of ZANU-PF at the time (it held 98 per cent of the seats in parliament) that most voters saw the result as inevitable. On the other hand, such were the party's resources (it got $3.4 million a year state finance, being the only party with the fifteen seats required to qualify) that its army of party workers could reach into the remote villages, promising villagers food and seed packs and offering them T-shirts. To an opposition party MP, the contrast was one where 'you campaign on a bicycle when they're campaigning by helicopter' (*Economist* 16/3/96). Given the eventual turnout figure of 31 per cent, the deleterious effect of a foregone conclusion seems to have had the upper hand.

It seems, therefore, that the ineffectiveness of political parties in mobilisation can be confused with apathy born of lack of competition. But it can also be confused with disenchantment born of government economic ineffectiveness. A fourth focus, therefore, is on government performance legitimacy.

PERFORMANCE LEGITIMACY PERSPECTIVES

Bratton outlined such a perspective to cover state/peasant relations in 1960–1994 in Africa. In his view, state/peasant relations have had a fourfold sequence that has followed the economic benefits to be had by engagement. First, there was mutual engagement, when state-sponsored cash-crop production and marketing schemes were introduced with great promises following national independence. Secondly, peasants disengaged following their disillusionment with these cooperative schemes and their pay-offs. Thirdly, there was a phase of state (or mutual) disengagement. As peasants reorganised themselves into informal or private production/trade networks, states faced a fiscal crisis and were unable/unwilling to support failing rural organisations. Consequently, peasants were left by the state to fend for themselves. The final phase has entailed a tentative re-engagement in a few cases. This has involved the reopening of dialogue between some state agents and social groups. Each stage in this general sequential perspective emerged not accidentally, but logically and out of the unresolved tensions present in the previous stage (Bratton 1994:231–54).

Certainly, the prospect of being able to have a share in national prosperity is a major attraction to participate in the political process, just as the strongly held belief that states hamper individual economic prosperity by taxes, over-regulation, corruption and mismanagement is a disincentive to participate. Nevertheless, the democracy movement that has swept Africa in the 1990s, whilst not touching all, has certainly drawn very large numbers into the political arena despite, or because of, the poor economic performance of governments. Some no doubt vainly imagined that democracy, as a system, meant Western prosperity. But others certainly sought freedom of expression and electoral choice, irrespective of economic outlook. New democratic systems that, with no improvement in economic performance, have seen a tailing away of voter turnout support Bratton's thesis. But those like Benin, Cape Verde, Comoro Islands, Côte d'Ivoire and São Tomé and Principe, which have maintained a high turnout despite the lack of economic take-off, argue for the presence of other factors in determining participation.

All these perspectives have their merits and in fact are not mutually exclusive. Much of the debate over whether societal norms or individual rationality are the chief factors in shaping behaviour can be synthesised within the concept of networks of influence (Knocke 1990). Individuals are neither totally isolated nor shaped only by the very broad social groups. Rather, they are members of small social networks, whose social composition may be predominantly of one category but is by no means uniform. By and large, it is within this group that norms are formed, reinforced and internalised. It is within this group that information and interpretation about the outside world and about the best course for maximising personal interest are disseminated. Alienation seldom develops in a vacuum; resources extend beyond the individual assets and can be borrowed or learned from the group; parties, like other ideological movements, initially recruit as much by friendship as by the power of persuasion; and knowledge of government performance is rarely achieved by self-investigation but by an assembly of material gleaned from the network.

How does political discontinuance relate to the propositions?

The propositions listed at the end of Chapter 1 covered all disengagement phenomena. In this section, their applicability to political discontinuance will be considered.

First, as regards the nature of disengagement, it was hypothesised that disengagement, is a universal phenomenon, a multi-scale phenomenon and a responsive strategy.

It has been shown in this chapter that political discontinuance is found in every historical period and amongst all social categories, though its higher incidence among the young, the poor, women and minorities has been noted. Among each of these groups have been found those who doubted they had the resources to effect, by formal politics, change in the ruling groups so as to bring benefits to themselves.

Political discontinuance has also been shown to be a multi-scale phenomenon, though the evidence suggests that formal political disengagement, unlike engagement, is much more likely to be an individual response, rather than a response as part of an organised movement.

As a responsive strategy political discontinuance does not show evidence of opportunism, for it is pursued when states are strong as well as weak. But it is a form of defensive disengagement: not the defence of running away from oppression, like that of political migrants, but the defence of not remaining in a fight against impossible odds. It might be argued that, in this case, disengagers are no more threatened by the authority than by a roadside brick wall. But a brick wall inflicts hurt if one repeatedly strikes one's head against it in the process of trying to get through it. And those undertaking political discontinuance have come to fear, as the politically impotent, the pain of dashed hopes and futile activity.

Secondly, as regards the pattern of disengagement, it was hypothesised that disengagement depends on macro- and micro-scale factors.

Both have been seen to play a part in political discontinuance. At the macro level, it is rare in Africa for there to be penalties for non-registration on electoral lists or for non-voting; hence the strategy of discontinuance is seen as freely available. This is in strong contrast to the widespread use of coercion to intimidate people from contemplating migration or being members of counter-culture or secessionist groups or engaging in the illegal second economy. Even in the states where these other forms of disengagement face threats of strict sanctions, electoral discontinuance is permitted. If electoral discontinuance attracts little response from the political authorities, it is also unremarkable in the view of society. Unless this strategy is paraded by way of explicit protest, when it provokes the most ardent political activists, it is, of all disengagement strategies, the least threatening to authorities. This is due to its largely invisible nature and the infrequent occurrence of elections.

The micro-scale factors that shape its occurrence are more numerous and complex. In the early decades of independence, low electoral turnouts were likely to be due to cynicism, as individual politicians and their ruling parties were seen as unable or unwilling to deliver the promised generation and redistribution of wealth. As the policies were despised, so also the politicians themselves were increasingly mistrusted and perceived as self-interested, exploitative and corrupt. But, with the institutionalisation of this corruption in one-party states, normlessness was added to cynicism. That is, individuals were alienated with respect to the political system as a whole. Cynicism concerning politicians stimulated opposition politics as long as efficacy remained high. When efficacy withered, apathy and then normlessness took hold. The emergence of normlessness argued for a more radical response. For the minority, with access to resources such as time, organisational skills, wealth, military equipment suppliers or military personnel, revolutions or coups were a possibility. For the majority, who had little access to such resources, the obvious option was a complete severance with formal politics. These micro-scale factors of personal efficacy and available resources have been promoted, reinforced and sustained by networks of influence. The most specific and explicit networks have been the activities of respected leaders, whether traditional chiefs, political patrons or religious clerics. Their sanctions to engage or disengage may vary from social ostracism and taunts of disloyalty to the clan, which may suffer the withdrawal of economic benefits following electoral discontinuance, to excommunication and loss of spiritual well-being, which can have both an eternal and a material dimension. In each case, the dominated individual/client is under severe constraints to disregard personal feelings in the matter of participation. When discontinuance comes at the bidding of traditional chiefs, political patrons and mainstream religious leaders, it tends to be a strategy of opposition (that is, engagement). But, when it comes at the bidding of a politically weak Sufi Marabout, Zionist 'bishop' or Watch Tower elder, it is part of a larger strategy of life withdrawal. The religious separatist leaders are doubly constraining, not just because of the nature of spiritual authority, but also because of the manner in which the communities they lead uphold/withhold their own members.

Thirdly, as regards the significance of disengagement, it was hypothesised that it provides a measure of political authorities, threatens the power balance of political systems, delays democratic consolidation and usually initially provokes resistance by force.

There is no doubt that the extent of political discontinuance, especially as measured by voter turnout, is seen by voters and authorities alike as a measure of government legitimacy. Thus, Mugabe and his ZANU-PF party may have been totally victorious in Zimbabwe's 1996 elections in terms of trouncing the opposition, but everyone knew that a 30 per cent turnout made it a hollow victory. Behind the words of one top party official, as he sought to shift the blame on to the voters, one can hear concern and tension: 'What we are seeing is not pleasing at all and we realise that people do not seem to appreciate what government [sic] has done for them' (ARB 1996, vol. 33 (4):12230). This amounts to an admission of a wide gulf in values between the ruling party/government and society. And, in view of the energy spent by the former on encouraging people to vote, it must also question the effectiveness of their hegemony.

The answer to the question of how much electoral discontinuance threatens the power balance in society appears to be: relatively little. No evidence has been recorded on engagers showing any reaction to disengagers (except political activists closely allied to the authorities). It is true that the attitude of the authorities themselves can easily turn hostile, particularly where the disengagers are a readily definable and a relatively small compact group. Thus, small separatist communities have been demonised and persecuted by the majority in a manner quite out of proportion to their numbers, threat or 'crime'. If political discontinuance has in particular circumstances provoked repression, there is only scant evidence that it has promoted reform, let alone seriously threatened the political system. Even the 75 per cent non-participation in the presidential elections of Dahomey (Benin) in 1968 only secured from the military their own candidate and a rerun. Perhaps more successful was the 97 per cent boycott by Bugandans in the Legislative Council election of 1961 in that it seems to have produced from the subsequent London Conference of 1961 the compromise deal for Buganda of a federal relationship within the unitary state (Low 1971; Ch. 6).

The significance of electoral discontinuance to democratic reform and consolidation is still under debate. As far back as ancient Greece, Thucydides argued that those who hold aloof from participating in public life are not simply 'quiet', but 'useless'. Or, according to Tocqueville (1968), they are mere 'colonists' in their own country, enjoying the benefits of society rules but not attempting to shape them. Not only do people fail to realise their own capacities in a political context but, says the argument, they open the door to, at best, folly and corruption and at worst, tyranny. Apathy, therefore, for Neville was a 'political debauch, which is a neglect of all things that concern the public welfare' (quoted in Parry 1972). According to this conventional wisdom, therefore, low turnouts in Africa's new democratic regimes would be expected to be giving room for authoritarianism to continue. Likewise, this electoral discontinuance should be undermining the authority of the states genuinely committed to democracy and threatening their chances of consolidating the new regimes. The evidence, however, is inconclusive. At least fourteen African countries that practise multi-partyism have autocratic leaders who try to squash dissent. These fourteen might be expected to be those with low political interest; yet only four of them have electoral participation rates of less than 50 per cent (in bold in Table 3.4).

Table 3.4 Authoritarianism and electoral turnout in selected countries

Type of rulers	Country	% Turnout	Year
Civilian autocrats	Côte d'Ivoire	62	1995
	Kenya	68	1992
	Zambia	**40**	**1996**
	Zimbabwe	**31**	**1996**
Ex-military autocrats	Benin	87	1996
	Burkina Faso	**44**	**1997**
	Chad	77	1996
	Ethiopia	no figs for 1995	
	Gambia	73	1996
	Ghana	77	1996
	Guinea	78	1993
	Niger	**39**	**1996**
	Togo	68	1998
	Uganda	73	1996

(Figures from *ARB*)

From the figures in Table 3.4, therefore, it appears that authoritarianism does not exploit low electoral interest (though some figures, like the 68 per cent received by Eyadema, President of Togo, are clearly inflated).

Were, then, those 'democratic' countries whose national election turnouts were less than 55 per cent, amongst the most fragile of the twenty-eight 'democracies' (Table 3.5)? Determining the democratic fragility of the countries listed in Table 3.5 is obviously a subjective exercise, but it is interesting to note that, in its list of 'democracies in trouble', *The Economist* (29/6/96) gave Burundi, Cameroon, Djibouti, Equatorial Guinea, Gabon, Kenya, Mauritania, Tanzania, Zambia and Zimbabwe. In other words, only three listed countries appear amongst those with low turnouts. In their judgement, at least, low turnouts are not threatening young democracies.

With no apparent published material on or social surveys of those who have withdrawn from political politics in sub-Saharan Africa, they must remain largely hidden within a sea that contains the excluded, the politically engaging boycotters and those never engaged in the first place. Just as the invisibility has reduced the force used against them, so also has it weakened any impact they may have had as agents of reform. Few of those who find reason to disengage from formal political participation will find that it is the only step they wish to take away from unacceptable authorities. The truth is that, though discontinuance will not play with the authorities at their game, it escapes very

Table 3.5 Countries with multi-party elections and low turnouts

Country	% Turnout	Year
Burkina Faso	44	1997
Cape Verde	45	1996
Mali	22	1997
Madagascar	45	1996
Mauritania	29	1997
Niger	39	1996*
Senegal	51	1993
Sierra Leone	46	1996
Zambia	40	1996
Zimbabwe	31	1996

* A functioning democracy prior to the military coup of 1996.

(Figures from *ARB*)

little. For the more radical, nothing short of tearing away their homeland and its people from the control of the current authorities is sufficient, even if this entails joining a mass organisation and condoning or
using violence. Secession, therefore, is the subject of the next chapter.

Secessionism

Most northerners seem to believe that the south must remain part of Sudan, but that southerners must accept that they are not the equal of northerners and that the north must remain in control of the country. They simply refuse to believe that southerners can take the fate of the country as a whole as seriously as they do themselves.
(Sudanese secessionist)

Introduction

In its willingness to use armed force as a last resort to escape unacceptable domination, secessionism is atypical among the disengagement strategies. Conceptually, this is untidy, since it is as if engagement is undertaken to achieve disengagement. Further, the sense of powerlessness among disengagers, which has been emphasised previously, is limited in the case of armed secession, for a successful military solution is anticipated, even if the campaign fights shy of launching a national revolution. The ambiguity is highlighted by the fact that some armed movements that set out to break away from the national government end up taking them over, as happened in Chad in the 1970s and 1980s. But, of course, not all secessionism is armed conflict. Besides, whether using force or not, the essence of disengagement is there: a minority ruled in a way that is unsympathetic, or even hostile, to its needs and unable to conceive of bringing about a change in policy either by revolution or electoral politics will invariably resort to some method of withdrawing from the tyranny of the majority.

For those political authorities that rule socially heterogeneous domains, the challenge of political integration is ceaseless. The question is, how are they to bring together culturally and socially discrete groups into a single territorial unit and establish a common identity? The issue is never more intractable than when domain boundaries fail to coincide with distinct cultural-social groups, whether it be a case of multi-group domains, for example Sudan, or multi-domain groups, for example the Touaregs. Legitimacy crises and a corresponding disregard of decrees issuing from the centre are the common experience of poorly integrated political communities.

In every age, cultural-social groups have sought to escape domination, not only by moving away physically from territory subject to misrule or by seeking as revolutionaries to overthrow and replace the central authorities, but by a policy of seeking to restrict the jurisdiction of those authorities from what they see as their own territory. It is not so much that they deny the rulers an authority over some territory, but that they vehemently deny it over the territory they themselves occupy (Buchanan 1991). It is their intention to escape control, whether legally by negotiation or by violent struggle; their declaration is the manifesto of secession.

Secession is the formal withdrawal from membership of a polity by a section. It is the attempt by an ethnic/regional group(s) to withdraw its region from the control of the state of which it is part. Loyalty, expectation and service are abandoned. It is a process which, as Wood observes, 'can best be understood as the antithesis or the reversal of political integration ... It involves dismemberment' (Wood 1981: 110–11).

As an escape strategy, secession is not a modern innovation. Of the precolonial Savannah kingdoms that constitute modern southern Democratic Republic of Congo (Zaire), northern Angola and western Zambia, Vansina writes:

> Another common feature of the major kingdoms was a system of territorial rule whereby the outer provinces were considered as tributaries, often enjoying an internal autonomy ... The practice of 'indirect rule' and the concomitant ubiquitous fading away of power and authority of the central government in the outlying provinces ... [meant that they] could break off from the kingdom whenever circumstances were favourable. (Vansina 1966:246–7)

Their disputes with the central authorities sound very familiar. The Ndongo on the southern periphery of the Kongo Kingdom seceded in 1556 over the right to conduct their own lucrative trade with Portuguese merchants, as opposed to yielding to the Kongo king's claim to a monopoly and insistence on the use of only his approved traders. The Ndongo were not prepared to see all the profits and 'development' stay in the hands of the north (Vansina 1966:59–61). For the Lualaba in the Lunda tributary kingdom of Kazembe (Zambia/Shaba, Democratic Republic of Congo border), the issues were the cruelty and greed of the central rulers, plus their failure to provide protection against Luba raids. When a foreign entrepreneur/adventurer offered protection and a better life, they readily allied under his banner and established their own independent kingdom in 1865, which was successful for twenty-five years (Vansina 1966:235).

Since the Second World War, at least twenty-three significant secessionist movements have troubled African states.[1]

SUMMARY OF SIGNIFICANT SECESSIONIST MOVEMENTS IN AFRICA 1946–98
Afar
There have been calls for a 'Greater Afar' embracing the Afar community of Djibouti, Eritrea and Ethiopia since the late 1970s. However, despite the Djibouti Government's attempt to portray the FRUD (Afar Front for the Restoration of Unity and Democracy) as secessionist rebels, its guerrilla campaign since 1991 (though one faction made peace in 1994) has had a reformist agenda.

Anjouan
In 1997, the simmering resentment at the federal government of the Comoros' neglect of the island led to demonstrations and violent clashes, culminating in a declaration of independence. Following the failed attempt of federal troops to recapture the island, a referendum gave almost universal backing to independence and a government was appointed.

Bakongo
The Bakongo ethnic group spans the Angolan, Democratic Republic of

---

[1] Though this study will focus on secessionism by state regions intent on forming recognised separate states, or at least autonomous provinces, there have been other attempts, at a local level, to assert a practical form of independence. Schatzberg gives an example of attempted subnational secession from the 1970s in Zaire. In the Bongandanga zone of the Mongala subregion, the Mongo comprised 15 per cent of the population, whilst the Ngombe comprised 85 per cent. There had been a long history of strife between the two ethnic groups, but things came to a head in 1974:

> the Mongo in Bongandanga wished to dismember the zone and attach themselves to ... [one of three] zones enjoying a healthy Mongo majority. Threatening letters were sent to the territorial authorities ... over this matter, and the writers claimed that if their demands for secession were not met, the sub-regional commissioner would not be welcome in the zone. (Schatzberg 1981:465)

At the still more localised level, whether the forming of urban no-go areas can be legitimately called secession is problematic. They hardly constitute a formal withdrawal from the state and there is no understanding amongst their members of being a putative micro-state. Not only would this be regarded as quite unachievable, but it is unlikely that the community has anything but a minimal coordinated administrative structure. On the other hand, one cannot question the lack of integration with the state and the achievement of autonomy at the level of policing/rule of law, if not economically. Since the members of these communities are more intent on withdrawal than change, it seems better to regard their actions as disengagement rather than rebellion.

Congo and Republic of Congo borders. In all three countries, it has shown restlessness and expressed a desire for autonomy over a long period (it briefly established an independent state in Congo Democratic Republic (DR) in 1960). An armed group, the Armed Forces for the Liberation of Kongo (FALKO), has been active in Angola throughout the 1990s.

Barotseland
Since 1946, Lozi leaders have been contesting the forced amalgamation of Barotseland with the state now known as Zambia. Secessionist demands continued up until independence in 1962, with calls for semi-independent status up to 1967. Discontent is still expressed, but over the years separatism has increasingly appeared to be largely an elite concern to preserve their status.

Biafra
Following discrimination and then the 1966 pogroms against Nigerian southerners living in the north, they fled to their homelands and pro-claimed an independent state of Biafra. It incorporated Ibo and others. The ensuing year-long war was won by the Nigerian federal state.

Bubi
The original inhabitants of Bioko Island, Equatorial Guinea, have been overwhelmed by mainland Fang immigrants. The Movement for the Self-determination of Bioko Island (MAIB) began armed attacks on the army in 1998.

Buganda
The large and ancient kingdom had always had a dominant and favoured status under British rule and hence they were extremely reluctant to go into an independent unitary state of Uganda. From 1953 to 1961, there was a clear majority of the Baganda people against an independent state, but, apart from minor concessions in the indepen-dence settlement, they were overruled.

Cabinda
The Angolan enclave was a separate colony under the Portuguese and has retained its sense of separateness. From 1975 to the present day, several small groups, such as the Front for the Liberation of the Cabinda Enclave – Cabinda Armed Forces (Flec-FAC), Front for the Liberation of the Cabinda Enclave – Renewed (Flec-R) and Cabinda Democratic Front (FDC), have been pursuing an armed struggle.

Casamance
The Catholic and animist Diola and other peoples of southern Senegal have never felt part of the independent, largely Muslim, state. Armed

groups, led by the Movement of Casamance Democratic Forces (MFDC), have been fighting state forces since 1982.

Chad

The conflict between Muslim northern peoples and Christian southern peoples is long and complex – at times, a civil war for control of the state, at times, secessionist withdrawal from the state when it is under the control of the 'other side'. It is difficult to put dates to the changing conflicts, but separatist sentiments prevailed in parts of the north in 1964–78 and 1981–7, and in parts of the south in 1979–84. Since then, though there have been many military groupings, few have had secessionist aims.

Eritrea

Eritrea is a multi-ethnic grouping that owed its self-consciousness to Italian colonialism and Ethiopian discrimination. First the Eritrean Liberation Front (ELF) and then the Eritrean People's Liberation Front (EPLF) fought a long and bitter war in 1955–95. This was ultimately successful in securing independence.

Kenya (North Eastern Province)

This Somali-inhabited region, like other Somalis, found itself outside the boundaries of the independent state of Somalia. Led by the Northern Province People's Progressive Party (NPPPP), it vigorously sought union with what was regarded as the homeland. The protests took a violent form between 1960 and 1967. Today, any unrest is largely vocal and spasmodic.

Kivu

There has been unrest on the eastern borders of Congo DR since independence. Periodic bouts of fighting with state troops have taken place ever since 1960, though apparently subsumed in the wider fighting of the 1997 civil war. The rebels operated under the name of the Parti de Libération Congolais and appeared to want a separate socialist state, although there were inter-Bembe overtones in the conflict as well.

Kwazulu

During the negotiated end of apartheid in South Africa from 1993, the party known as Inkatha made a bid for secession or autonomy in the name of the Zulu people. Much of the secessionist language has been posturing to win concessions from the central government, although there is no doubt that some would sooner see a separate state.

Ogaden

This is another secessionist movement based on the desire of ethnic Somalis to be reunited with the state of Somalia, which colonially agreed boundaries have separated them from. The Ogaden is the far eastern portion of Ethiopia. The conflict has been going on since 1960 and the Ogaden National Liberation Front is still conducting a low-level guerrilla campaign.

Oromo

The Oromo, Ethiopia's largest ethnic group (and independent until late nineteenth century), have contested central repression since the mid-1970s, although the civil war gave a strong boost to anti-centre groups like them. The current Tigrean domination of the state has further fuelled unrest and an armed movement, the Oromo Liberation Front, has been formed.

Somaliland

Currently, Somaliland acts as an independent state in northern Somalia, and has done so since 1991, after Somalia fragmented during the civil war. Ruled separately by the British and discriminated against by the Somalia state, it seized the breakdown of central control to assert its independence. Unlike Eritrea, it is not recognised by the international community.

Southern Cameroons

This slice of north western Cameroon was formerly part of British Cameroon, as opposed to the rest of the state, which was French Cameroon. The linguistic and ethnic divide has fuelled secessionism since the merger in 1961. The Southern Cameroons National Council still leads an active political campaign.

Southern Sudan

Racial/religious differences between the north and south were exaggerated by British rule and exacerbated by Arab discrimination against non-Muslims. Armed groups (fighting both the central government and one another) were active in 1951–71 and have been so from 1983 to the present. Led by the Sudan People's Liberation Army (SPLA) their objectives have fluctuated between autonomy, secessionism and government overthrow.

South Kasai

Of all the groups that proclaimed independence when Congo (now Democratic Republic of Congo; formerly Zaire) was unravelling in 1960–2, this Baluba-dominated one was one of the more likely contenders for survival. It had its own army and government and, above all, sat on large diamond mines that could finance the project. The end came in 1962 after a leadership split and mutiny that gave the central troops the opportunity to retake control.

South Katanga

The Katanga movement is a Lunda nationalist project. In 1960, in the wake of the breakup of Congo, it established a largely viable independent state with the aid of Belgian mining businesses. It successfully held off national and United Nations (UN) forces for three years. Secessionist armed groups have appeared periodically since and secessionist sentiment still seems attractive to many in the chaos of the post-civil-war period.

Stanleyville

This short-lived movement in north-east Congo, in 1960–2 and 1964, was not ethnically inspired, but was an attempt to preserve the socialism of ex-president Lumumba. Its attempt to set up an independent state in the midst of the disintegration of Congo's central government succumbed to state forces.

Touareg

The Touareg people are nomads living on the northern boundaries of Niger and Mali. Having long felt abandoned by the central authorities, they took up arms in 1990 to secure greater autonomy or separation from the two states. Many of the armed groups made peace in 1993, but others continued their struggle until 1998 and still have not disarmed.

As Map 4.1 shows, the secessionist movements have been spread across the continent.

Currently, Somaliland acts as an independent state in northern Somalia, and has done so since 1991. Groups of varying strength calling for self-government have had largely unimpeded movement through much of Ethiopia since 1990 and within large sections of southern Sudan for nearly forty years. On a smaller scale, discontented peoples seeking to detach themselves from state control are engaged either in contentious negotiations – for example, Anjouan of the Comoros Islands – or in military and terrorist operations. The latter are found, or have been until very recently, in anglophone Cameroon; Kivu Province, Democratic Republic of Congo (Zaire); the Cabinda enclave, Angola; the Bakongo area in Republic of Congo; the Touareg areas of northern Niger and Mali; parts of northern Chad; the Afar areas of Djibouti, Eritrea and Ethiopia; Ethiopia; Bioko Island, Equatorial Guinea; and the Casamance region of Senegal.[2]

---

[2] Also coming to light recently was the planned Boer secession in South Africa in 1994, which intended to create a *volkstaat* through military force (*ARB* 1996, vol. 33 (12):12516).

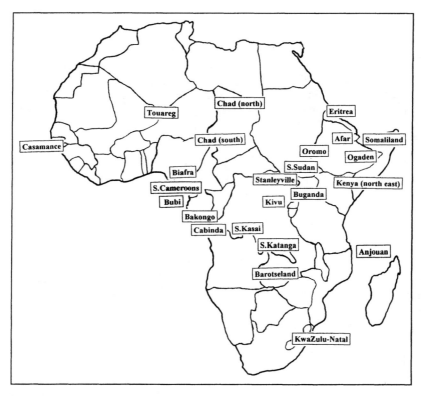

Map 4.1 Regions of significant secessionist movements

The characteristics of secessionist movements

Secessionist movements share a number of characteristics, some of which are unique and some common to other political collectives, whether social movements, guerrilla movements or political parties.

CAMPAIGN STRATEGY

Secessionism is 'not an amorphous cluster of sentiments drifting towards a haphazard end' (Premdas 1990:14). Rather, under determined leadership, there is a two-pronged campaign. First, there is active mobilisation. This commonly entails manipulating social cleavages, whether by fanning the flames of discontent or by creating an image of an ideal independent domain where group interest will be protected. Secondly, there is a vigorous negotiation with the authorities. But, if this is unproductive, this is dropped in favour of the use of force, terrorist or military.

SHARED VALUES AND EXPERIENCES

Secessionists have a consciousness of themselves as distinct identities based on their belief that they possess distinguishable primordial values, such as language, beliefs and race, and/or that they possess a common history of discrimination and neglect, or even of repression and persecution. So, to distinguish between the indigenous Lunda and the immigrant Baluba, who came to form the majority in Katanga, Tshombe, the leader of the secessionist movement, spoke of 'authentic Katangans'. Whether factual or mythical, secessionist assertions are believed by the movement to be true and they sustain its objective to put distance between it and the authorities. Typically, they are negative – that is, stronger on defining what the new domain will not be like than what it will be like – and amorphous – that is, sufficiently vague to be 'an aggregative device meaning all things to all alienated people' (Wood 1981:123).

THE OBJECTIVE OF TERRITORIAL SELF-GOVERNMENT

Secessionists see their uniqueness as contained within a territorial space or 'homeland'. (In the case of irredentism, such as the Kenyan Somalis, this includes the territory of the neighbouring state.) To preserve their way of life, it is necessary to have political control of that space. This may not necessarily mean full sovereignty, as in the narrowest sense of secession, but can entail resistance to further incorporation or subordination and/or demands for local control and subsidiarity in decision-making which might properly be called separatism.

One southern Sudanese leader, Joseph Lagu, said: 'I never believed in secession from the north. My only aim was to obtain recognition for the southerners. I had resorted to force because I concluded that the successive governments in Khartoum were not willing to concede the point' (quoted in Raghavan 1990:132–3). Others in the southern Sudanese movement, however, have taken up a secessionist line, arguing that federalism is unrealistic. 'At times one or another of these themes was ascendant; at other times both were heard simultaneously even from the same quarter' (ibid). This mixture of objectives within a single movement, or sometimes a switch from one political objective to another, has also been a feature of other movements, such as the Touareg and Lozi. A pedantic distinction, therefore, between secessionism and separatism obscures rather than enlightens analysis. Underlying either policy is the affirmation of the right of self-determination. In Premdas's view, the enshrinement of this doctrine in the international moral order since the 1940s has facilitated, if not created, many modern separatist movements (Premdas 1990:15).

THEY ARE STRONGLY CONTESTED
The alleged right to self-determination is not an uncontested moral claim. In Kenyatta's words in 1962 concerning the Kenyan Somalis: 'It is a very touchy question ... we regard Somalis who live in NFD [Northern Frontier District] as part and parcel of Kenya. This is a domestic affair of Kenya' (Hoskyns 1969:25). In other words, it clashes head-on with another alleged right, namely that of a state to safeguard its sovereignty and territorial integrity. Ottaway has developed the latter argument by insisting that the right of groups to determine their own destiny by having their own state is very different from the right of individuals to determine their political destiny by choosing their own government from among competing political parties. The former, she argues:

> is a non-democratic, monopolistic interpretation of self-determination, because it gives greater importance to the creation of a separate exclusive state than to the question of how such a state will be governed: invariably, a focus on group self-determination supersedes the idea of individual choice. (Ottaway 1995:238)

Her elevation of the state to a sacrosanct status is debatable, but indisputable is the fact that in secessionist conflicts both sides claim the moral high ground.

Setting aside moral rights, the fact is that an authority rarely gives away, without a contest, its resources, which in the case of a state are land, revenue, manpower, mineral reserves, strategic/defence requirements and perhaps prestige. In the twenty-four secessionist movements shown on Map 4.1, only five saw negotiations as the first response of the state, namely Buganda, Somali-inhabited Kenya, KwaZulu-Natal, Barotseland and Southern Cameroons. (It is thought that secret negotiations between the president elect of South Africa, Mandela, and the Boer leader, General Viljoen, caused the putative secessionists to pull back from their planned politico-military venture (*African Research Bulletin, Political Series (ARB)* 1996, vol. 33 (12):12516.) And the first two of these began under colonial rule as it was in the process of handing over control – in other words, under authorities with far less emotional interest at stake. In Hechter's view, serious negotiations will only occur where high costs are required to buy off or militarily defeat the secessionists; where the region is of low strategic and/or economic value; where international actors side with the secessionists; or where the host state is weak (Hechter 1992:277). None of these factors, however, are central to the five African cases.

The state's fear is that conceding secessionist principles opens the door to other groups to follow the example of the vanguard movement. Nothing stirs up the anger of the state more than an assertion of independence. It can tolerate hatred, as long as the disaffected pay their taxes; it can accept non-participation in political life, provided it is silent; it can even, for the most part, let the disgruntled migrate, provided the troublemakers do not remove resources, skills and secrets; but it will not accept those who stand up where they are and shout 'we will not have you rule over us'. Before intransigence or, at best, largely cosmetic concessions, determined secessionist movements see little alternative but to resort to force. The resulting tragedy, in Premdas's words, is that:

> The mother country must be dismembered. Maimed factions must now become healthy wholes, territory is lost and with it, tenacious memories, people and vitality. Prolonged struggle demoralises all sections in the conflict equally, polarises and demoralises all members, creates a garrison mentality, cripples democratic institutions, breeds fanaticism and helplessly accepts a distorted existence as normal and inevitable. (Premdas 1990:13)

IMPERMANENCE

Being often products of young ambitious (male) leaders, secessionism is not always an ideological movement, or even a popular movement, but more a pragmatic means to a self-serving end. This was all too apparent with the Lozi aristocracy, who were the driving force behind the secessionist struggle in Barotseland from 1946 to 1967. Self-interested strategies tend to be short-term. Shifts from secessionism to separatism or even the co-existence of the two positions within a single movement's leadership have already been mentioned, but sometimes the demands of realpolitik may even bring the abandonment of secessionism altogether for a policy of engagement. Pressing the war beyond the old South and embracing groups where secession was not seen as an option, the southern Sudanese leadership reaffirmed in 1997 their 'principal task is to create the conditions for a fundamental change in Khartoum' (Garang, quoted in *ARB* 1997, vol. 34 (3):12625), when resources were enhanced with external support. [3] And, in Nigeria in the 1960s, both the Ibo and Hausa actually reversed their previous stands:

> The Ibo were the most prominent proponents of one Nigeria. With a considerable investment in human capital they had migrated all over Nigeria in their quest for employment. Perhaps one Ibo in four or five lived outside the Eastern Region before 1966. But when recurrent violence, culminating in the massacres of September–October 1996 drove the Ibo back to the east, then, and then only, did the Ibo become secessionists. Meanwhile, the Hausa travelled the opposite direction, from their openly secessionist inclination of mid-1966, to their strong role in suppressing the Biafra secession and preserving an undivided Nigeria. (Horowitz 1992:122)

VARIABLE POPULAR SUPPORT

It should not, of course, be assumed that secessionist movements necessarily have the universal support of the regions they seek to detach. Rarely are people and territory readily disaggregated into two homogeneous sections. For its part, the Katanga movement, both in the 1960s and in its recent form, has by definition been principally a movement by a minority tribe, the Lunda, and that not with total support from them. In the case of the Lozi separatist movement, the problem has not been one of ethnic diversity but of class. It has always been largely an elite concern to preserve their status, with little widespread support from the general public for anything beyond special status within Zambia and a mild form of autonomy (Caplan 1968). Thus the electorate gave overwhelming support for the nationalists at independence and have never been interested in any proposals for a tribal political party with a secessionist agenda. Even in 1995, talk of the Lozi cutting ties with the Zambian government until it withdrew laws giving the state authority over its land, on closer examination turned out to be the traditional leadership fighting to preserve its non-democratic powers. The laws enabled freehold ownership of land and the government veto over tribal leaders' distribution of it. The statement issued by the leaders in the name of the Lozi people is revealing: 'The Litunga [ruler of the Lozi] needs land. Without land there is no Litunga. Therefore the

---

[3] Or, again, both the Tigrinya of Eritrea and the clans of Somaliland began by supporting federal union in the 1950s, before switching to secessionist policies in the 1970s and 1980s.

people of Barotseland reject the Land Act of 1995 since it is aimed at taking away the powers of the Litunga' (*The Herald*, Harare 7/11/1995). Nor are levels of support static. The Eritrean nationalists moved from being the preserve of a few Muslim fighters in the 1950s to securing the overwhelming support of the Muslim and Christian populace by the time of their triumph over the Ethiopian forces in 1991.

The nature of the underlying friction

A number of attempts have been made to explain secessionism other than in terms of disengagement.

ETHNIC CONFLICT
Some see secessionists as essentially a racial group antagonised by rule being in the hands of another nationality. In this view, secessionism is at root the result of ethnic conflict. Certainly, most African states have many internal fault lines, based on race, which are often deliberately manipulated for narrow political ends (some would argue, for class ends, namely to divert attention from capitalist exploitation). For example, tribalist policies have been pursued by governments where state ministers, ambassadors and local commissioners all come from the state leader's ethnic group, as in Kenya with Kenyatta's preference towards the Kikuyu and his successor Moi's preference for the Kalenjin. For Fanon, 'this tribalising of the central authority ... encourages regionalist ideas and separatism ... all the decentralising tendencies spring up again and triumph and the nation falls to pieces, broken in bits' (Fanon 1967:184). But is racial group identification, especially where enhanced by language and religion, the prime mover behind secession? One can certainly see anti-Amhara sentiments in Eritrea and anti-Arab sentiments in southern Sudan. Likewise, the secessionists of Biafra were clearly defending Ibo identity in the face of the pogroms by northerners, and the self-styled 'authentic Katangese' were doing likewise for the Lunda when immigrants threatened to overwhelm them numerically and economically. In almost every African secessionist movement, there is certainly an ethnic dimension (or sub-ethnic in the case of the clans of Somalia and the Bembe of South Kivu). Some would argue that ethnic bonds are invariably more intense than those emanating from associations of class and interest. Says Geertz:

> Congruities of blood, speech, custom, and so on, are seen to have an ineffa-ble, and at times overpowering, coerciveness in and of themselves. One is bound to one's kinsmen, one's neighbour, one's fellow believer ipso facto; as

the result not merely of personal affection, practical necessity, common interest, or incurred obligation, but at least in great part by virtue of some unaccountable absolute import attributed to the very tie itself ... For virtually every person in every society, at almost all times, some attachments seem to flow more from a sense of natural – some would say spiritual – affinity than from social interaction. (Geertz 1963:109–10)

But is racial group identification a sufficient cause? There are clear exceptions. Firstly, not every secession is connected with race. Southern Sudan has dozens of distinct ethnic groups and Eritrea at least nine. Other cases can be given where the process is due to elite division alone, for example, the Toro Kingdom of west Uganda separated in the early nineteenth century when one of the sons of the ruler of Bunyoro-Kitara grew tired of waiting for the succession struggle and decided to carve a kingdom for himself from the western borderlands of his father's dominions. Though Bunyoro was able to restore its former authority after his death, it was itself destroyed by the British and Toro became part of the Uganda protectorate (Ingham 1995). Likewise, the Stanleyville secession of 1960–2 was essentially a movement in support of the deposed president Lumumba. Secondly, not every ethnic group or even the major ones are calling for regional autonomy or sovereign independence. Take, for example, the Yoruba of southern Nigeria and the Baganda of Uganda. Though both, as relatively advanced groups within the state, considered secession (the Yoruba prior to independence and the Baganda both prior to independence and after Obote removed their ruler as head of state), both came to see the advantages of staying within it to maintain access to the markets of the entire state. In the end, they found 'the attractions of exerting influence and reaping rewards in a large undivided state were stronger than the temptations of a more homogenous contracted homeland' (Horowitz 1985:249). Nor is secession a case of disenchantment by those ethnic groups that have relatively recently been incorporated into the state and therefore least identify with it. Otherwise, it would not have been Tigray that resisted the Ethiopian state, for it had formed part of that state over a very long period. Instead, one would have predicted conflict to have broken out first in the more recently incorporated south and west regions.

ECONOMIC CONFLICT

Others have seen secessionism as primarily group withdrawal to avoid economic dominance (for example, Hechter 1992; Sangmpam 1994). Secessionism in their view is not competition between ethnic groups *per se*, but where there is unequal distribution between available resources. This is especially likely where close juxtaposition of unequally successful groups is brought about by mass communications and urbanisation. Thus Lijphart writes, 'if modernisation leads to rapidly increasing social transactions and contacts among diverse groups, strain and conflict are more likely to ensue than greater mutual understanding' (quoted in Premdas 1990:18). Certainly, there is clear evidence of economic stratification along racial lines in many African states. For example, the black southern Sudanese ethnic groups have always been subject to northern Arabic economic hegemony. Between 1954 and 1965, 505 northerners were commissioned as army officers, but only sixteen southerners. In 1969, the south had only twelve secondary schools compared with the north's 178; no southerner held a rank above Deputy Commissioner, nor were there any permanent under-secretaries or directorships of government departments in southern hands. It is not hard to understand a sense of injustice when backward groups see others, whether indigenous or immigrant, benefiting and themselves neglected in their own homeland. They naturally fear domination by the better educated, better skilled 'others', who monopolise the commanding heights of the economy and bureaucracy. When calls for proportionality in public appointments and distributed resources fall on deaf ears, separatism or secessionism may appear the only answer. 'We want more fairness in the distribution of resources ... we insist on the fact that Katanga, which provides the biggest share of the Congolese budget, should not be deprived of its share of the cake,' said the Lunda leaders (Sangmpam, 1994:171). Other examples in this category of backward and abandoned groups include the Tubu of north Chad, Somaliland, the Somali of Kenya and the Touareg. Compared with those who controlled the centre and/or their region, they have been severely disadvantaged, whether by carelessness or by wilful neglect.

Yet not every disadvantaged group calls for secession. Further, the difference between the secessionists and the rump state has not always been to the advantage of the latter. The seceding Ibo of Biafra and the Baluba of south Kasai were in fact the privileged groups. Indeed, as they migrated into other regions, it was their economic success and prosperity that were the precipitant of conflict. Their secession began, not with their own envy and resentment, but in being envied and resented and becoming the butt of harassment. This made them retreat to their homeland and seek to withdraw that homeland from the state that harboured their antagonists. (On south Kasai, see Willame 1972:35–48.) Thus patterns exist of both economically advanced and economically backward groups withdrawing.

COLONIAL DIFFERENTIATION
The contradictory experience of economically defined groups might suggest that shared historical-political experiences transcend both

ethnic and socio-economic factors. It is striking that nine significant secessionist movements in Africa experienced regional differentiation during the colonial period. British rule in Sudan in 1898–1946 quite deliberately fostered and accentuated differences between the north and the south. In the south, it promoted Christianity and restricted Muslim entry; introduced the English language; and organised a different pay structure for government service. In their hasty departure, the British did seek to revoke the twin administration policy and to leave behind a unitary state. However, at independence in 1956, there were still only six of the 800 government junior posts and four of the seventy-four commissioned army positions held by southerners, though they had 25 per cent of the population.

Likewise, the British were not slow to acknowledge the separate identity of the Somali of north-east Kenya. The British Commissioner for the East Africa Protectorate wrote in 1905:

> If it were possible to detach the districts inhabited by Somalis it would be an excellent thing to form them into a separate government as they are different in population, economic and physical conditions from the other provinces: but unfortunately, they are too small to form a separate administration, and adjoining Somali territories are not British. (Quoted in Hoskyns 1969:23)

In 1924 much of the Somali population (Jubaland Province) was in fact transferred to Italian Somaliland. The remainder, however, was kept in isolation within Kenya. They were not allowed to move outside the region without a special pass; were allowed no political parties and were largely ignored in terms of development, such that by 1960 they had only one intermediate school, compared with the rest of Kenya's 600, despite being 2.5 per cent of the population (Hoskyns 1969).

It was deliberate British policy also that led to differences in the timing and intensity of Western education in northern and southern Nigeria. To uphold indirect rule through the Muslim emirs in the north, hardly any opportunity was given to Christian missionaries and Christian schools in 1900–10, so that inevitably southerners rose to the highest ranks in the administration in both regions. In 1947, there were only 251 northerners attending secondary school – that is, 2.5 per cent of the total number of secondary pupils – even though the north had 54 per cent of the population. Even in 1957, there was only one government secondary school throughout northern Nigeria (Nwankwo and Ifejika 1969:27–8).

Then again, Eritrea was separately administered from Ethiopia because of the Italian occupation in 1890–1941. Under the British, anglophone Cameroon and Somaliland also had a colonial experience distinct from the lands they were subsequently united to. For its part, northern Muslim Chad was neglected by the French compared with the Christian south, whilst Biafra and Katanga received privileged attention under British and Belgian rule compared with most of their regional neighbours. Finally, Casamance was under Portuguese rather than French influence until 1886. Do the roots of separate conscious identity lie, therefore, not in ethnicity, but in colonial history? Did regionalism precede ethnicity? The evidence is inconclusive. In Eritrea, with its nine or more nationalities, one would be inclined to say yes; but, in Katanga, where it was only the minority Lunda that became secessionist and not the majority Baluba-Katanga (nor the immigrant Baluba-Kasai population), the answer has to be no.

IMMEDIATE SECURITY THREAT

What of more recent history? Is there a pattern in the specific and direct modern precipitants of the movements? Wood argues that most armed confrontations are 'triggered by some action or event which is construed as a direct threat to the security of the other side' (Wood 1981:28). Common themes are actual or potential central discrimination/neglect; central assimilationist policies; and severe repression of the movement in its initial stages. Aggressive assimilationist policies were certainly pursued by the Ethiopians in Eritrea, the Chad government in the Muslim north and centre and the Sudanese government in the Christian south. Almost all other secessionist groups endured discrimination/neglect within (or, in the cases of the Ibo and Baluba, outside) their homelands, which quickly turned to persecution after the initial protests. Beyond this point, subsequent development may be affected by a host of factors, including the capability and ingenuity of the ruling regime and the ideology, organisation, international support, unity and leadership of the movement.

One must question, however, whether the immediate precipitating cause is sufficient. Is this not a flame that sets alight prepared tinder? Assimilation is only a threat to a group that is already self-conscious and defensive. The Hadiya of Ethiopia, for instance, in the nineteenth century, welcomed absorption by the expanding Oromo to the point of actively expelling their kinsmen who refused to submit to the suzerainty of the Oromo (Baxter 1994:175). Then again, neglect may be perceived, not as discrimination against a group *per se*, but as regional disadvantage that warrants migration. Secessionism, therefore, is more complex than it might appear at first. Movements may be uniform or mixed racially; backward or advanced economically; privileged or neglected politically; central or peripheral geographically; majorities or minorities in their homeland demographically; and, compared with those who control the centre, they may have similar or different racial identity, religion and colonial experience. Some could clearly be viable successful states, others appear extremely dubious, casting doubts on rational choice theorists, who argue that people will only desire to secede if they expect to profit from it personally (Hechter 1992:273).

DISENGAGEMENT

Returning, therefore, to the argument of this book, it would seem better to broaden this contemporary political explanation and to see secessionism as essentially withdrawal from unacceptable domination, whether this is imminent (as a result of constitutional change), of recent duration or embodied in the long-term experience of the group. For groups that perceive their uniqueness and that have that very uniqueness threatened by those in authority, secessionism may constitute the most attractive form of escape. The alternatives may look bleak. Given that they recognise their distinctiveness from the centre and from much of the rest of the state's population, the attraction of revolution to seize central power as a minority is strictly limited. Where democracy is not in place constitutionally, or at least in practice, there is little space for representing their appeals for more sympathetic rule, little opportunity as a regional minority for securing new national legislation and, above all, few restraints on human rights abuses against them. One southern Sudanese described this official 'deafness' as follows:

> most northerners seem to believe that the south must remain part of Sudan, but that southerners must accept that they are not the equal of northerners and that the north must remain in control of the country. They simply refuse to believe that southerners can take the fate of the country as a whole as seriously as they do themselves. (Quoted in Malwal 1994:96)

Nor is electoral discontinuance by a minority within a democracy a sufficient lever to change the attitude of the centre so as to resolve the crisis threatening the group. As for migration, this is no more than a temporary solution in these days of tight border control and immigration quotas. And, even if irredentism is an option, political ambitions are very likely to be as confined in the new state as in the previous situation, or, as in the case of Somalia, circumstances may so deteriorate as to make this an unattractive proposition. From this broad political viewpoint of the underlying friction, the issue for secessionists is not so much how they differ from the centre – it may be on the grounds of ethnicity, religion, colonial heritage of language and customs, economic prosperity and development, or any other factual or mythical basis. The issue is that, the collective consciousness having been established, the group wants to preserve itself and knows how to acquire the resources needed for challenging the centre. In this context, preservation means to escape from unjust rule, such as unequal and inadequate distribution of resources, assimilationist policies, religious proselytisation, repression or even ethnic cleansing. Faced negatively with the withholding of resources for development facilities and/or protection and positively with forces that would undermine and overwhelm their existence as a distinct group, the instinct is to disengage. This will be so whether or not it is to their obvious economic advantage. Those that imagine that cold cost–benefit calculations are primary (e.g. Hechter 1992) are mistaken. Not that reason and calculation are totally abandoned, but that preservation of the group within which individuals find their identity is as much a factor in the decision-making as personal gain.

Listening to the secessionists of the Southern Cameroons, one hears the historical-political argument of separate culture arising from their distinct colonial experience and the economic argument of neglect and exploitation. Yet, in the following quote from the 1994 memorandum of the Southern Cameroons National Council to the Secretary General of the Commonwealth, there is something more; there is a condemnation of hegemony and perhaps an unexpressed fear of near extinction:

> Within the past 33 years ... we have been disenfranchised, marginalised and treated with condescending suspicion. Our interests have been disregarded. Our participation in national life has been limited to non-essential functions. Our natural resources have been ruthlessly exploited without any benefit accruing to our territory or peoples. The development of our territory has been negligible and confined to areas that directly or indirectly benefit Francophones and their mentors, the French. (*ARB*, 1995, vol. 32 (10):12006)

Given that they had been promised a federal structure if they accepted unification, only for a unitary state to be imposed upon them in 1972, their fears were not unreasonable. In a similar vein two Sudanese protested in 1963:

> the administration, the army, the police, the judiciary and the trade in the south [are] all in Arab hands; Arabic is the official national language as well as the medium of instruction; Friday is the day of rest etc. Could domination be better expressed? (Oduho and Deng, quoted in Horowitz 1985:239).

As Horowitz argues, since the individual sense of identity, where one fits into a coherent and valued order of things, is the feeling of self-worth, affiliations are crucial:

> A threat to the value of those affiliations produces anxiety and defence. For this reason people often express hostility towards those who create uncertainty about the correctness of their own behaviour and that of the groups to which they belong and they often do so out of all proportion to

the character of the threat that presently confronts them. (Horowitz 1985:181)

The expression of this hostility in the attempt to withdraw persons and land from the powers of domination will be examined in two case studies. The fact that the two have significant differences – namely, over whether they are advantaged or disadvantaged economically and homogeneous or heterogeneous ethnically – highlights the contention of this chapter that these factors are of secondary importance. That both experienced discrimination and/or persecution and colonial distinction in terms of treatment (preference/neglect) or separation underscores the argument that these are primary factors. The crucial role of international actors in bringing failure or success to the movements also runs through both cases.

An unsuccessful and a successful secession

FAILURE IN BIAFRA, NIGERIA

If the Ibo were not specifically given preferential treatment by the British, they certainly enjoyed, along with the other southerners, the benefits of education that were denied the north and took advantage of the new opportunities better than most other groups. As independence drew near, they were well placed to benefit more than most. Following the 1951 Constitution, the leading independence movement, the National Council of Nigeria and the Cameroons, under its leader Azikiwe, was perceived to become more and more an organisation catering for the Ibo- and Ibibio-speaking peoples. As a result, it began to lose the support of a number of Yoruba- and Hausa-speaking people. As an Ijebu trader perceived it: 'In 1948 it was clear [that Azikiwe's] great objective was to set himself up as a dictator ... and to make the Ibo nation the master race' (quoted in Rotberg 1965:358). Even a neutral observer like Rotberg concedes that the Ibo were promoted by Azikiwe to the forefront of the movement (Rotberg 1965).

The Ibo, like so many advanced groups in economically backward regions, had migrated to other regions, using their educational benefits to secure economic advancement. With so much to gain from being part of a unified state, such groups are reluctant seceders. Only discrimination that curtails those economic opportunities and/or violence that threatens their lives are likely to overcome their natural reluctance to secede. In the case of the Ibo, mounting discrimination and pogroms in the northern cities combined in 1966 to drive a strongly pro-union group, which had previously borne collective violence (at Jos in 1945 and Kano in 1953), to take the secessionist road. The discrimination in employment, work contracts and business licences had been going on since the 1950s as a result of the 'northernisation' of administration and business by the Northern Regional Government. Angered by alleged Ibo nepotism, northerners had made a concerted effort to remove Ibo from high positions in government and universities. The military coup of January 1966 by mainly Ibo officers and their unification decree abolishing the regions were both interpreted in the north as attempts at Ibo domination. The result was a counter-coup by Gowon and the widespread rioting of September to October, when more than 10,000 Ibo were massacred. Following the pogroms, about one million people abandoned everything they possessed and trekked back to their home region of Biafra (de St. Jorre 1972:85–7).

In mid-1966, it was Gowon who had been talking of secession, saying 'the basis for unity [in the country] is not there ... I therefore feel that we should review the issue of our national standing' (quoted in Buchheit 1978:166). Nor was he the only one to raise this issue. The Ad Hoc Conference on the Constitution in September saw all three regions suggesting the inclusion of a right of secession. Secession, therefore, was in the air as a peaceful and legitimate possibility when the northern city massacres of Ibo began (Buchheit 1978:174).

The only functioning political bodies in eastern Nigeria at the time of the deepening crisis were the Consultative Assembly and the Advisory Committee of Chiefs and Elders. At a joint session of these bodies in May 1967, they claimed that the lack of the provision of security meant that the federation had forfeited any claim to their allegiance. They further mandated General Ojukwu to declare 'eastern Nigeria a free sovereign and independent state by the name and title of the Republic of Biafra' (Buchheit 1978:173).

Horowitz claims that, though the emergence of a secessionist movement is determined mainly by domestic politics, the success of such a movement is determined by international politics (Horowitz 1985:230). Only in a minority of cases, however, mainly as a result of strategic, economic or ideological motives overriding natural conservatism, do foreign governments side with secessionists (Wood 1981:132). It was unusual, therefore, for Biafra to have received various forms of military and diplomatic support. Gabon, Côte d'Ivoire and Zambia recognised Biafra; France was sympathetic and sent arms covertly; China gave verbal support; and Portugal, South Africa, Israel, Haiti and Tanzania were sympathetic. But the international support for Biafra did not match that received by the rump state. The international community as a whole, including the Organisation of African Unity (OAU), reiterated the familiar line of respect for territorial integrity and non-intervention in internal affairs. It refused to contemplate change to the nation-state status quo.

Military defeat and surrender for Biafra finally came in January 1970, but bitterness continues concerning the envy, hatred and destruction of lives and livelihood that began the war. The pogroms rapidly, and possibly permanently, turned a regional group (the Ibo) who readily emigrated from their homeland and defended federal unity, into a group not only conscious of its identity as never before, but longing still, in the case of many, for the propitious events yet to arise which would permit successful secession. Since 1970, the exploitation of the east's oil reserves largely for the benefit of the central government/ruling elite has added the dimension of discrimination and neglect to that of fear for their preservation. Should their demand for a larger share of the benefits from their resources be met with central repression, the flickering flame of secession could still flare up again. So far, it has only ignited amongst two minority groups in the east, namely the Ogoni and the Ijaw (*ARB* 1995, vol. 32 (12):12054), both of whom have aspirations for political autonomy and a fair share of the oil wealth; but it could easily spread.

SUCCESS IN ERITREA

Many have argued that no state will readily hand secessionists their demands. There is one exception in Africa, namely Ethiopia. The current Ethiopian government, themselves installed after a successful rebel conquest of the Ethiopian state, not only kept its promise to allow its Eritrean allies to hold a referendum on independence, but freely granted that independence upon the overwhelming evidence of the electorate's wishes. This single successful post-independence secession in Africa is an apparently unlikely one. Eritrea is not a homogeneous region, either in ethnicity, religion, development or history. There are at least nine nationalities, who in total split more or less evenly between the Christian and Muslim religions. The eight Muslim nationalities were never subject to Ethiopian rule before the federation of 1952 (by which the UN established a self-governing state within Ethiopia). The Christian Tigrinya, on the other hand, experienced many attempts to assimilate them, which at times they accepted and at other times resisted.

The movement for secession began with the Muslim nationalities' vain opposition to the proposals after the Second World War for the former Italian colony to be united with Ethiopia. As the federal government began to encroach on daily life, the Eritrean Liberation Movement organised demonstrations and strikes in the late 1950s. Faced with severe repression, they turned in the 1960s into an armed secessionist movement, the ELF. One could characterise the eight nationalities as backward groups (many being nomadic) in an advanced society, in that most of the benefits of Italian industrialisation and education had gone to the more settled Tigrinya. The secessionist movement might have stayed as a Muslim concern, with little prospect of success, but for the central authority's response of indiscriminate repression upon people throughout Eritrea, especially following their annexation of the self-governing state in 1962. The counter-insurgency measures included a scorched-earth policy, which drove 28,000 to flee to Sudan; the detention of 3,000 civilian prisoners; reprisals and atrocities against villagers and nomads; and on-the-spot fines and punishments. Just as alienating was the process of enforced adoption of Amharic, which is not the indigenous language of any Eritreans (Cliffe 1989:136). The effect was to drive the Tigrinya, who in the 1940s and 1950s had widely supported the union, to join the ELF in growing numbers.

The union was not a success and, almost inevitably, the Tigrinya broke away in 1974 to form the EPLF, which had 'a more clear-cut national democratic programme and more coherent and centralised structure' (Cliffe 1989:138). With armed conflict confined to the peripheral areas, the EPLF might have stayed the minor partner in the secessionist cause but for the events of 1974–7. That period, when the Ethiopian military were weakened by the revolution of 1974 and the Somali war of 1977–80, saw the ELF and EPLF gain control of the entire Eritrean territory, save Asmara and Massawa. For the EPLF, this had a dramatic effect, for it brought them into close contact with the Tigrinya peasantry for the first time and, with the introduction of land reform, they were able to win over the vast majority to their cause. Gaining the peasants as their supporters and their youths as fighters transformed the EPLF into the larger movement. Fresh clashes with the ELF, as both retreated before a Soviet-revitalised Ethiopian army, left the latter severely weakened and less able to withstand the ruling military council's onslaught of 1979–89. The ELF eventually lost even its peripheral bases and withdrew into Sudan, where it split into several factions.

This turn of events left the EPLF as the dominant secessionist force. Yet it was conscious that it needed to convince non-Tigrinyas that it was no exclusive Christian organisation. By and large, the balance it maintained in its leadership and fighting units between nationalities and religious groups was successful in providing, for the first time, a united Eritrean national secessionist movement. It was a demonstration that Herder's *'Blut und Boden'* (blood and soil), with its emphasis on a shared organic (particularly linguistic) inheritance, is not the only valid concept of a nation state. There can also be the state based on what Renan calls *'la volonté de vivre ensemble'* (the will to live together). This makes a nation the result of a conscious historical process and goes some way to overcoming ethnic factionalism (Prunier 1994:73).

It is a long way from military success in a disputed territory to becoming an internationally recognised sovereign state (as Somaliland has found: as of 1998, no nation had recognised it). A number of favourable events in the regional and international political scene, however, combined to facilitate the transition to independence in Eritrea's case (see Pool 1993). First, the alliance with the Tigray People's Liberation Front (TPLF) proved too much for the Ethiopian army, weakened as it was by the withdrawal of Soviet aid in the late 1980s, and the political centre collapsed. Whilst the TPLF-dominated forces filled the vacuum in Addis Ababa, the EPLF filled it in Asmara. The alliance meant that there was no opposition from the Ethiopian authorities to a referendum on independence and subsequent secession. (Ironically, the friendship has subsequently broken down and, in 1998, they were involved in a border war.) Secondly, on the international front, the region no longer held its former strategic significance, following the end of the linking of Gulf oil security to Red Sea security and the close of the Cold War. Further, the EPLF's abandonment of Marxism in 1987 and its de facto recognition by Western governments throughout the famine relief operations of 1985–6, 1988 and 1990 meant that Western support for independence was not withheld. In 1993, two years after the collapse of Mengistu's rule, Eritrea formally became an internationally recognised nation-state.

How does secessionism relate to the propositions?

Ten propositions (see the end of Chapter 1) were made earlier about all forms of disengagement. Their applicability to secessionism, in particular, will now be considered.

Under the heading of the nature of disengagement, it was hypothesised that disengagement is a universal phenomenon, a multi-scale phenomenon and a responsive strategy.

It has been shown in the discussion above that secessionism, like other forms of disengagement, is a universal phenomenon, though, unlike the others, it only exists in a collective form. Historically, attempts by social groups to exclude themselves from the control of central power have gone on continuously since precolonial days, although geographically it has been concentrated within peripheral groups. Though typically led by young educated men, secessionist movements have nevertheless attracted all ages and classes and both genders.

As a responsive strategy, most secessionist movements represent defensive disengagement against authorities that are hostile by design or neglect. However, some of the examples have suggested that, at times, opportunist disengagement plays a part, such as in collapsing states. For instance, in the chaos of Congo (Democratic Republic of Congo) in 1960, regional strongmen made their bids (in vain, as it transpired) to head states of their own. Writes Willame:

> By the end of [1960] centrifugal pressures had produced the separatist movements of ... Bakongo Alliance ... Bayanzi Alliance and the Democratic Assembly of Lac-Kwango-Kwilu in the province of Leopoldville [west]; the proclamation of the 'Mining State' of S. Kasai [south-central]; the secessionist attempts of Equateur Province [north-west]; and the creation of an autonomous government in the Maniema district [east]. Most of the dissident groups were limited to the formation of paper governments ... S. Kasai, S. Katanga, and Kongo Central [west], though, were able to create functioning local governments and thus establish their independence from Leopoldville. (Willame 1972:35)

Under the heading of the pattern of disengagement, it was hypothesised that disengagement depends on macro and micro factors.

This is indeed the case with secessionism. Despite the common perception, withdrawal from the state is rarely, if ever, solely because the regional groups were different from the central authorities in the primordial sense. The crucial factor is the pattern of domination. Secessionists perceive themselves to be dominated in an unacceptable and often threatening way. Thus, even where distinct social identity already existed, it provoked little or no collective action to escape. Ethnicity by itself is rarely a sufficient mobilising force. What did produce a high degree of collective social identity and action, however, was where a region, whether of single or multiple ethnic groups, had a shared experience of differentiation, followed by discrimination, neglect or persecution. Collective action readily became secessionist in nature when the central authorities were unwilling to concede the need for distinct policies to redress the discrimination and neglect, but rather took steps to suppress the demands for fairer government. Insensitive responses lit the fires of antagonism, whilst severe militaristic reactions only added further fuel. Another key macro-scale factor has been the availability of the secessionist strategy, which, in the case of armed secessionism in particular, concerns access to external suppliers of military equipment.

Micro-scale factors weigh heavily against individual participation in secessionist movements. There is the question of the normative illegitimacy of using violence and that of the unlikelihood of success in the face of superior military power (the odds being very low to those who know their history). The normative and practical obstacles mean that it is the rarest of disengagement phenomena. Any success in mobilisation, therefore, falls heavily upon the networks of influence. These have to promote and sustain appropriate norms to undertake a strategy that is so risky and time-consuming (of vital concern to agriculturists). These must interpret the events of society to them and promote a secessionist response. Clearly, secessionist leaders have a prominent role in this. They have been most successful in winning hearts and minds where they have nurtured both fear and hatred of the central authorities and dreams of a prosperous future in a new state. The few cases where the entire adult population has had the opportunity to demonstrate its support have shown that effective secessionist leadership can win support across the social divides. Thus Eritrea's 1993 referendum saw 99 per cent in favour of independence; in the 1961 Legislative Council election in Uganda, there was an electoral boycott of 97 per cent by the Bugandans, representing their near total opposition to a loss of all autonomy within the unitary state; and a UK Government Commission found that 87 per cent of the Somali-inhabited region of Kenya favoured secession (Hoskyns 1969:33). As noted above, however, not every elite-led separatist movement can secure such a broad popular base, especially, as in the case of the Lozi, where the selfish ambition of power is ill-disguised.

Even popular movements face a near-insurmountable challenge in translating their level of support into effective leverage to secure 'release' by the central authorities. Rarely have bare negotiations achieved anything, with the possible exception of Buganda in the 1961 London Conference. And this exception was more the result of tactical support by the leading Legislative Council opposition party, so as to ensure an alliance that would secure the independence election (Sathyamurthy 1986:386). Secessionists throughout history have found that only weapons talk when it comes to powers giving up territory, people and resources. Limited arms purchases and guerrilla tactics may not be enough for outright victory, but they can secure military stalemates even against modern armies. Such may be sufficient for previously reluctant central authorities to open negotiations, though the concessions in these circumstances tend to be minimal. For example, after fourteen years of failing to impose a military solution, President Nimeiri of Sudan offered the south self-government, the recognition of English as its principal language and equal rights for Christians and followers of African religions. Had this policy of recognising southern distinctiveness been translated into corresponding action by the bureaucrats administering the south, those desiring to disengage might have settled for autonomy. But the evidence of only the slowest change, capped by Nimeiri's apparent U-turn when he announced that Shariah law would henceforth be the basis of all law, undermined the fragile peace and exposed the unresolved problem of racism.

Apparently more sincere concessions have been made to the Touareg and the peoples of Casamance. But the overall picture confirms

Horowitz's contention that, although the emergence of secessionist movements is determined by domestic politics, whether they succeed is a matter of international politics (Horowitz 1985:230). This external dimension becomes central when there is sustained leverage by outside powers, whether assisting or restricting military support to either the secessionist or government side, and/or concerted action by the international community to bring antagonists to the negotiating table or to act as peace negotiators themselves. In the end, major structural factors outweigh all other determinants. Thus, for all that individual Eritreans may have enjoyed personal efficacy, normative agreement, supportive cultural networks, regional self-consciousness, manifest threats from the central authority and a ready-made, highly efficient, political and military organisation, in the end it was the action of external powers, especially Soviet strangulation of aid to Ethiopia, that undermined the centre's resistance and opened the door to the secessionists' fulfilment. For the Congo seceders, there may have been fewer positive social and personal factors, but, even so, the crucial element in their defeat was US-sponsored UN interventionist forces. Or, again, the Somali armed secessionist movement in Kenya dried up after a new Somali government withdrew support.

Under the heading of the significance of disengagement, it was hypothesised that it provides a measure of political authorities, threatens the power balance of political systems, delays democratic consolidation and usually provokes resistance by force.

Secessionism can be seen as a measure of an authority's failing legitimacy. It denies the right of the authorities to continue any longer as the rightful powers of the contested areas. The characteristic intransigence of their response to seceders can also be seen as a measure of the authorities' weakness, in that it is born, not of power, but of fear – a fear that has nothing to offer the disaffected other than threats and violence. The shift in the power balance threatened by secessionism very much depends on the size and prosperity of the putative breakaway region and the influence its people have had in central government prior to the conflict. The longer the conflict continues, the greater the danger to the central authority of imitation by other disaffected groups. Perhaps even reciprocal separatism will occur: secession in the south of Katanga quickly produced an equal and opposite secession among the Baluba of north Katanga; the secession of the Sara in southern Chad when certain northern Muslim groups were dominant was followed by the secession of the northerners when the Sara took power, and then again renewed northern control led to a second Sara secession; in Congo (Brazzaville), when the Bakongo of the south were dominant, northerners planned secession, but, after a coup brought northerners to power, the Bakongo planned the same strategy (Horowitz 1985:278).

The perceived danger to the world nation-states system of secession has already been flagged by the UN. Boutros Ghali, when Secretary General in 1992, warned that:

> The new danger which will appear in the world in the next ten years is more fragmentation. Rather than 100 or 200 countries, you may have at the end of the century 400 countries and we will not be able to achieve any kind of economic development, not to mention more disputes on boundaries ... [In Africa] there are 5,000 tribes. Suppose each tribe would say it has the right to self-determination, you will have a kind of new micro-nationalism with small states of 50,000 or 100,000 people. (Quoted in *The Times* 21/9/92)

Whether or not he is correct about mini-states being powerless and economically crippled or whether economic development must always be the prime concern of people, the lament is widely shared in the world body and reportedly in the OAU, who would rather live with the colonial mismatch of peoples to frontiers than see more Eritreas.

This situation highlights the fact that disengagement is not simply a bipolar conflict between political authorities and dissenters, but a triangular conflict between the authorities, the disengagers and also the non-disengagers. Secessionist movements, especially if seen through government propaganda, may be perceived to be people of wanton and unjustified violence, holding an ideology that endangers the central authority's very existence. In addition, any cost of waging a war against them, in terms of lives lost and expenditure entailed, simply adds to the resentment (a resentment that may last long after the dispute has been resolved). That resentment spills over into violence against those perceived to be socially related to the secessionist movement (for example through ethnic/regional identity) is not surprising. Hence, southern Sudanese living in northern Sudan have been harassed by the local population (African Rights 1995a).

Secessionism within a state that has a democratic constitution is a protest that the institutions of representation and distribution are not working properly. The minority has no confidence that its distinctive voice is adequately heard and that its distinctive needs are adequately met. Whilst the central government is committed to crushing their withdrawal by force rather than listening and negotiating, the mutual antagonism precludes the building of a democratic union. Even without military conflict, no democracy can be consolidated whilst the very boundary of the constituency is disputed.

It has been observed throughout the chapter that secessionism is usually resisted by force as the first resort. Negotiation has rarely been the first response of the state; rather, the norm has been that, when arms are taken up by the secessionists, negotiation only follows a military impasse. In the shadows of any conflict, also, is the military. If an armed secessionist movement is met by force and a military conflict ensues, then the military authorities not only become a more influential voice in the central government, but may themselves become a semi-autonomous focus of power that is not readily reined in.

The attraction of secessionism is that its withdrawal strategy promises more than a negative avoidance of the worst excesses. But, given its poor record in keeping its utopian promises and the high practical costs, it is the rarest of disengagement phenomena. Indeed, without outside help strengthening secessionists and/or weakening the core authority, it is probably doomed to failure, whether it uses political or military methods. The next chapter moves from the least popular and the least successful disengagement strategy to one much more shaped to providing autonomy within the current parameters of struggles to survive economically and militarily, namely cultural withdrawal. The battle for the mind can at times be a bloody affair, but, as will be shown, it is often an undeclared war, and a war, for all the inequality of the sides, which is unwinnable and where the combatants frequently settle for a decree nisi.

Cultural withdrawal

*Exile, the informal economies, magic and religion are
the most obvious paths to physical, economic
and spiritual survival.* (Lemarchand, 'Uncivil States and Civil
Societies')

The hegemonic dream

The goal of those involved in the hegemonic quest is to create a 'unified moral order' in which 'a certain way of life and thought is dominant, in which one concept of reality is diffuse throughout society'
(Williams 1960:587). For leaders of political authorities, the aim is to
bring the diverse outlooks and beliefs found across their domain into
subjection to their own, not by using force, but through persuasion,
integration and co-optation. The project is, of course, as Young
reminds us, 'a mere incubus, images of absolute power etched in the
minds of its promoters, managers, and beneficiaries. Even at its zenith,
the empirical state fell far short of its extravagant designs' (Young
1994a:40). Cooper (1980:111–24) describes eloquently the failure of the
British in Zanzibar to eradicate 'idleness' and establish a new order of
industriousness, self-discipline and sobriety. Nevertheless, the ambition persists. In Fatton's definition, based on Gramsci, a ruling class is
hegemonic when it:

> has established its material, ethical and political leadership over society, and
> when the relationships of superordination and subordination are accepted
> by all as organic and not contradictory, and as legitimate and not exploita-
> tive. When such a situation crystallises, the ruling class has achieved hege-
> mony. (Fatton 1989:52–3)

In precolonial societies *par excellence*, there was a strong reliance on
ideological coercion. This was because, given the non-separation of the

producers from their means of production, economic (class) methods to ensure the extraction of surplus were inappropriate. This dependence on ideological coercion for extraction purposes explains, in the view of Sangmpam, the 'exceptionally high number of ideological rituals in lineage societies' (Sangmpam 1994:95).

The approaches of the ruling classes, both under colonial rule and since independence, have largely centred around statism. This has three pillars of belief. First, state power represents the will of the people (in the singular) and rules in their collective interest. It is, therefore, entitled to rule by diktat. Secondly, state power promotes unity and is therefore entitled to expect consent, or at least acquiescence. Criticism and appeals to traditional and manifold cultures are not acceptable. Thirdly, state power promotes economic well-being ('development') and is therefore entitled to extract resources from the populace and to distribute those resources as it sees fit (see Chazan 1994b:75).

> The goal has been to penetrate society deeply enough to shape how individuals throughout the society identify themselves, and the organization of the state has been to effect such far-reaching domination. It has included vertically connected agencies, designed to reach to all pockets within the territory, and specialized components to promote the state's system of meaning and legitimacy (for example schools), to make universal rules (legislative bodies), to execute those rules (bureaucracy), to adjudicate (courts) and to coerce (armies and police). (Migdal 1994:24)

On this basis of nationalism, authoritarianism, communalism and materialism, the power elites attempted to construct a unifying national culture or, to put it more cynically, to justify their continuance in rule. The attempt to coalesce attachment to the state and attachment to the leader are illustrated clearly in Mobutu's presentation methods as head of state in Zaire. What he at first called 'authenticité' (authentic nationalism) later became the quite explicit 'Mobutism', with its ban for a time in 1974 on the press using the name of any state official other than himself (Callaghy 1980). Young describes the process as the dominant class transforming society according to an image of themselves (Young 1994b:247–9).

Such a project, however, does not go unchallenged. A whole array of social organisations maintain distinct popular political cultures or, in reference to the surrounding dominant culture, develop 'contra-cultures'.[1] Thus, despite all the resources at their disposal to disseminate

---

[1] The concept of contra-culture was introduced by Yinger. He writes that the set of norms of a subculture 'derives from standard socialization in a sub-society', whereas the set of norms from a contra-culture 'stems from conflict and frustration in the experience of those who share many of the values of the whole society but are thwarted in their efforts to achieve those values' (Yinger 1960:632–3).

their ideology and suppress alternatives, such as 'organic intellectuals' acting as 'managers of legitimation' (Fatton 1989:52), the hegemonic schema has rarely been able to achieve symbolic ascendancy. What Mbembe calls society's 'historical capacity for indiscipline' ultimately undermines and defeats them all (quoted in Young 1994b:279).

> Thirty years of authoritarian rule have forged a concept of indiscipline as a method of popular resistance. In order to survive and resist laws and rules judged to be antiquated, people have had to resort to the treasury of their imagination. Given that life is one long fight against the state, the collective imagination has gradually conspired to craftily defy everything which symbolizes public authority. (Monga 1994, quoted in Diamond 1994b:14)

As Monga notes, this is broader than withdrawal from participatory politics, which only briefly seized the people's imagination at independence; rather, it is withdrawal from authority and community.

Popular political cultures can be defined as 'a people's predominant beliefs, attitudes, values, ideals, sentiments and evaluations about the political system of its country and the role of the self in that system' (Diamond 1994a:8). The cultural arenas in Africa's young, heterogeneous states are typically ones of conflict rather than consensus. Indeed, Kamrava takes hotly contested and fragmented political cultures to be the defining feature of the Third World (Kamrava 1995). Chazan captures this graphically when she writes, 'A constant tug of war exists between competing institutions and orientations, between alternative explications of consciousness and meaning' (Chazan 1994b:60). And it may be that no single ideology has a total monopoly even within a single individual. The Zimbabwean politician, Joshua Nkomo, tells how his Christian father, a mission teacher and opponent of traditional medicine, turned to it to cure him as a baby (Nkomo 1984:8–11, 20–1). As Bayart reminds us, when referring to Nigerian and Kenyan city dwellers:

> The members of African societies pursue family, therapeutic, economic, or political strategies which transcend the usual divisions to which we try to assign them. Someone who is ill, will one after another, consult the doctor in an Abidjan hospital, the faith healer in the suburbs and the witchdoctor in his village, because he simultaneously inhabits these different worlds. (Bayart 1989:12)

The absence of adequate political institutions that could integrate ideas and accommodate differences exacerbates the situation. The conflict itself is, of course, a productive interchange (Comaroff 1985:154–5). It will convince some of the inadequacy of the current values, or the expression of those values, and may lead to innovative experiments with superstructural reconstruction so as to offer better meaning within the changing circumstances. But one must not assume that the process is simply one of social change producing ideological change, whereby it is brought to correspond to the new reality. Newly emerging ideas and beliefs may constitute a negation, as much as a reflection, of the penetrating new order and further, new ideas may precede and precipitate social change, rather than always superseding them (van Binsbergen 1981:40; Fields 1985:15–21).

Counter-hegemonic values are not only expressed through organisations and movements. As Schatzberg reminds us, it is vital not to miss the dispersion of political ideas over a much wider area of African life:

> To understand the full range of African political thought ... we must examine the diverse means by which people voice political ideas indirectly. In other words African political thought must be redefined to include the works of novelists, dramatists, poets, musicians, journalists, theologians, philosophers, social scientists, proverbs, fables and oral literature. (Schatzberg 1993:445)

And, one could add, the constant debates and discussions of African life. Nevertheless, it is still true to say that ideological movements, both secular and religious, and their leaders play, in their more organised way, a vital role in redefining norms, beliefs and the appropriate expressions of these in relation to authority. 'These articulations have symbolically emancipated individuals and groups from official restraints, recast political norms and culturally reinforced the economic dimensions of civic restructuring' (Chazan 1994b:82). These associations and associational leaders act as those who frame alternative, counter-hegemonic agenda. Specifically of religious innovators, but relevant to a wider field, van Binsbergen says:

> Three categories are suggested to form a potential avant garde of religious innovation: those who are, more than others, involved in the new economic and political opportunities that arise during the period covered; those who are, as religious specialists, more than others involved in the religious forms of a previous stage of religious innovation; and those who belong to segments of society previously oppressed and who now, under changing political and economic conditions, stir with hope (initially expressed in a religious idiom) of improving their social position. (van Binsbergen 1981:30)

For many organisations the techniques of resistance and opposition to cultural domination are no more than self-enclosure, evasion, impassivity and indifference, or perhaps ridicule. Others will engage in a more active promotion of an explicit counter-culture. Those most opposed to the promotion of a single cohesive cultural framework are those groups that are 'holistic in aim'. These:

> seek to deal with all the needs of their members and consequently demand total allegiance ... [Such] fundamentalist groups, ethnic associations, parochial networks, or ideological movements either ignore the state or seek to replace it, leaving little leeway for ideas or interests beyond their own particular purviews. (Chazan 1994a:273)

In view of their bounded nature and explicit aims, these holistic organisations will be the primary, though not the exclusive, focus of this chapter.

The process of resistance and withdrawal from the dominant classes reaches, therefore, into the realm of ideology, morality and social customs. As in the other areas of disengagement, so disengagement from cultural domination is a responsive strategy. It is a spiritual withdrawal – spiritual in the sense that it offers a future millennium or a present self-enclosed community, rather than a destination for emigration; it turns its back on the authorities' values and beliefs rather than simply on their laws and institutions.

Cultural disengagement can be differentiated by its outlook – religious or secular – and by its social pattern. The latter may entail actually physically withdrawing from society in autonomous communities (what I call communalism), or maintaining a measure of daily social and economic links, but holding ideological views and practices distinct from the majority (what I call separatism). The categorisation can be represented in tabular form (Table 5.1).

Since separatism and communalism have blurred boundaries and groups in time can move from one to another, the chapter will follow the twofold division of outlook, namely religious and secular, whilst illustrating the separatist/communalist distinction.

Table 5.1 A typology of cultural disengagement

Outlook	Social pattern	
	Separatism (within society)	Communalism (outside society)
Religious	Quietism	'New Jerusalems'
Secular	Delinquent and criminal, stigmatised, primordial, and mobile subcultures	Self-help organisations and networks that seek self-sufficiency

Religiously motivated withdrawal

Religion has always been central to ideological conflict and subsequent withdrawal. But not all religious movements must be seen as political, let alone counter-hegemonic. Certain belief systems, for example many spiritist and animist cults, have never taken a large-scale organised form and have rarely related their precepts to issues of political control. Further, even those religions that are influential because of their mass support, or certainly their leaders, often offer regime support. For example, the spirit mediums have, since precolonial times, legitimised new rulers in the name of the ancestors and, more recently, leaders of the mainstream Muslim and Christian organisations have often been keen to be part of, or closely allied to, the ruling elite, with its benefits of wealth and influence. This is true even when regimes do not share their world-view. Thus the Islamic emirs of northern Nigeria chose to enter into an alliance with the British colonialists in the early twentieth century largely for temporal gain.

Religious movements and the factions within these movements have covered the entire spectrum from political engagement to disengagement; from legitimisation and accommodation, through quietism,[2] to providing a regime critique or even leading rebellion. Their appeal to ordinary Africans has been, first and foremost, in their role in providing religious meaning: a fact surprisingly overlooked by those many political scientists and historians who place African religious movements into a proto-nationalist/nationalist sequence and see them as little more than anticolonialism in religious disguise (Ranger 1986:51). But often there is an additional political appeal. This can range from offering a way of sticking the tongue out at authority to setting out a serious counter-ideology and alternative political programme; from providing comfort and an ideology of resignation in the midst of politically induced suffering to self-contained communities that escape all other authority; from offering welfare hand-outs and social advancement now to promising a future kingdom of material prosperity or spiritual bliss; from granting individual salvation from witchcraft or judgement to supplying an alternative 'family' support network and sense of belonging. As Ranger observes, 'Once we take into account the full range of religious responses, and the full range of problems facing those who responded, we can see a much more complex pattern of religious politics' (Ranger 1986:51). Indeed, one might go so far as to say that such is the overlap of religious, political and social objectives in African religious movements that neat separation of motivations is

---

[2] Quietism is taken to be a preoccupation with the divine and divine matters, to the exclusio of all but a minimal interest in secular life.

decidedly difficult. For Haynes, the 'spiritual and material concerns interact with highly fluid boundaries in a context where many Africans relate to religion as a means of solving a number of personal problems, some of which will be material issues' (Haynes 1995a:101).

Before looking at examples of religiously motivated withdrawal, both within and outside society, one last caution for analysis must be heeded. In studying the social phenomenon of disengagement, the concern must be not with what the official orthodoxy of the various movements have to say about political authority, but with the views and practices of popular religion. Popular religion is the product of the interaction of the original doctrine (that is orthodoxy) and the cultural conditions of the community of converts (which are likely to be very different from that in which the religion was born) (Laitin 1978:572–3). The same point is illustrated very clearly in Ranger's excellent essay on the Mwana Lesa movement of 1925:

> Nyirenda brought the Watch Tower message to the Lala. But the Lala brought many things with them when they responded to the Watch Tower message. The Mwana Lesa movement was formed through the interaction of the two – of Nyirenda's particular Watch Tower teaching and of Lala religious beliefs ... The Lala wished to assimilate Nyirenda to their mythical system and sought through him to realize their [pre-existent] millennial expectations. But they also wanted to draw upon the new things he had to offer. (Ranger 1975:53, 65)

The resultant practical religion of the converted makes for a diversity of responses, even within a single theology, and responses that vary over time. Haynes's caution is to be heeded:

> To speak of theology, Islam or Christianity, or the church, in the singular is to fail to appreciate that such concepts only have meaning in the class context within which they are viewed. Religious unity is a chimera. Religious 'universality' in fact masks diversity, a result of the stratification of social classes and groups. Clerics' theology is the official philosophy of their religion, yet it transmogrifies into a number of forms which pertain to the level of life at which the recipient of the ideas exists. 'Popular religion', that is religion as it is lived, is thus quite different from that of the professional articulators of the religion's philosophy. (Haynes 1995a:106)

Such popular religion may become a potent symbol of opposition to the authorities. This is especially true where oppressed minorities have a different religious as well as ethnic affiliation from those in power. Religion can play an important part in mobilising the people to support separatism. Thus, the people of both southern Sudan and Casamance have used Christianity as part of their defensive ideology, that is, to 'provide the ideological basis for action against representatives of a dominant (Islamic) culture' (Haynes 1996a:14). In both cases,

Christianity had a significant, but not overwhelming, presence in the regions prior to the armed conflict. Yet, in the course of the resistance to Islamic rule and its fierce retaliation, Christianity has grown rapidly. A very large-scale conversion to Christianity is reported, for instance, among the Dinka and Nuer of Sudan, such that, whereas in the early years of the conflict Christians made up about 10 per cent of the population and were subject to repression even by the secessionist movement (then Marxist in orientation), it now constitutes the majority. It seems clear that an element in this conversion is that Christianity is seen as a more powerful religion than animism, one providing a stronger political, social and cultural bulwark against the northern Islamisation. Such is the desire for a distinct and united identity in contrast to the north, that one civil official in the south argued: 'Most importantly, Christianity is needed to stand firm against encroaching civilisations. We need a Christian Fundamentalism. There is an intrinsic feeling that there is something other than Islam. But if the Northerners became fundamentalist Christians, we will become Moslems' (quoted in African Rights 1995a:39; cf. African Rights 1995b:49). The growth of Christianity is less dramatic in Casamance, but still the mobilisation against Islamic domination was led by a Catholic priest. In both cases, 'popular Christianity, closely linked with ethnicity concerns, is the main symbol and vehicle of opposition to a putatively hegemonic state and its religio-political allies' (Haynes 1996b:17).

The use of religion as a symbol of opposition is not to say that it is all self-consciously politically motivated. Yet authorities are inherently nervous of even the smallest sects, seeing threatening wolves in religious clothing. Traditional, colonial and postcolonial rulers have all suspected revolutionary or counter-establishment aims and have feared religion's potential to mobilise and provide a focus for opposition. Bayart summarises the state-religion rivalry succinctly:

> The coexistence is not completely peaceful because the state cannot officially agree to the existence of [religious] movements which refuse all civic obligations, such as respect for the national colours, censuses, electoral participation, incantation of party slogans, purchase of party cards, payment of taxes or of health care ... If [churches, temples and mosques] do not set out to subvert the space of the state, very few of them commend themselves to the authorities, payment of taxes or the expectations of the ideology of development and national unity. In their actions they double up the statist root system with their own networks and provide logistical support to the 'exit' option ... Like the prophetic movements of the colonial period, contemporary sects ignore rather than contest the state. (Bayart 1989:256–7)

Before looking at Christian and Islamic movements and their offshoots, something will first be said about African spirit religions and their role in cultural withdrawal.

ANIMIST WITHDRAWAL

Animists are normally characterised as apolitical, but this is not strictly correct. In traditional African societies, spirit religion played a crucial role in the legitimisation of rulers. A senior medium of the Tandi chiefship, Zimbabwe, told Ranger in 1981: 'A Chief **must** have a spirit medium. The spirit medium **is** the chiefdom' (Ranger 1984:317). Though rulers claimed descent from original ancestors/clan founders, their confirmation in office by those very ancestors came through the spirit mediums. Through these mediums, the leaders of the past expressed their will to the present. Rulers ruled, therefore, not only by the ancestor's election but on behalf of their interests. As a result, rulers and religious leaders lived in harmony in a unified world controlled by their ancestors.

The entry of the colonialists drove a wedge between the two, by undermining the legitimacy of the chiefs in the medium's eyes. The European authorities did this by interfering in the selection of the chiefs themselves. And, even when the true descendants were retained as chiefs, they deflected the people's obligations from the ancestral will to the imperial will. In response to such compromised leadership, there was a widespread move to withdraw allegiance 'from the chiefs of the present, to the chiefs of the past' (Lan 1985:140), who could only be made available to them by their mediums. 'The chief who held his legitimacy as a representative of the ... [ancestors] through descent, lost it to the representative of the ... [ancestors] through possession' (Lan 1985:141). For example, when chief Kago 'publicly refused to join the 1901 Shona insurrection, the spirit mediums successfully appealed to the local population to disregard his pronouncements' (Isaacman 1976:129).

For their part, in contrast to so many chiefs, the mediums were implacable in their hostility to the colonial authority and culture. One medium's pronouncement was transcribed as:

> The spirit disapproves of certain developments introduced in modern days. For instance it does not care for contour ridging because it causes too much work and has introduced features that were not in the landscape in former days. His spirit declares that there is no pleasure in walking the fields or bush as the contours make movement difficult. This innovation makes the tribal spirit angry and as a result people are short of food. The tribal spirit ... dislikes the rising rates levelled by the rural councils. (Gelfand 1971:140, quoted in Ranger 1984:318)

Some took to organising and coordinating rebellions, or raising support and providing ritual approval and divine sanctions for secular leaders of uprisings (Isaacman 1976:128; Chingono 1996:164–5). Others chose symbolic disengagement, such as ritual prohibitions.

They refused to have contact with whites and the artefacts of polluted white society. To them it was a society vastly inferior to the world of the dead.

This was the position of the spirit mediums in the Rhodesian Zambezi Valley in the 1970s. Disengagement from white culture and chiefs who had absorbed it had been the only possible recourse in the face of the overwhelming force of colonial power. But, with the arrival of the Zimbabwe African National Liberation Army (ZANLA) guerrillas and their pledge to free the land from white control, the mediums, whose chief duty was to protect the land of their ancestors, thought again. They switched from passive disengagement to support for the guerrillas in their violent engagement to retrieve the lost lands and lost autonomy. To the mediums and their followers, the guerrilla leaders constituted the legitimate successors of the chiefs (Lan 1985).

Only after the Zimbabwe African National Union (ZANU)'s election victory was there a falling away of the ritual prohibitions that had made a symbolic protest against the exploitation of blacks by the European cultural invasion. 'The mediums feel that under [ZANU's] control, the beneficial aspects of white society should now be absorbed,' wrote Lan after independence (Lan 1985:214). He recorded that, in the main, they were enthusiastic about Western education, medicine and technology. Their previous rejection had been based, not so much on the threat of these novel methods to traditional ways, as on their association with those whose fundamental outlook threatened in a much more significant way their cultural foundations. They could only embrace technological change when it was within the parameters of their cultural priorities.

When the new state of Zimbabwe, in its turn, threatened those same priorities, it met a predictable resistance. In 1981, a government agency was established to declare who was and who was not allowed to practise traditional medicine. This attempt, in effect, to pronounce who was and who was not a legitimate and authentic medium encroached, like the colonialists before them, on the ground of legitimisation, which was the sole right of the ancestors, who expressed their will through the mediums. That the protest of the mediums was no hollow threat was shown the next year. Lan (1985) quotes a medium who accused the government of failing in its promise to bring development aid to the people of the Zambezi Valley and their ancestors. If this persisted, he threatened, the ancestors would transfer their legitimation elsewhere. Once again, in the face of cultural hegemony which they had no effective means of overcoming, they were threatening disengagement.

The attraction and inherent dangers of harnessing the counter-culture of spiritism has similarly appeared in Mozambique. The Mozambique National Resistance (Resistencia nacional Moçambicana or RENAMO) commanders quite specifically couched their motivating ideology in terms of disengagement from state-propagated secular values and a return to traditional ancestor worship. Thus the conflict with the Liberation Front of Mozambique (Fronte da libertaçao de Moçambique or FRELIMO) government was portrayed as a 'war of the spirits', a crusade against a cultural invasion that was forcing people to abandon their ancestors and accept foreign 'communist' ideas. Certainly, following independence, FRELIMO, under the slogan of 'Down with feudalism; down with obscurantism', opposed spirit possession, exorcism by traditional healers and those practices which perpetuated the prominence of chiefs. RENAMO, on the other hand, attempted to mobilise the support of the disgruntled mediums and thus to secure the legitimisation of the ancestors. Hence no major military decisions were made without prior consultation with the spirits. In Roesch's opinion:

> There can be little doubt the Renamo's religiously based propaganda, which calls on people to abandon communal villages and to return to their ancestral lands and traditional way of life, finds considerable resonance in the consciousness of the rural population of Gaza Province. (Roesch 1992:478)

The threat of state communalisation to their cash-cropping was real. RENAMO's violence, however, may have crossed the boundaries of acceptability to spiritist culture, for all its rhetoric and ritual:

> The ancestral spirits are now beginning to speak out against the violence being practised against their descendants by Renamo. Speaking through local spirit mediums, the ancestral spirits are letting it be known that they no longer want their 'children' to be troubled by Renamo and no longer want fighting between Frelimo and Renamo forces in their area. (Roesch 1992:478)

In the face of this threat to delegitimise the RENAMO movement, its leaders were pressured to consider peace moves. Spirit religion may not promote autonomous communities, but under spirit mediums it knows how to construct a social withdrawal that can carry a serious threat to local powers.

ISLAMIC WITHDRAWAL
The initial response to European (Christian and foreign) penetration of traditional Muslim areas, such as the Sahel, was commonly to undertake jihads. These were frequently led by what Coulon (1985) calls 'warrior prophets'. Despite their bravery and some temporary successes, the outcome of their holy wars was never in doubt and, in time, the military option was abandoned. Many reformist Muslim leaders found they had more to gain by close alliances with the French

authorities. It was an alliance that offered benefits to both. For the Muslim leaders, it offered them the opportunity to have a place within the power structure; for the French, it provided them with the intermediaries they need to maintain control over an 'alien' society. But, in popular Islam, there persisted a vigorous anti-authoritarianism (whether against the colonial or the independence authorities).

For most, this meant (and still means) separatism – a measure of social withdrawal from Christian educational systems and reliance on Islamic self-help organisations and networks, such as the popular Sufi brotherhoods.

> In many urban settings there is a sense of Muslim community that offers a welcome structure of solidarity and serves to replace networks of social solidarity which before urbanisation were based on kinship structures and on clan and age groups ... Muslim community organisations ... serve to 'rescue' those who come to the urban centre for economic betterment but instead find themselves cut off from family and community. For them religious-community organisations offer an alternative 'family'. (Haynes 1995a:105–6)

The popular Islamic organisations in Muslim states and even non-Muslim states (which are commonly in alliance with Muslim reformists) offer the opportunity to affirm the autonomy and identity of a religious or etho-religious community.

But communalist responses are also to be found. Under the charismatic leadership of some remarkable 'preacher-prophets' some strands of popular Islam have undertaken internal escape within counter-societies. These have openly defended alternative values and proclaimed a new social order within the European or independence government domains. Of the period of French rule in Senegal, Coulon writes that, like Mohammed's flight with his followers from Mecca to Medina (the 'Heijira'), they too, in their own way:

> organized their Heijira by regrouping their disciples into religious and labouring communities which were far from colonial towns and which, in time, became real townships themselves. Moreover when they set up their organization in pre-existing towns, they endeavoured to show their independence by creating separate neighbourhoods ... relationships with authorities were limited to paying taxes, recruiting soldiers, participating in compulsory public works projects ... and later also groundnut cultivation. Aside from these obligations, the Marabou's village lived its own life, at least on the ideological level. (Coulon 1985:358)

They thus successfully demarcated their own religious and social territory within the French colonial order. Also during the colonial period, many Mahdi movements arose within Islam. Their hope was that, when injustice reached its zenith, the Mahdi, the rightly directed one, who was to be a descendant of Mohammed (or Isa Jesus), would reconstruct past glories and start a reign of abundance and justice. From them, self-proclaimed Mahdis arose, who, in Sudan and northern Nigeria between 1880 and 1920, in some cases formed separate settlements.

Later, in the 1930s, a Sufi brotherhood leader, Ibrahim Niass, proclaimed himself the 'Saviour of the Age'. His message of anticolonialism and concern to keep Western education at bay (whilst encouraging the learning of Arabic) attracted a large following throughout West Africa, many of whom gathered in distinct communities (Cruise O'Brien 1988:24). Even outside the colonies with Islamic majorities, a few separatist communities developed, such as Chinsala, 'which emerged in Malawi at the end of the nineteenth century in reaction to the hegemonic policies of the Presbyterian church and to taxation' (Shepperson, quoted in Haynes 1996a:36).

A recent example of an urban community under the authority of a Marabout was that led by Muhammadu Marwa in Kano, northern Nigeria, in the 1980s. Known as the Yan Tatsine Movement, it particularly attracted young men who had migrated from the countryside:

> Their numbers swollen by land shortage, their casual occupations supplanted by modern technology, their survival threatened by inflation and their appeals for charity neglected by oil-rich townsmen, gardawa [a derogatory term for itinerant Islamic students] turned to a prophet who made them proud of their poverty ... [in] an elect community, introverted and paranoid, its members created a 'private republic' in the streets of Kano until destroyed by the army [in 1983]. (Iliffe 1987:245)

Their counter-culture was clear not only in their social isolation, but in their doctrine, which condemned affluence to the point that anyone wearing a watch, riding a bicycle, driving a car or sending their child to a state school was an infidel destined for hell.

CHRISTIAN WITHDRAWAL

Christianity and para-Christianity[3] ran parallel to the developments in Islam. That is, where it represented the prevailing religion, the majority of the mainstream denominations courted and were courted by the authorities. On the other hand, 'popular' Christianity and its offshoots were more prone to separatism. Negatively, this could be a reluctance either to join political parties, to honour the symbols of the state, to

---

[3] By para-Christianity are meant movements with a significant content of Christian and biblical symbolism and metaphors, but departing from some of its fundamental tenets.

accept inoculation, to send children to school or to utilise state courts (Ranger, in Crummey 1986:391; Lan 1985:41); or, positively they could set up parallel institutions, such as their own schools or courts (Rotberg 1966:150; Lan 1985:41).

Some argue that much of the modern-day 'Christian fundamentalism', which has seen such rapid growth across Africa in the last twenty years (estimated at forty-eight million church members and children (Johnstone 1990:45)), follows a pattern of cultural separatism and promoting disinterest in practical politics or even in tackling the impoverished 'earthly' conditions of Africans (Gifford 1991). This interpretation, however, is based on faulty logical deductions from certain fundamentalist beliefs and overgeneralises about a complex movement. It cannot be assumed that the call for members to set their minds on 'higher' things is necessarily incompatible with a concern for earthly affairs, any more than a hope of a 'brighter tomorrow' guarantees passivism today. Some streams within the movement certainly come close in their discourses to sneering at social involvement. One Liberian denomination (the Potter's House) circulated a tract in which Satan is presented as saying, 'I'll get you to dedicate your life to all kinds of enlightened causes. I must keep you away from God's true and original purpose' and one of their leaders was heard to preach, 'I'm not too concerned about the cities of the world. I'm a spiritual nomad, a pilgrim' (quoted in Gifford 1991:12, 16). But popularist presentations to highlight members' priorities are a long way from proving that members' practice is one of being so unconcerned with this world as to be indifferent to poverty alleviation, as Gifford would have us believe. A more sophisticated analysis of the movement as it is found in Nigeria, by Marshall, shows that their beliefs do not necessarily promote indifference to material circumstances at all. Religious conversion is experienced by fundamentalists 'as a liberating and empowering personal re-birth, and ... the new spiritual power possessed by the born again individual cannot be disassociated from the "practical" power to transform his/her social and economic world' (Marshall 1991:36). Not only does this involve a critique of government action from the Christian perspective, but even the focus of fundamentalists on the role of evil spirits in the political system, which might appear to be a total distraction from more relevant earthly causes of societal problems (Gifford 1991:15), is not quite what it seems. Far from promoting disengagement, it causes believers to turn their face towards politics, focusing their attention on the corrupt political practices and even inviting them to play an active part in the destruction of the evil forces, though most might not regard prayer as being as practical as the believers hold. An official of Nigeria's Pentecostal Fellowship (which speaks nationally for all 'born-again Christians' and is the most powerful voice in the

Christian Association of Nigeria, the interdenominational organisation representing the interests of the Christian population to the government), summarised the relationship of fundamentalists to politics as follows:

> Many Christians believe it is wrong to want to be in politics. But we are teaching them in our sermons, in our lectures that if we don't take active part by helping to choose the right person, you will see that it is the enemy that is coming to rule us again ... we have to do that to get the next President; we will do it. Because the suffering is enough. (Pastor Ladele, 1991, quoted in Marshall 1991:35)

If elements within fundamentalism have been inclined to separatism, it seems that this is unlikely to hold in the future.

Cases of Christian groups resorting to autonomous communities have been much less common. The predilection of the radical stream of Independent African Churches in the colonial period to call their physically and socially separated communities 'New Zion' or 'New Jerusalem' (imitating the influential African mission of the black American sect called the Christian Catholic Apostolic Church in Zion) has led to them being called Zionists.

There was little attempt on the part of these Zionists to make a rational analysis of the current political and economic scene or to challenge colonialism. Their prime intention was to withdraw from colonial power. Like the Maraboutic communities, they offered to those who saw their socio-cultural norms being destroyed an ideological alternative to the dominant assumptions (Buijtenhuijs 1985; Ranger 1986). It was not, therefore, just a case of rejecting white leadership, like the so-called 'Ethiopian' churches.[4] Rather, it contested the very structure of the colonial order, its values and the Protestantism that condoned it, along with its world-view that separated state and church, secular and spiritual. Zionism offered a God and prophets concerned for material well-being (particularly in healing and bounded holistic communities), self-rule and unsophisticated ritual for the illiterate. They might be economically dependent, but they were ideologically separatist.

In her study of Zionism amongst the Tshidi peasants in South Africa, Comaroff writes that the movement marks:

> the emergence of a systematic counterculture, a modus operandi explicitly associated with those estranged from the centers of power and communication ... Its adherents have seldom directly resisted the mechanism of [South

---

[4] A title adopted by many in South Africa on the basis of the Bible, Psalm 68, verse 31: 'Ethiopia shall soon stretch out her hands unto God.' It was subsequently applied more widely by some analysts.

African] politico-economic domination – a formidable prospect in such coercive contexts – but they have contested the logic of the sociocultural system of which they are part... Its very existence is an exercise in determined estrangement from an effacing world, a holistic stance ... that has been judged as a purposive attempt to defy the authority of the hegemonic order. (Comaroff 1985:191, 254)

In the case of South Africa's nationwide Zionist Christian Church, the rejection of the external (and evil) society in which they live is incorporated in the ritual of aggressively stamping their feet as if to crush and discard it. This, then, is not mere escapism, but in effect a political act against the dominant culture and the state (Ranger 1986:23). In Zululand, Sundkler sees the Zionists not just as separate communities living on relatively viable collective estates, but as attempts to create:

a third race over against both the heathen and the Christian community ... the kingship pattern of Zulu society is imprinted on the leadership in all the independent churches. The leader is a king, 'inkosi', and the church is his tribe. (Sundkler 1961:95, 102)

Baeta's study of the separate communities of Zionists in Ghana makes the same point about their self-encapsulation and the development of such distinctive cultures and comprehensively efficient organisations that their members feel themselves to be virtually new tribes. The largest of the groups, for instance, the Musama Disco Christo Church (the Army of the Cross of Christ Church), has a leader who is called and acts like a paramount chief, its central community is a sizeable village that practises mutual aid like a common family, and the sense of belonging is enhanced by the use of a distinct self-made language to express greetings and common phrases (Baeta 1962:63).

By and large, the marabout and Zionist communities that have confined themselves to withdrawing from political power have escaped violent clashes with the authorities. It is relatively safe in the legitimate world of ritual action to act out defiance. When religious groups go beyond ritual and explicitly denounce the hegemonic order, however, the consequences are not so peaceful. The Israelites of Bulhoek, South Africa, after the First World War, were a case in point. Their hostile stance towards the South African government and refusal to move from the land earmarked by the government for European settlement led to a military conflict in 1921, when more than 163 were killed and 129 wounded (Wilson 1975:61–3; Davidson 1994:26). A similar clash occurred with the Lumpa Church in north-east Zambia in the late 1950s and early 1960s (Roberts 1970; van Binbergen 1981; Fields 1985). Led by Alice Lenshina, its assertive stand on indigenous leadership, organisation, worship and values naturally tapped anticolonial feeling. The rapid growth not only provoked hostility on the part of the colonial authorities but, in due course, the jealousy of the nationalists. Faced with an increasingly hostile environment, with arrests and forcible removals by the authorities and arson attacks and murders by the nationalists, the church became progressively encapsulated from the world as a self-sufficient community living in stockaded villages. In the eyes of Kaunda, who was shortly to become the first president of Zambia, Lumpa:

> disassociate themselves with the activities of the ordinary people ... and have gone to the extent of setting up separate villages and to an ever increasing degree have demonstrated their unwillingness to abide by the normal laws of the land ... they are bent upon pursuing their own independent ways in defiance of orderly and good administration ... These people have gone out of their way to become anti-social. (National broadcast, 28/7/64, quoted in Legum 1960:104, 106)

Given Kaunda's and the nationalists' view of the state, they saw little option but to break the counter-culture. The final conflict began in 1964, a few weeks before the creation of the independent state. It arose over a dispute about schooling. Lenshina forbade her followers to send their children to school. It was an action, however, that united government and non-Lumpa villages against the movement. For the nationalists, education was the key to the Zambian state's future; for the villagers, it was the path to prosperity for members of their extended family. When an uncle/guardian assaulted a nephew for not attending school, Lumpa members ransacked his village. The village brought in the police, who made several arrests. Their action provoked Lumpa attacks on police patrols. The government's response was to give Lumpa seven days 'to abandon their segregated way of life and take their place within the society of the District'. Unwillingness to cooperate led to attempts to enforce it by the police, which only stiffened resistance. Finally, two police were fatally ambushed and armed clashes between the two sides left 600–700 dead. The church was subsequently banned in Zambia and what remained fled to the Democratic Republic of Congo (Zaire).

For a story of the conflict between religion and political authority on a large scale, however, we must turn to the Watch Tower movement. This not only brings into focus the dynamics of disengagement, but illustrates change over time as disengagement strategies adapted to local circumstances, or met particular opposition.

THE WATCH TOWER MOVEMENTS

Originating in the USA in 1874, the Watch Tower Bible and Tract Society (now more commonly known, in its orthodox version, as

Jehovah's Witnesses) was introduced into South Africa in 1906–7 and, through incoming or returning labour migrants, into the whole of central Africa over the next thirty years. So successful was it that, in some areas, whole villages and even complete or near complete tribes were converted. Though these mass movements continued to be influenced by the parent organisation's imported literature, they were without official supervision. Left to the direction of their own prophets, they quickly developed, in response to each local situation, their own distinctive rituals, doctrinal emphases and lifestyles. It was not until the 1950s and early 1960s that most of the independents were brought within the effective control of the Witnesses' bureaucracy (Cross 1978:307–8).

The popular versions of those early years (and today) appealed to Africans for a number of reasons. Firstly, they offered a church run by and for Africans – that is, free of European teachers, who were accused of practising trickery in their Bible instruction for their own ends. European churches were also disliked for the fees they charged for schooling, for the long probationary period that was demanded before baptism and membership and for being in league with the colonial authorities. Secondly, there was the Watch Tower movements' teaching of a black millennium.[5] In the hands of the African prophets, the Watch Tower promise of a bright earthly millennium in the future became the means for transcending the intolerable conditions that Africans were powerless to change. It was a vision of 'the last' becoming the 'first'. 'God will clear all the Europeans back home to England and everything will be ours and we will be rich as they are,' claimed Sindano in Abercorn District in 1923 (Rotberg 1966:138). George Kunga, a Nyasa preacher, assured his listeners in Bulawayo in 1923:

> Goliath was a big man. David was a small man. The white race are now powerful but it will be the same as happened to Goliath. David the small man rose up and killed him. So it will be with the white and black races. The king of the white man will cease to be king and we shall reign. (Hodges 1985:7)

Such a future, where every wrong was righted and every dream fulfilled, won converts in their tens of thousands. Only in the urban and mining centres was the reception initially lukewarm. Van Onselen, accounting for this among the mineworkers of Southern Rhodesia, attributes it to two factors. First, Watch Tower was primarily an ideology promising socio-economic mobility, which appealed more to the

---

[5] Millenarianism is a movement inspired by hope in a 'salvation that is [to be] collective (enjoyed by the faithful), terrestrial (not to be realized in some other worldly heaven), imminent, total, and miraculous' (Welch 1980:26).

small group of semi-literate (especially the mission-educated) in the mines than to the unskilled underground mineworkers. Secondly, the challenge of Watch Tower to the colonial state was too diffuse; it failed to challenge or respond to the specific evils of the mine compounds and forced labour (as the burial societies did) or to directly confront the mine owners (as the fledgling unions did) (van Onselen 1976:204–9).

Underlying their withdrawal was the belief that the world and secular government was the work of the Devil. 'All those who worship in the names of kingdoms, nationalities or under the symbol of secular rulers are idolatrous,' preached Kamwana in Nyasaland (Ranger 1986:14). Watch Tower's value system was at total variance with secular society. The authority of the movements alone, of their leaders and elders, was the only legitimate form of authority. Translated into practice, however, this amounted not just to a call to separation, like the Zionists, but to the rejection, with varying degrees of severity, of the authority, not just of colonial officials, but of traditional chiefs and later trade unions, nationalist bodies and the independence governments. It was not a proto-nationalist movement, it was an anti-systemic one. It was not fighting against authority to change it; it was withdrawing from it because it could not change it (and did not have to, since God would).

In the words of Hanoc Sindano, a Northern Rhodesian preacher in 1923:

There they are, they who over burden us with loads and beat us like slaves, but a day will come when they will be the slaves ... God only is to be respected and obeyed, nobody else on earth has any right to it: no more the European than the native chiefs. The English have no right whatsoever in the country, they are committing injustice against the natives in pretending to have rights. (Quoted in Rotberg 1966:134)

Similarly, Kamwana appealed to his congregation in northern Nyasaland in 1939:

We are the children of God and must therefore pay no attention to the laws of the boma. The time is at hand, do not respect the boma, that is earthly, if we obey the laws on earth made by the boma, then we are worshipping the Devil ... People must not be afraid to break government laws. Nobody should remove his hat to the Provincial Commissioner or the District Commissioner. These gentlemen ... are pretenders. (Quoted in Rotberg 1966:150–1)

Under this sort of anti-authoritarian teaching, it is not surprising that there followed both disengagement and active rebellion against traditional and state authorities. In Northern Rhodesia and Nyasaland, it is reported that members, on the one hand, ignored and, on the other, insulted and assaulted traditional chiefs and headmen (Rotberg 1966:139; Fields 1985:144–62, 243–5) and even, on occasion, overthrew these state-sponsored and collaborating customary rulers (Fields 1985:256; Isaacman 1990:55). One can understand, too, their refusal to acknowledge symbols of secular rule ('idolatrous elements', as Kamwana called them), such as singing the national anthem and observing Armistice Day and Empire Day, and, in many, though not all, cases, their refusal to vote or to send children to state schools. Beyond that, a whole list of disturbances of an anti-state nature are attributed to Watch Tower incitement.

Concerned as they were to have as little as possible to do with a Satan-controlled world, the Watch Tower movements had three alternatives for maintaining religious purity: first, to rid the world of those things that make the world evil – that is, to undertake witch-hunting and/or killing; secondly, to separate physically – that is, isolationism; and, thirdly, to separate symbolically – that is, quietism. The first course was that followed by Mwana Lesa ('Son of God'). Under, let it be said, incitement from the Lala chiefs and encouragement from the people, he moved from detecting witches to assuming by 1925 the right to execute them by drowning. (For a detailed account of the Mwana Lesa movement, see Ranger 1975; Fields 1985:163–92.)

Mwana Lesa was concerned to regulate existing villages on Watch Tower lines, but others responded with communitarian withdrawal from traditional village society. Some early Watch Tower preachers argued that, since the Apocalypse was at hand, they should forsake their huts, fields and livestock and go to the forest to watch and pray for Judgement Day (Rotberg 1966:136). Others withdrew Watch Tower adherents 'to erect unauthorised settlements which they labelled "Jerusalem" ' (Assimeng 1970:103; Fields 1985:154). 'One preacher, Hanoc Sindano, was allowed to form a village ... This Jerusalem survived intact into the 1950s' (Fields 1985:160). Roberts refers to another group, led by Anok Simpungwe, among the Mambwe in 1917–39, where 'the church set itself apart from other Mambwe by the highly abstemious conduct of its members. Eventually they rejected all authority and the head village was burned down on government orders' (Roberts 1970:520). Hodges describes converts, faced by the Depression, which hit the Copper Belt mines in the 1930s, returning to their birthplace in Luapula Province. Apparently they were reluctant to go to their home villages:

> where they felt the opportunities for social and economic advances were few. Instead many turned to mass separatism through the establishment of Watch Tower villages. Here, based on nuclear or small extended families, the movement's adherents made use of the Watch Tower's ethical precepts

... to satisfy the aspirations for advancement which urban life had aroused. (Hodges 1985:8)

The best-documented case of communal isolationism is that of Jeremiah Gondwe. In 1941, he received permission to build his own village for the exclusive use of the large number of his followers (Cross (1970) gives more details). Having already become a Lamba hero, the village grew rapidly. By 1969, there were 1,048 inhabitants, compared with less than 100 for most local villages. Nor was it just Lamba subsistence farmers that were attracted. People came from all over Northern Rhodesia, along with sizeable groups from the Luba of Katanga and the Luvale of Angola. Together, this intertribal community emphasised peaceful, harmonious living, economic cooperation and self-sufficiency and community values. Many of his followers, even up to Cross's interview in 1970, still refused to allow their children to go to school, where singing the national anthem and saluting the national flag were compulsory, though this was not Gondwe's personal position. Indeed, by this time, his nationalism seems to have overcome, or at least mellowed, his anti-authoritarian reservations. Hence, he successfully appealed to his followers to register as voters and vote 'yes' on the 1968 referendum on the constitution.

Meanwhile, the orthodox Jehovah's Witnesses, following their capture of most of the movement after 1955, followed a third response to the teaching of owing no allegiance to earthly powers. It can be characterised as one of symbolic or partial withdrawal from the state. Although they participated in mainstream society economically and, to a degree, socially (though in Zambia they still tend to live outside the village in rather small settlements), they refused to participate in elections and military service (national conscription or liberation armies, such as ZANLA) or to sing the anthem and salute the flag. In addition, Witnesses began withdrawing their children from schools, which were one of the state's primary means for propagating their nationalist ideology. As they displaced the independent Watch Tower groups, they:

> substituted a passivist millenarianism for their overtly rebellious and nationalist spirit. A European Jehovah's Witness in charge of Northern Rhodesia said in the late 1950s 'Jehovah's Witnesses are not called to change the social structure lest they attract people who are interested in social reform rather than the kingdom of God'. (Hodges 1985:8)

With the young independent states conscious of their unconsolidated hold on both the structures of power and the political culture, they were understandably anxious. This was particularly true in Zambia's case, faced with the Witnesses' transtribal challenge (estimates of membership in the 1960s and 1970s range from 41,000 to 135,000 members).

The state–Witnesses tension was never more conspicuous than at elections, when ruling parties, seeking legitimation, met a refusal to vote or indifference to party (which is 'national' in their eyes) support. Normally the non-participation was practised passively, but on occasion it could be active and provocative. On one notorious occasion, during the Zambian election of 1968, Witnesses 'flouted party [United National Independence Party, UNIP] discipline by walking past a voters' queue in the pouring rain with an elaborate display of umbrellas and indifference' (Cross 1978:309). Not surprisingly, the authorities and political activists in Zambia, Uganda, Mozambique and especially Malawi have clashed violently with Witness members.[6]

The Watch Tower movement in central Africa has for ninety years kept at arm's length every force of domination as a matter of theological conviction. Although its strategies have varied across the strands of the movement, it has consistently challenged the legitimacy of authority. To rulers unsure of their hold on their claimed domain, this was not something that could go unnoticed (for Kaunda's personal antagonism, see Assimeng 1970:111–12). Hegemony's clash with those who run counter to state absolutist tendencies is evidenced in the proscription of the organisation in Malawi in 1967 and public threats by ministers of state in Mozambique and Benin (Hodges 1985:4–11).

Zionism and Watchtower represent more than the culture of a millenarian minority. As Comaroff says of South African Zionism: 'we confront the collective response – the distinct order of value and practice – of a large sector of the population on the cultural and economic fringe. This is the universe of the modern world system' (Comaroff 1985:263).

Secular-motivated withdrawal

The evidence of groups withdrawing from political authorities because of a conflict with their non-religiously inspired values is much more slight and ambiguous than for the religious groups considered above. Indeed, with a few exceptions, the area has hardly been examined by researchers. Three types of communities suggest themselves as possibly

---

[6] The continuing independent Watch Tower movements are rather more isolationist than the orthodox Witnesses and hence have met similar responses. Kamwana's Mlonda Mission came under violent attack for refusing to buy ruling-party cards and was finally banned as 'dangerous to the good government of Malawi' in 1967. During the 1973–4 cholera vaccination campaign, it also had force applied against it (Ranger 1986:14–15). Or, again, in Democratic Republic of Congo (Zaire), African Watch Tower (Kitawala) was rigorously suppressed following its unresponsiveness to Mobutu's legitimation campaign in 1975 (Callaghy 1980:478).

containing distinct secular subcultures, which are pitted against that propagated by the authorities. They are (i) localised self-help groups; (ii) delinquents and criminals; and (iii) mobile communities.

LOCAL SELF-HELP GROUPS

These can be formal or informal, based on kin and lineage (e.g. ethnic associations in regions or cities, home-town associations, burial societies, etc.) or common interest (e.g. food and artisanal production groups, women's groups, saving associations, neighbourhood security groups, community improvement groups, market associations, trade unions, cooperatives, church/mosque member support networks).

Specific provision of a social improvement or service by voluntary groups may have political implications, but it would not normally constitute political action, let alone a withdrawal in a separatist or communitarian form in response to the dominant elites' cultural values. They are, rather, the natural arrangements made by people sharing common needs who believe that shared activity is an appropriate way of meeting them.

As regards kinship organisations, there is a long history of individuals looking to them for safety and welfare. In the precolonial period, 'it was within kinship organizations that individuals more fully realized their private and political needs, turning kinship into public institutions' (Ekeh 1989:192). Developments since then have only entrenched this pattern. First, colonial indirect rule only canonised kinship structures, making them bolder, whilst its unwillingness to provide services outside the administrative centres compelled individuals to rely on them still more. Secondly, the increasing failure of the independent state during the 1980s to make social/welfare provision made individuals turn to associations, whether they were ones that had survived suppression or co-optation by the independent state or were newly formed. The associations took up where they had begun in the early twentieth century – that is, providing the services required by their members but not offered by the state. Areas such as education, health, infrastructure construction, relief for acquired immune deficiency syndrome (AIDS) victims, adjudicatory systems and even policing have all been undertaken in the last decade.

How are such kinship associations to be understood? Is this an expression of civic virtue, with individuals coming together to provide for the community what is otherwise unobtainable from the state? Is this a manifestation of no more than sentimental attachment to a place and culture? Is this essentially the formation of local lobby groups with agendas that are brought before the authorities for assistance? Or is this about the establishment and operation of a parallel state? In other words, is this about engagement or disengagement (Barkan et al. 1991)?

McNulty and Lawrence (1996) and Warren *et al.* (1996) favour the view that they are about engagement, acting as intermediary brokers between the local community and the state (and international actors with power/resources as well). The development projects and social service provision by the home-town associations which they studied among the Yoruba in Nigeria were not so much withdrawal from a predatory state, or even the enthusiastic seizure of an opportunity to replace the state in the wake of its failure; they were, in their opinion, about mobilising financial and human resources to promote and protect common interests. Far from disengaging from an irrelevant and inadequate state, they found official delegations from the local communities that approached government offices and ministries so as to put forward their development needs and the case for government support, or even umbrella development organisations that incorporated local government councillors. And, though the state was often unable to help practically, it was keen to maintain the link with these associations through official registration so as to ensure that they did not become autonomous.

Others, however, argue that something more significant is happening at the cultural level. 'People are organizing themselves in order to limit their vulnerability to a predatory state, to improve rudimentary social welfare networks through community efforts and to improve their material well-being. [There is] ... a turning away from the state' (Ake 1991:37). In other words, kinship associations entail a conscious withdrawal from an unacceptable state and not just survival techniques in the situation of an absent state. Likewise, Chazan claims that groups such as kinship units, ethnic associations, local development societies and traditional political systems have not only supplanted the state's socio-economic roles, but have 'carried a strong protest against the symbolic codification of ruling class dominance' (Chazan 1994b:81). She views them as relishing the establishment of autonomous niches whose 'alternative notions of authority, community, distributive justice and conflict resolution are then defined in particularistic terms. Each social group has amplified its own set of operative norms and endowed them with symbolic and practical meaning' (Chazan 1994b:83). But, though she believes that such social networks, especially primary associations, are 'breeding grounds for the construction of alternative value systems' (Chazan 1992a:134), she is nowhere specific. Ekeh, too, seems to hold that it is particularly the primordial self-help groups, in which (unlike the state) ordinary Africans do feel a strong interest, that threaten to form autonomous units.

The trend for several centuries in Africa's history led to the creation of kinship as an alternative public institution, existing side by side with the formal state. They constitute ... two public realms ... the 'civic public', operating on amoral codes of behaviour and using the apparatuses of the formal state, and the 'primordial public' whose value-premises are moral, binding together members of the same natural and assumed kinship (including ethnic) groupings. (Ekeh 1989:192)

When wronged by the state the natural response is not to engage the state through opposition, but to withdraw to this primordial public realm.

Certainly, what makes kinship associations potentially significant politically is their holistic approach and their role very often as the apex organisation in the community, coordinating all the other organisations. Single-issue organisations, with their parallel services, are far less challenging to the state than multiple-issue groups, especially if the latter have a territorial base or coalesce around a recognised political constituency. But it is not just the number of the issues but the nature of the issues that makes a group politically disturbing to the state. States are far more likely to see 'political' challenges from organisations that encroach on areas where they still claim a monopoly, rather than from those who work in areas where the state does not work, has abandoned its work or commonly works in association with others. This applies to all organisations, kinship or not. Take the negative reaction of the Mozambican authorities to the Maforga Mission, near Gondola (Chingono 1996:187–92), which provides basic health care, training for women and disabled men, care for the elderly, the disabled and orphans and provision of food and clothing. Sometimes, they feed up to 400 and treat 1,000 people a day. Being unregistered with the government, operating a clinic for prematurely born babies, which is the responsibility of the Ministry of Health, and concentrating large groups of people in one place, contrary to government policy, they are the cause of great concern. Said the Provincial Director of Planning: 'They don't seem to recognise us. They just do what they want ... Well it's a question of money and power.' Apart from the state's fear of dependency, it is the power issue that is at stake. Chingono comments: 'It seems the government is worried that the concentration of large groups of people, apart from providing an easy basis for organised opposition, will highlight its own weaknesses' (Chingono 1996:188). Or, more generally, as Bratton puts it: 'In the quest for order, most African governments endeavour to eliminate independent centers of power. The universal trend of political centralization represents an attempt by political leaders to enclose an unruly environment within the confines of manageable political institutions' (Bratton 1989b:573).

The best example of single-issue kinship groups that threaten the state by their self-provision and withdrawal are the vigilante groups. States see this as clearly encroaching on instruments of social control, such as policing and courts, in which they claim a monopoly. Where they fail to provide security and punishment for offenders, however, kinship groups are very likely to take action themselves, as the following examples show. For the Gisu in Uganda in the 1960s, the dilemma was how to control serious crimes against the person (in their mind, primarily, theft and witchcraft) in a context where state law enforcement had been transferred from local chiefs to distant and alien magistrates' courts and far-away police posts (Heald 1998). Given the impotence of the state in the rural areas, gangs arose who used intimidation, curfews, 'trials' and murder to eradicate the criminals and ran protection rackets for the villagers. This institutionalised system of law outside the state law comes close to Hobsbawm's definition of a mafia organisation (Hobsbawm 1959:5–6). Yet, while the vigilantes saw themselves as a direct alternative to the Ugandan state apparatus in the rural areas (a 'Gisu government'), the movement was not primarily rebellion but disengagement, and disengagement not because of the threat of the dominant but because of their failure. It was 'a local form of self assertion', an attempt, largely successful, 'to establish a viable parallel apparatus of social control in the community' (Heald 1998:252). But the disengagement was far from complete. The combination of the support of local leaders and chiefs and the connivance of the police (who were too under-resourced to stamp them out and so often preferred to work with them so as to forestall lynch law and to effect arrests) meant that 'they could be said to straddle the divide, a foot in both camps of community and officialdom' (Heald 1998:252). By the late 1960s, some of the vigilante groups were co-opted by the ruling party and its local strongmen to intimidate and terrorise rival candidates and, by the 1980s, they were largely incorporated into the people's militia organised to protect the rural areas against the incursions of the civil war.

Village vigilante groups also arose in the early 1980s in rural northwestern Tanzania to deal with cattle-rustling and other crimes (Abrahams 1987:179–96; Tripp 1992:235–7 covers their appearance in Dar es Salaam). In part, the spontaneous appearance of these village groups, armed with bows and arrows, who sought the culprits and frequently enforced a fitting punishment, was meeting the perceived failure of the state. The police were seen as under-resourced, inept and, worse still, possibly in collusion with the criminals. But, beyond state inadequacy, there was a rejection of state values in determining what was criminal, in defining conclusive evidence, in fixing punishment and even in the method of protection used by law enforcers. For the vigilantes, crime included witchcraft, evidence of guilt could be obtained from divination, punishment carried out by the groups themselves could range from social ostracism and fines of cattle to exile or even death, and the vigilantes frequently used traditional medicines to protect themselves from harm when they went after thieves. The state was intensely wary of these groups, although its official line was to praise them for their initiative whilst insisting that they hand over suspects to the police and leave the determination of guilt and punishment to the courts. Ultimately, the Tanzania state, like the Uganda state, used co-optation to neutralise the threat, formalising them in 1990 and announcing its intention to empower party cells and wards to form councils to deal legally with criminals.

The South African townships, though multi-ethnic, nevertheless under apartheid functioned as if they were a single 'black' race. In the face of inadequate state policing, a judicial system that was too expensive and inaccessible, high crime rates, gang activity and ill-disciplined youth militants, townships commonly responded from the mid-1980s with their own street patrols and an informal justice system of 'people's courts'. The latter could be formal, run by civic organisations and street committees, informal, run by local-level youth congress activists, or more violent one-off acts of summary justice by the 'com-tsotsis'. 'Township courts, and informal justice more generally, have a profoundly jekyl-and-hyde character: some operate with laudable procedures, local support and participation, and limited sentencing [fines, community service and counselling]; others provide summary justice based on high levels of apparently arbitrary violence [including torture and killing]' (Seekings 1992a:194).

Initially, the government saw this development as undermining its formal legal and policing system and the 'courts' were severely repressed. But, by the mid-1990s, the more responsible groups were being tolerated and even welcomed in the fight against crime, and there was talk of formalising the alternative system.

Concerning holistic kinship associations, three examples show the variety that their form can take as they seek to recapture control over their own existence and destiny and to become power centres, following norms that may be distinct from the state (e.g. gender-chauvinist, gerontocratic, non-democratic and explicitly religious).

The Wazaramo Union was one of fifty-one ethnic associations established in Dar es Salaam in the early part of the twentieth century to provide social services for the new urban immigrants. Whether it was burial (previously taken care of by relatives in the village) or the need for loans, accommodation, job vacancy news or recreation, the societies enabled the newcomers to adapt more easily to the strange city environment. The Wazaramo Union, perhaps because it represented the peoples of the immediate hinterland of Dar es Salaam, was the largest ethnic organisation in the city in 1955, with 3,500 members. Its prime concern was the development of their rural area of origin. It 'lobbied the colonial authorities to withdraw their support of certain discredited local leaders and to replace them with leaders chosen by the Zaramo. The union also owned trucks to transport passengers and agricultural produce between town and country' (Tripp 1992:225). Like all other associations organised on the basis of ethnicity, it was banned in the early 1960s by the independence government, since it was feared that such groups would raise 'tribalistic' demands and undermine national unity. Yet ethnic-based welfare associations re-emerged around 1987 in Dar es Salaam to raise funds for food relief, orphanages, AIDS victims, health and educational facilities in their home regions and to serve as burial societies. The state has chosen to legalise some and to turn a blind eye to others, seeing their contribution to social welfare as out-weighing any national divisiveness (Tripp 1992:237, 239). Kinship associations like the Wazaramo Union serve as vehicles for community self-preservation and have the potential to develop as organisations that grow away from the state, whether ignoring it or replacing it.

The Fiditi Progressive Union is a home-town association centred on a Yoruba town of 42,000 in western Nigeria. (The following account is based on McNulty and Lawrence (1996).) Like many others in Nigeria, it was founded in the 1920s by migrants in Lagos who wanted to see the benefits of the urban and European environment, especially in health and education, come to their own local communities. Its membership, therefore, has always extended beyond the residents of the town itself. Today, it not only includes migrants living in all the main cities of Nigeria, but their children and children's children who have never resided in the town. Unlike localised voluntary organisations, it claims to speak for all members of the community, rather than representing the specific interests of just the town's inhabitants or particular social, political or religious factions within the community (although it is clearly led by educated, male, city dwellers). Primarily, it sees its role as one of speaking for the community and representing it before the Nigerian state, in a way the traditional authorities have failed to do. In the words of its current president, it is 'a government at the grassroots level' (quoted in McNulty and Lawrence 1996:30). Through that lob-bying and through self-help, they have established primary schools and a technical college, dispensary, postal agency and telephone service, and they are currently building a town hall. Yet, though the focus is developmental, there is a political agenda as well as a cultural one in this (as probably in every) Nigerian kinship association. In the event of civil strife and the failure of the state to ensure security of life and prop-erty, the locality represents a refuge for the members. Unfortunately, this is not an implausible requirement in Nigeria. It was well noted that, during the civil war, the Ibo fled back to their eastern homelands, only to find nowhere to live and no equivalent of a home-town association to receive them. And, given the current political instability in Nigeria (and many other African states), it is not hard to see the attraction of having a haven of refuge amongst one's kin in the event of economic and political collapse in the future. If the role of the Fiditi Progressive Union is engagement now, it also has the potential to follow an effective disengagement role should circumstances necessitate it.

In South Africa, the apartheid regime provoked a non-traditional ethnic network (i.e. multi-ethnic, non-regional and largely urban) through its classification of all blacks as a single 'race' and its subsequent discrimination against this majority group. The state policy created what has been described as a 'veritable explosion in associational life' (Price 1992:15, quoted in Diamond 1997:12), whose agenda was clearly more than economic self-help. It has been argued that the 'civics', as the residential associations were called in the black townships, developed more along totalist and exclusivist lines and still largely retain a 'resistance and hostility to state authority' and a desire 'to displace the state as alternative authority structures' (Diamond 1997:13), but this is an exaggeration which takes their 'people's power' rhetoric at face value. Their prime strength, from their formation in the late 1970s/1980s, was in fact their ability to engage the apartheid state, lobbying over civic issues, such as rent increases, and leading protest action. In a situation where local government collapsed under rent strikes, councillor resignations and general lack of legitimacy, and where political parties such as the African National Congress (ANC) were banned, civics represented township residents and organised intermittent campaigns. The degree to which they were able to provide alternative services was severely limited by their own lack of resources, their less-than-total support, the limited and passive participation even of supporters and their weak organisation. Generally speaking, they were preoccupied with national issues and bringing apartheid to an end or with acting as a watchdog on local government, rather than providing alternative institutions of local government. As Seekings points out, where they did attempt the latter, it was short-lived and often within the context of 'negotiating for greater formal participation in local state decision making' (Seekings 1992b:222). His conclusion is that, despite the impression of a strong dynamic movement, they were usually too weak organisationally to effect much and their 'people's power' involved unrealisable ambitions. The one exception is their involvement in informal justice through the 'people's courts' discussed above.[7]

---

[7] The white settler communities make an interesting comparison as minority groups largely excluded from political power. In Zimbabwe, 'white racism' is regularly raised

DELINQUENTS AND CRIMINALS

Delinquency and criminality do not necessarily constitute immoral or amoral behaviour. It can be that it is society's values that have changed, leaving behind those who have not changed as a non-conformist minority. In other words, 'delinquent' and 'criminal' constitute highly political concepts, frequently used by the power elite to characterise those who oppose them. As Chabal observes, 'delinquency may or may not be the political expression of a gagged under-class, but the state's reaction to it is undoubtedly an indication of this perception of the political nature of apparently anomic behaviour' (Chabal 1992:95). Only a closer examination of the actual and perceived intentions of those 'criminal and delinquent elements' and 'agitators' which, in the authorities' eyes, lie behind riots, vandalism, arson attacks and shootings in modern African cities, will determine their political significance, if any. One would assume that most of what could be called politically motivated riots come into the category of engagement. But, where the state has taken the initiative in rejecting the values of a subordinate group, it may well be disengagement.

Take the cases of the criminalisation of traditional African practices. Colonial decree outlawed hunting on communal land and called it poaching in state parks or private property; eating the fruit of the land became theft of agricultural produce from landowners; it made communal justice the conduct of illegal vigilantes; not having formal employment could be vagrancy; and even movement to traditional pastureland in some cases became the unauthorised crossing of international boundaries (Cooper 1980:111–24). (The redefining of legality also led to decriminalisation of evils held from time immemorial. Thus the capital crime of witchcraft was redesignated harmless superstition and anyone punishing witches was liable to prosecution.) Many of the decrees, unsurprisingly, had to be watered down or abandoned in the face of the widespread ignoring of them by the indigenous population. In Zanzibar:

> At most, the long campaign against vagrancy, produce theft, and petty crime added somewhat to the risks of wandering around and helping oneself to coconuts. The campaign may have made an ex-slave more likely to seek a

by state leaders, President Mugabe in the 1996 election accusing whites of establishing elitist racist clubs which excluded blacks, and Vice-President Nkomo accusing white farmers of ignoring state structures and forming white governments. From the other side of the fence, Roelf Meyer of the New Movement Process in South Africa has stressed 'his concern to counter the internal retreat of the whites, who were taking less and less part in public affairs' (*Africa Research Bulletin, Political Series* (*ARB* 1997, vol. 34 (7):12755). These do appear to be groups that are 'contained geographically ... and possess specific historical or mythical symbols that unite their members' (Chazan 1994b:79). Yet detailed case studies are awaited so as to provide an empirical basis for claims that their conduct constitutes disengagement from cultural hegemony.

plantation on which to squat but no more likely to work. In 1920, officials were still voicing their old plaint: ex-slaves 'live a life of vagrancy and indolence on the Arabs' plantations.' Twenty-three years of fighting crime and vagrancy had helped induce ex-slaves to lead such a life *on* Arab plantations rather than *off* them. (Cooper 1980:121)

The criminal status of runaway slaves is also obviously problematic. They became especially numerous throughout Africa during the nineteenth century. Cooper reports that viable communities were common in British East Africa from the 1870s and did not decline until 1903, by which time the runaways no longer needed the protection of a community (Cooper 1980:49–50). Elsewhere, communities of runaway slaves in Ningi in nineteenth-century northern Nigeria seem to have formed a semi-autonomous state within the political system of the Sokolo caliphate.

For groups to continue in these 'criminal' acts is clearly not of the same order as those who, by their crimes, prey on others for self-accumulation. Widespread continuance in outlawed traditional practices must rather constitute an act of group defiance, a communal rejection of the new culture introduced by the dominant (but not necessarily the majority) class.

Within more classic definitions of criminality, namely, practices long and widely held to be antisocial, cultural disengagement would only be an appropriate description where there was evidence of a distinct community that rejected state-purveyed social norms in favour of its own 'traditional' values of 'honour', justice/vengeance and mutual support. The published evidence in Africa for such communities is meagre. Austen (1986:94–5) apparently identifies distinct criminal subcultures in the nineteenth-century Sahel. He writes of occupational groups there that were regarded by the majority as semi-criminal communities. Metalworkers, leather workers and minstrels 'became the basis for socially and virtually segregated caste groups in the Sudanic zone of west Africa and in Ethiopia'. But this may be no more than the prejudice with which stigmatised groups are invariably treated.[8]

---

[8] Whether these stigmatised groups were criminal or not, their mobility certainly furthered their disengagement and may have attracted those who had reason to escape the authorities. There have been other low-caste groups whose very ostracism is their defence from interference. The Osu 'slaves' of Iboland, Nigeria (slaves in that they were bought for and devoted to that deity), lived in separate communities occupying the lowest possible social rank. Even their touch defiled and marriage to them was unthinkable for the Ibo. The interesting feature of their communities was that other marginalised groups, though otherwise free, could find refuge in them at the cost of remaining there for life. Thus criminals, widows anxious not to be inherited and the handicapped all used them as a means of escape from society. Not until colonial legislation in 1956 were the then 60,000 Osu legally protected from discrimination, whereupon their communities dispersed (Iliffe 1987:93, 145).

The single area of criminality that has been widely covered by researchers has been banditry. Hobsbawm (1959, 1969) argued for a distinct category of 'social bandits', namely, those who undertook to be protectors, redistributors and avengers on behalf of the surrounding peasants. These were held to be in contrast to those bandits who were wholly venal. His concept was taken up by many scholars and applied to Africa with varying success (Isaacman 1977; Crummey 1986). In practice, very few groups in Africa can warrant the epithet 'social bandits'. Clarence-Smith records that many 'deserters from the colonial army, escaped slaves and fugitive head porters' in southern Angola in 1840–1926 joined bandit groups and 'returned to wreak vengeance on their former masters' (Clarence-Smith 1979:37, 173). Often mentioned, also, are the bands of Mapondera and Dambukashamba on the Rhodesian/Mozambican border at the turn of the century (Isaacman 1977), of Chitokwa in Rhodesia in the 1960s (Ranger, in Crummey 1986) and of Mushala in Zambia in the 1970s (Crummey 1986). These, however, must be regarded as, if anything, engaging the authorities by opposition and perhaps attempts at influence. Their violence was aimed more at hurting the authorities than at pushing them away so as to be left to withdraw in peace. They certainly contested the values being deployed by the dominant class, but by confrontation rather than by disengagement.

MOBILE COMMUNITIES' SUBCULTURES

Nomadism has long been practised as an economic strategy. For some, it is a way of life adapted to the animals on which they live – for example, pastoralists and hunter-gatherers; for some, a way of life adapted to the necessities of cropping with limited tools and no fertiliser to replenish plant foods – for example, shifting cultivators; for others, a way of life adapted to trading and the sale of craft work. The nineteenth-century metalworkers, leather workers, minstrels and merchants of the Sahel, who 'tended to be more geographically mobile' than others, have already been mentioned (Austen 1986:95). Yet all these groups also value their independence and ability to ignore territorial authorities. Mobility is a challenge to political control and tax collection (Mamdani 1996:165–7). 'Untidy, uncontrolled movements over national borders make pastoral peoples natural anarchists' (Siddle and Swindell 1990:117). Authorities, therefore (especially those like states, which are paranoid about boundaries, suspicious of all vagrants and usually envious of nomad-occupied communal land), have increasingly pressurised them to conform to sedentary living. The process has, in some cases, politicised the groups and strengthened their resolve to move freely without consenting to any localised control.

Though many of those who were nomadic pastoralists in pre-colonialist times have since chosen sedentarisation and participation, either within state systems led by other groups or within states formed by themselves, a significant minority have persisted with their nomadic or semi-nomadic practices – for example, the Maasai, Turkana, Herero and Rendille. Since other groups, such as the Fulbe and Tutsi, have maintained pastoralism whilst shifting to a sedentary pattern, it cannot be maintained that the economic and ecological requirements of pastoralism necessitate nomadism. Its persistence therefore points to a valuation by these groups of their distinctive political system, which is decentralised, fragmented and largely egalitarian. Such a valuation, of course, cannot be maintained without a concomitant distancing of themselves from the state that promotes such contrary values. Azarya characterises the relationship of the Maasai to the Kenyan state, for instance, as one of 'insecurity, mutual suspicion and basic incongruence of needs and interests' (Azarya 1996:79). This retention of ancient patterns of social life is not necessarily an ethnic-wide cultural response. One small section of the Fulbe, known as the Mbororo, has, unlike the majority, retained nomadism. Van Raay describes them as:

> taking little interest in anything but their cattle … [they] keep aloof from the daily affairs of settled communities as long as these do not affect them. However intimate their knowledge of the area, familiarity with its occupants is rare. Frequent attendance at the markets of the area by [them] make them meet many people but these contacts remain superficial. (Quoted in Azarya 1996:82)

This refusal of some nomadic groups to integrate with the state, whether precolonial, colonial or independent, has led to strained relations. Whereas the nomads have wanted to maintain their autonomy, mobility and decentralised polity, the central authorities, for reasons of control, have wanted them within boundaries and preferably in one place. The conflict between the nomadic and sedentary cultures has led to the latter marginalising the former or seeking to impose their will by force. Violent conflicts occurred in the colonial period between the authorities and the Nandi, Nuer, Turkana, Somali, Herero and Touareg, as the nomads sought to resist land grabs, forced relocation to reserves, sedentarisation and crop cultivation projects.

Despite the overwhelming superior force of the state, the conflict between the centralised and decentralised political systems is still running. For instance, when the Touaregs of Niger and Mali began returning from Libya and Algeria in the late 1980s after their ten-year absence to escape drought, they not only received little help in resettlement, despite the promises, but it seems faced harassment at the borders about their right to enter in view of their uncertain citizenship.

The reception only highlighted for the Touareg the little they had in common with the state authorities and their need for autonomy. No doubt with outside prompting and assistance, they took to arms and a fierce rebellion broke out in 1990–5 in both Niger and Mali, which brought harsh repression by the state security forces in their attempt to restrain it. The uprisings were variously portrayed by the authorities as banditry and secessionist movements, although most of the rebels themselves explicitly said that they wanted greater autonomy within federal systems, rather than independence. Significantly, in the peace talks, central governments have been more willing to offer development funds and to talk of fully integrating the Touareg into the political and economic arenas. Even more indicative that they have not understood and do not want to understand the nomads' desire for freedom from control, the governments of Niger, Mali, Algeria and Libya, in their own discussions together, have talked of joint measures governing border controls, monitoring Touareg movements in the border region and returning the more than 100,000 refugees of the rebellion to their region of origin.

The case of Masowe's Apostles or 'the Basketmakers' is not one of cultural nomadism but enforced wandering. Their origins are in eastern Southern Rhodesia in the 1930s, under the leadership of Johana Masowe. They were one of the many African independent churches, but subsequently emphasised a political and economic agenda. Their message from the very beginning 'was profoundly inwardly-looking: the white system had reneged on its promises and Africans should turn their backs on it, contracting out of both peasant agriculture and labour migration' (Ranger 1984:327). White missionaries did not meet African needs, being unable to cast out devils. But nor did African tradition, with its chiefs' demands for tribute without providing services in return; its oppression of the young through the bride-price system; and its susceptibility to witchcraft. Thousands of converts joined the church in the 1930s in the Makoni district: children ran away from mission schools; young men and women married without bride-price; converts refused to perform corvée labour; and the leaders destroyed the regalia of the spirit mediums (Ranger 1984:327). Hindered from preaching what was seen by the colonial authorities as an anti-white agenda, they became for forty years a migrant people. A group of 150–200 moved to South Africa in 1943, finally settling in Port Elizabeth in 1947. With no government interference and accepted by the community for their industry and the quality of their craft work, they became a settled community of nearly 2,000. However, in 1955, they began to come under pressure from the state to return to Southern Rhodesia, on the grounds of their being illegal migrants. Finally, in 1962, they did return to Rhodesia, but quickly gained permission to move on to Northern Rhodesia. Yet even there they had conflict with the state authorities. Their encapsulated communities, which shunned healthcare, state education and integration with the 'unenlightened', elicited the veiled threat of the Governor of Lusaka in 1973 that 'they must be part and parcel of the society and not create their own empires' (Dillon-Mallone 1978).

How does cultural disengagement relate to the propositions?

The ten propositions listed at the end of Chapter 1 embraced all forms of disengagement. How far do they apply specifically to cultural withdrawal?

First, concerning the nature of disengagement, it was hypothesised that disengagement is a universal phenomenon, a multi-scale phenomenon and a responsive strategy.

The chapter has shown that cultural withdrawal too is universal; it crosses historical and social boundaries. Particularly striking are the transtribal and rural/urban nature of religious movements and the merging of status (class) and rural/urban origins in the urban ethnic associations. Having said that, it is particularly the rural population that has felt the most severe impact of the rapid postcolonial cultural change, and that has therefore been the most attracted to cultural disengagement. Even though movements like Watch Tower and the Lumpa had numerous urban congregations, the vast majority of these were labour migrants (Cross 1978:1–2). There is evidence, too, that religious disengagement, in particular, has appealed to women as articulating a sense of their opposition to male-dominated social systems and/or offering a vehicle to enhance female status. The Kubandina spirit-possession cult was a predominantly female organisation that fulfilled the former role, and Haynes argues that particular women have sought to enhance their own status in founding new religious movements, namely, Gaudencia Aoko (Maria Legio in Kenya), Alice Lenshina (Lumpa), and Alice Lakwena (Holy Spirit Church in Uganda) (Haynes 1996a:174). It is also remarkable how many women have come into positions of leadership in the Christian churches in southern Sudan (African Rights 1995a:19).

Though commonly found at the individual and organised collective movement level, cultural disengagement can take the form of a spontaneous mass movement. Whole village and/or tribe conversions to Watch Tower are recorded in Northern Rhodesia among the Lala (1925–6), Lamba (1925–35), Mambwe (1907–39), Bemba and Wiko

(1930s); in Nyasaland among the Tonga (1908–15); and in Belgian Congo among the BaKumu (1944).

Cultural disengagement was found to be a responsive strategy for those threatened by social upheaval and cultural hegemony. Organisations and communities that are reactionary, upholding traditional values, or those that are reconstructive, offering new and better meanings, are particularly appealing to those faced with what is seen as socio-cultural disequilibrium within their own or adopted communities.

Secondly, concerning the pattern of disengagement, it was hypothesised that disengagement depends on macro-scale and micro-scale factors.

Whether those withdrawing were separatists or communalists in their group form, they were the product of both macro- and micro-scale factors. On the macro side, the nature of the domination was obviously crucial, as was the willingness of the authorities to allow physically separate settlements. Likewise, the group's philosophy as to the source of legitimate authority and the degree to which they saw society as polluted and/or 'alien' were fundamental. Yet even the mass movements among social groups advocating withdrawal have had their detractors – those who were not swept up with the rejectionist programme. And even within the same movement there have been observed variations in time and place over the rightness or degree of withdrawal. Clearly, there is plenty of room for micro-scale factors at the level of personal belief, assessment of the material benefits/costs of communalism and the social costs to the individual and their family of being in the minority. In practice, it has been seen that individuals' choices have been shaped by their interrelationships in their communities and by charismatic or authoritative figures who have interpreted to them the condition of society and offered an appropriate withdrawal response. As the separatist groups grow, they themselves act as vital networks of influence in recruiting individual members to and sustaining them in the counter-hegemonic views and withdrawal patterns of behaviour. Very often, there is a pattern of development over time in the withdrawal ideology. Thus, exclusive self-sufficient communities were often arrived at via the more open form of cultural disengagement, namely, separatism. The subsequent step to total withdrawal was either the result of the degree of harassment by the power elite or a result of the increasing degree of alienation from the dominant ideology and values. The flow, however, has sometimes been in the other direction, when cultural withdrawal has been exchanged for engagement, as opposition actions are weighed as to their practicality and efficacy and ruling classes successfully co-opt those they have previously antagonised. Thus, for those with new expectations of bringing about change, it was appropriate to switch from Lumpa rejection to UNIP opposition, from spiritist withdrawal to ZANLA support and from vigilante disregard of the state judicial system to working with it .

Thirdly, concerning the significance of disengagement, it was hypothesised that it provides a measure of the nature of political authorities, threatens the power balance of political systems, delays democratic consolidation and usually initially provokes resistance by force.

Like other forms of disengagement, cultural withdrawal does provide a measure of the nature of political systems. In particular, its extent and time span are a measure of the weakness of power elites, whether colonial or independent. In the case of the British colonial power, the weakness was born of the contradictions of indirect rule. In this system, the British found themselves, on the one hand, committed to rationality and therefore, for example, decriminalising sorcery and yet, on the other hand, seeking to enhance the authority of collaborating chiefs, who nevertheless vehemently believed in the danger of witchcraft, as much as their people. With chiefs expected to uphold British colonial rules forbidding witch denunciation and punishment, their authority and credibility were undermined. Where such illegitimacy and inconsistency occur, a space opens wide for others to fill: in this case, for those who still offered unequivocal opposition to and eradication of witchcraft.

The weakness of the African independence governments was that they inherited the European-shaped state on a wave of anticolonialism, but that their attempts to provide a unity based on nationalism were inadequate and unavailing. They also lacked legitimacy, whether for class or racial reasons, and penetration, especially in the rural areas far from the capital. Hence, they readily allowed alternative ideologies and providers to spring up and offer unifying foci. When the centre's insecurity to such opposition brought the use of force to impose its values and customs, it only provoked still further cultural disengagement.

The significance of cultural withdrawal has also been apparent in the disruption it has brought to the power balance. Though small numerically and despite seeking to avoid the authorities rather than confront them, communities that disengaged caused almost as much consternation among the ruling elite as larger, explicitly political groups, or even rebels that sought to engage the state. Their open rejection of the symbols of cultural hegemony and allegiance to 'higher authorities' have proved intolerable and provoked denigration and persecution. In Zambia's case, it can be said that a total of no more than 150,000 religious separatists created two of the most serious internal crises in the last eighty years of the state's history.

Given that democratic values of tolerance of pluralism, mutual trust and willingness to compromise more often follow than precede democratic institutions, the area of cultural withdrawal marks a crucial testing ground for whether Africa's young democracies will be consolidated. It is often argued that autonomous associations are a vital balance to central power in a democracy, but this assumes that all these associations are engaged in dialogue with the state. As has been shown, many currently disregard or turn their back on the state. The challenge for democratic consolidation is to convince these separatists and communalists that their best interests are served by representing their alternative values and views and expressing their criticisms of state policies and abuses to the state itself. An alienated pluralism will only undermine democratic consolidation.

The isolation of most cultural disengagers reduces conflict with mainstream society, but, where their paths do cross, discrimination is not uncommon. It may be the result of straightforward prejudice and suspicion against non-conformist behaviour or because a conflict of interest is perceived – for example, over a third party receiving (or not receiving) state education, blood transfusion or immunisation. Thus, the state-controlled press in Zimbabwe widely reported and supported human rights activists' condemnations of parents who denied their children vaccinations and medication on religious grounds. Their inaction was described as a gross violation of children's basic human rights, and both activists and the press called for state intervention to proscribe the practice (*The Chronicle*, Bulawayo, 18/10/96).

The battle for the control of beliefs and values is vital to authorities, since it touches their legitimacy. The battle for the control of economic activity, which is the subject of the next chapter, is equally crucial to them, since it touches their revenues – that is, their ability to pay their agents and patrons who keep them in power. If disengagement in the cultural arena undermines the right to rule, disengagement in the economic arena undermines the ability to rule. Perhaps surprisingly, not all who deny authorities the right to rule withhold financial dues; nor do all who withhold financial dues deny the authorities' values and right to rule. The reasons for similarities and divergence in the populations making up disengagers in the two arenas will now be explored.

Illegal
Activity
in the Second Economy

Most Africans tend to view the state and its development agents as hostile forces to be evaded, cheated or thwarted as opportunities permit (Ake, 'Rethinking African Democracy')

Introduction

Every day, Africa farmers are found working their smallholdings to grow food for their families or bartering their surplus with other villagers or merchants in exchange for requirements they cannot meet themselves. Where they are involved in the cash economy, it is often in selling their produce to unlicensed traders out of despair at the inadequacy of state producer prices and delays in payment. In the cities are innumerable artisanal and commercial enterprises whose workers produce goods and services concealed from the state, except for officials bribed to keep silent. In places, there is not even the pretence of secretiveness, as informal transport operators and market traders know the state relies on them for basic services and supplies. For these workers and self-employed persons, as for those in open waged employment, scarce commodities must be obtained from the extensive distribution network that illicit producers and traders or smugglers supply with almost everything legal, or illegal, at a price. At their desks sit public officials supplementing their meagre wages by demanding remuneration for their 'free' government services. Meanwhile, their bosses use their access to and influence with the business community, lawful and criminal, to obtain, hoard or sell goods and commodities on the market. And, at the very top, political elites siphon off money from government budgets and international aid or offer contracts, monopolies and licences, along with the appropriate protection from 'interference', in lucrative trading opportunities.

This is the second economy – the production and exchange activities which are not measured by national accounts statistics. This is that part of the total economy in and out of which step, with varying regularity, probably the majority of farmers, traders, workers, business owners, officials and politicians in their search for subsistence or, in some cases, fabulous wealth.

Hart was one of the first to draw attention to the informal income opportunities outside the formal wage economy, in his study of urban workers in the 1970s in Accra, Ghana.[1] Writing of those who took second jobs or established petty enterprises to supplement their incomes, he said: 'Denied success by the formal opportunities structure, these members of the urban sub-proletariat seek informal means of increasing their incomes' (Hart 1973:67). Since he wrote, there has been extensive research on alternative economic systems, although only since the 1990s has the complex interlocking connection between Africa's first and second economy begun to be explored (for example, Turnham *et al.* 1990; MacGaffey *et al.* 1991; Sangmpam 1994; Reno 1995a; Chingono 1996).

Although there has been this renewed interest in the second economy, it is not a phenomenon that only arose in the 1970s as a result of failures in agricultural production, world market prices, government economic mismanagement, rapid population growth and local scarcities in the legal sector of the economy. Techniques of survival on the margins by craft and ingenuity have their roots in Africa's precolonial history. Iliffe writes:

> Like pre-industrial Europe, Africa was and is a harsh world for the weak. By protecting themselves from famine, by exploiting the resources of the bush, by hawking or begging or stealing, by endurance or industry or guile, by the resourcefulness of the blind or the courage of the cripple, by the ambition of the young or the patience of the old – by all these means the African poor survived in their harsh world. (Iliffe 1987:8)

In precolonial Mozambique, it appears that: 'many women and alienated youths were able to shield some portion of their labor and produce from expropriation by male household heads. The strategies they adopted were strikingly similar to those employed against the colonial capitalist system' (Isaacman 1990:47). And, after the Portuguese took Sofala in 1506, they tried to impose a royal monopoly on trade, but 'instead an unofficial private trade developed ... [which avoided taxation and] was difficult to detect' (Beach 1983:239).

This inheritance served the poor well as the European powers

---

[1] The size and importance of the informal sector are said to have been first officially noted by the International Labour Organisation (ILO) in Kenya in *Employment, Incomes and Equality*, (ILO 1972).

erected their colonial states. Most of the widespread withdrawal of labour from state-designated commodity production and anti-erosion schemes was resistance (albeit quiet and everyday) that engaged rather than disengaged the state (Jewsiewicki 1980:29; Isaacman 1990:35–7). But some of the activities were clearly illegal second-economy ones, such as smuggling and illicit mining or evasion of price controls. For example, tobacco growers of southern Nyasaland in the 1930s were in the habit of illegally selling their produce off the private estates whose land they rented. They paid their rent in the tobacco they had grown, but much of the highest grades was sold at the outside markets for higher prices. The necessity of being a registered grower at these markets was circumvented by 'renting' registration cards (White 1987:178–9). Or, again, traders, especially women, sold 'Kaffir' beer to industrial and mining workers in the cities long after it was criminalised (Bozzoli 1991:142–64). To gain access to the lucrative, but closed, mining compounds of Southern Rhodesia, it is reported that they would sign on for a 'soft' overground job and, while going through the motions of that, would earn the bulk of their income from their beer selling (van Onselen 1976:101–2). Even in colonial times, the state was not averse to tacitly accepting illicit trading for the sake of political gain, especially the peace and security offered by traditional chiefs who 'let out' their land to illegal miners (Reno 1995a:28–54).

Herbst is therefore justified in complaining that, in the light of Africa's long tradition of informal activity:'It is therefore extremely difficult to see the informal sector as representing a dramatic new avenue for escape for Africans facing new economic and political hardships' (Herbst 1990:195).

Today, the second economy is flourishing and is thought to exceed more than half of the non-agricultural labour force. One survey in the mid-1980s in Tanzania revealed that 33 per cent of urban traders and 54 per cent of urban workers had secondary informal economic activity, providing 28 per cent and 47 per cent respectively of their incomes. In rural areas, 43 per cent of household heads had secondary activity and 83 per cent of their basic needs were met from the unofficial market (Maliyamkono and Bagachwa 1990). MacGaffey claims that, in the late 1980s in Kinshasa, Democratic Republic of Congo (Zaire), only about one million of the estimated four million labour force was employed and earned any wage in the official economy at all (MacGaffey 1992:246). She quotes a household survey that revealed that only 25 per cent of income came from wages and salaries (MacGaffey et al. 1991:13, 37). (For figures of estimates of the proportion of the non-agricultural, non-wage-earning labour force in several African countries in 1976–88, see Charmes, in Turnham et al. 1990:19.) Some of the second economy quite deliberately seeks to avoid the eyes of the law, implying a rejection of the state that made the laws, for its venality, inequity, inefficiency, inadequacy, greed and illegitimacy. But, equally, much of it straddles the legal–illegal, state–society, economic–political boundaries, blurring analytical divides.

Economic disengagement is the most problematic of all the forms of political disengagement. Though it is commonly applied to the second economy, it is hotly debated as to what exactly the second economy includes, whether any part of it is truly political and whether any or all of it is disengagement anyway. Further, much of the discussion concerning it has failed to acknowledge adequately its extent, the divisions and contradictions within it and its political aspects.

Naming the second economy

The preferred generic term in this discussion is the 'second economy', since this does not prejudge its nature, or else the descriptive term, the 'unrecorded economy'. As the latter suggests, the discussion will take a very broad view of its scope – namely, all economic activity that is neither reported nor measured by the state. MacGaffey favours a narrower definition that makes some degree of illegality an essential part (MacGaffey *et al.* 1991:12). This would exclude from the debate, however, the household and subsistence economy, which for some political analysts is a significant part of self-encapsulation and, therefore, of disengagement from the state.

In some circles, the term 'illegal economy' is popular, but legal is a relative concept that varies between countries and even within a country over time. For instance, in the colonial period, Northern Rhodesia in the 1920s criminalised home beer-brewing. Far from eradicating it, it meant that women had to pay the additional 'taxes' of bribes to the police to leave them alone. It highlighted, however, the ambiguity of the concept of legality. What was illegal by colonial decree was so widely approved by the population and unenforced by the local authorities that it never lost its legitimacy. Later, in 1983, the Democratic Republic of Congo (Zaire) decriminalised artisanal gold and diamond mining and the sale of its produce, although this remains illegal in many other countries.

Though 'underground economy' and 'hidden economy' are commonly used titles, this book takes the view that they are not adequate, since much of the activity is carried out quite openly and known to the authorities, or at least to sections of them. In Kenya, there has even been a special government department since 1988 to register and promote the unregistered and unlicensed artisans and traders, in recognition of the vital part they play in economic activity, if not in tax revenue (King 1996)! In Kinshasa in the early 1990s, half of the 57,000 daily bus passengers travelled on buses that operated outside the law. According to MacGaffey, 'controls are ineffective and the gendarmes and transport authority officials seek to extort tolls rather than make drivers respect the regulations' (MacGaffey 1992:248). Very often, such accommodation is the first step to legislation. The most open of all second-economy activities is, of course, that performed by state officials themselves.

Equally misleading as descriptive terms are the 'parallel economy' and the 'irregular economy'. The former suggests that the two economies run as separate entities, when in fact they are interlinked, with goods and persons now in one arena and now in another, even within the course of successive transactions. As for irregular, its connotations of haphazard and unorganised could not be further from the truth. MacGaffey even goes so far as to say that:

> Second economy activities operate in a more regular and predictable manner than is generally the case in the official economy ... it operates according to a system of rules known and subscribed to by all participants. Examples include standardized equivalents observed for barter transactions, set rates for bribes at unofficial border controls, arrangements set up for terms of clientage and the reciprocal obligations of other personal ties. Reliability in this system is ensured by the trust and confidence that come from relying on personal relationships of kinship, ethnicity and clientship. (MacGaffey 1992:254)

Finally, the use of the term 'informal trading' implies that the second economy is only concerned with small-scale backstreet enterprises, though these and petty commerce from people's homes are very common. (An International Labour Organisation (ILO) survey in Kinshasa in the mid-1980s recorded 12,000 artisanal and commercial enterprises (MacGaffey 1992:249).) But the size and scale of the activity is not relevant to categorising an activity as being in the first or second economy. There can be very large-scale operations in terms of quantity and value of goods. Secondly, the second economy is not an activity confined to the poor. Certainly, there are those small operators who use it as a coping strategy to overcome appallingly low wages and producer prices or as their only means of entry into economic activity, in view of the legal, bureaucratic and financial barriers to entry into the formal economy or even its virtual collapse in places. But, as Table 6.1 shows, there are large-scale operations where business people take advantage of second-economy market opportunities to accumulate considerable wealth (MacGaffey 1983:352). The difference is that between the individual hunter selling ivory prior to 1990 to small-scale traffickers and white store-owners (Rukarangira and Schoepf 1991:89) and

Table 6.1 Roles of the first and second economy

	Criminal	Venal	Unlawful	Semi-legal	Legal (unrecorded)	Legal (recorded)
Small scale	Poaching	Illegal use of minor state position for profit	Unlicensed and unrevealed trade, production and services	Federated but unlicensed trade	Subsistence farming	Salaried occupations
	Sexual services			Cooperative house building on invaded land	Crafts	Taxed and licensed services production, trade and services
	Drug sales	Public theft and embezzlement	Petty smuggling of legal goods		Bartering	
	Sale of stolen goods				Scavenging and resale for recycling	
			Mining enclaves	Federated but unlicensed public transport		
Large scale	Smuggling arms, drugs, stolen cars	Illegal use of major state position for profit	Gem and mineral dealing		Hoarding of scarce goods (up to certain limits)	
			Currency dealing			
					Speculating	
			Credit associations			

the Zone Commissioner in Kisangani who 'was temporarily removed from his post in 1979 after allowing passage across the river of a truck containing three tons of ivory valued at $100,000' – a man almost certainly working for politicians even further up the hierarchy (MacGaffey 1983:358).

Is economic disengagement political?

For many, 'political' implies ideology and organisation – that is, shared principles of governance and joint actions for achieving them – whereas, to them, the salient feature of the second economy appears to be that of business people in search of profits (Maliyamkono and Bagachwa 1990) or at least survival (ILO 1989). The case for seeing those involved in the second economy as primarily motivated by self-centred economic improvement, not principled political opposition to the state, appears to be self-evident: a case of avoiding rules so as to make their living, rather than a case of avoiding the state to undermine its living. If their conduct in the illegal second economy is anti-state, it is born of necessity or desire for wealth and is incidental to their main objective. Their activity is a pragmatic economic strategy, not an idealistic political statement. In support of this non-political interpretation is cited the sensitivity of the illegal second-economy supply and prices to market conditions. Though state rule might continue to be predatory, where formal markets do make provision – for example, tea in Tanzania or currency-dealing in Zimbabwe following the Economic Structural Adjustment Policy – the illegal second economy is virtually non-existent; and, where markets collapse, as with ivory after the world ban on ivory trading in 1990, the illegal second-economy production inevitably fails.

But the economic interpretation does not exhaust the dimensions of what is taking place in the second economy. It is hard to exclude the political when the activities being considered entail production, distribution and services that are either illegal in and of themselves or activities which, though legal, are carried out in a manner intended to avoid state taxes and dues. Certainly, most states would interpret the systematic evasion of their control of the economy as a challenge to their legitimacy and hence commonly prosecute people under the emotive term of 'economic sabotage' or have periodic crack-downs on the more visible activities. It was following the shock that President Nyerere of Tanzania had in 1983, when inspecting a private warehouse in which he found enough stored goods and spare parts to 'make the central government's store look like a joke' (quoted in Kasfir 1983:101), that he declared 'the war on smugglers'. Surely President Mobutu was an exception and courting popular support at any price when, to huge crowds in Kinshasa in 1974 and 1975, he enjoined them to 'steal cleverly, little by little, and invest your money in Zaire', and 'to those who have stolen money and put that money into houses here in Zaire, and not abroad' his message was, 'I congratulate you for putting money into these houses and these houses will remain yours because you have improved our land' (quoted in Young 1984:303).

Others would see the second economy not just as illegal activity challenging particular rules of the state, but as a manifestation of the class struggle, challenging the state elite's right to rule. From this perspective, illegal second-economy activity is not just a coping strategy in economically hazardous times, but a form of non-violent resistance to those whose revenue extractions and production controls would strangle the right to live at or rise above the subsistence level. MacGaffey argues that:

> Participation in the second economy can be seen as a political option. By their actions, people are contesting what is legitimate. By refusing to comply with regulations and restrictions, they confront and resist, in a non-violent manner, a predatory state and the class that controls it. By mounting such resistance, the subordinated classes not only challenge the state by evading its exploitation, but also undermine the power of the dominant class by contributing to state decline. (MacGaffey 1994:172)

De Soto sees it not just as resistance but, positively, as a silent revolution by which an alternative system offers a freedom of opportunity and provision that the state would never have conceded. People operate in this economy, he writes, not 'to live in anarchy, but so that they can build a different system which respects a minimum of essential rights' (De Soto 1989:xiv). Chingono seems to reach a similar conclusion, following his interviews with those in Mozambique who had voluntarily left their jobs in the formal economy to become self-employed in the second economy:

> One such young man vowed that he would never work for anyone, the government or private company, because it was, in his words 'working for the *chefs* all the time'. 'I want to be my own *chef*', he confidently declared, and, he confided, it was because of his philosophy that he had avoided military call-up throughout the war. In other words, the grass-roots war economy ... had offered the participants involved *relative* freedom from the suffocating grip of the state and from (direct) exploitation by big capital, as well as freedom of movement across national boundaries in spite of the celebrated sanctity of the nation-state. (Chingono 1996:109)

This extension of the usage of 'political' founders, as far as traditional views are concerned, on the failure to distinguish a political act from an anomic act. Critics would ask whether all those in the illegal second economy are really explicitly reacting against the state and the class that controls it. Where are the common/public goals, as opposed to straightforward self-interest? Where is the evidence of coordinated action? Individuals who act alone, to avoid state regulations concerning their production, with no concern but their own survival, do not possess, in this view, the ingredients of political actors. But is there another, looser, sense of counter-hegemony, asks Chabal, that:

> is only noticeable in the failure of a given course of state action or even the absence of action ... for example rural dwellers, atomised and seemingly passive, do not overtly challenge the state. Yet, their decision to increase or reduce production, surely one of the central economic factors in the life of African countries today, is, very largely, the consequence of their response to state politics. (Chabal 1992:84)

This takes us into the realm of implicit political opposition, where economic disengagement is a statement, albeit undeclared and anonymous, of rejection, and, being made by thousands across the land, even though they are isolated and uncoordinated, amounts to something very akin to a political act.

Other political scientists (for example, van Onselen 1976; Scott 1985; Adas 1986; Lichbach 1994) elaborate this point still further, arguing that simply the presence of implicit common goals and implicit common action is sufficient to warrant an act being political, no matter whether there is a self-interested motive as well or whether the acts appear to be individual. In their view, to expect coordinated campaigns might be appropriate for the elite, the intelligentsia and the urban middle classes, with their personal networks and institutional skills and access, but it is not realistic for the lower classes. They quite deliberately avoid confrontation, because, as the weak, they could not survive the ferocious response it would provoke. Their tactics, therefore, employ everyday, but largely hidden, responses. In his work on the African proletariat, Cohen (1980) highlights what he calls the hidden responses to capitalist labour processes, such as desertion, internal migration and working to rule. Similarly, concerning the workers who lived in the oppressive mining compounds of Southern Rhodesia between 1900 and 1930, but with wider relevance, van Onselen argues:

> The analyst who seeks for an index of worker consciousness or an outright demonstration of African resistance should not ... look for dramatic responses. Compound police, spies, censorship and the sjambok [whip] do not produce an environment conducive to the development of public ideologies, organizations, meetings, petitions or strikes. In tightly controlled situations, such as the compound undoubtedly was, the patterns of

resistance among black miners should in the first instance be sought in the nooks and crannies of the day to day situation. (van Onselen 1976:239)

Resistance, in this view, is found in unorganised practical defiance, desertion, 'loafing' and poor-quality production. Because peasants have little consciousness of being a unified social group and are scattered across the countryside, they are extremely vulnerable to repression and the institutional means to act collectively are extremely restricted. But this is not to say, in the view of these analysts, that they are apolitical – rather, that political culture inevitably takes a different form. Atomistic acts should be considered political, according to Brown (quoted in Lichbach 1994:414), where 'they were made thinkable by the consensus and support of the community': in other words, where there is implicit cooperation, a supportive subculture akin to a social movement – 'a social movement with no formal organisation, no formal leaders, no manifestos, no dues, no name and no banner' (Scott 1985:35).

As for implicit social goals, amidst what appear to be the self-indulgent actions of individuals, these same writers argue that the very essence of peasant politics is to combine the self-indulgent and the selfless:

> It is precisely the fusion of self-interest and resistance that is the vital force animating the resistance of peasants and proletarians. When a peasant hides part of his crop to avoid paying taxes, he is both filling his stomach and depriving the state of grain [etc.] ... To require of lower-class resistance that it somehow be 'principled' or 'selfless' is not only utopian and a slander on the moral status of fundamental material needs; it is, more fundamentally a misconstruction of the basis of class struggle, which is, first and foremost, a struggle over the appropriation of work, production, property and taxes. (Scott 1985:296)

Is this creating mythical persons who are unwittingly involved in a peasant-wide policy of disengagement against an illegitimate state? Peasants or diamond miners, selling their excess to the highest bidder, indifferent to the trader's legality, might appear apolitical. But research has repeatedly found that these selfsame peasants and workers are far from politically naive (for example, Mathiason and Powell 1972; Barkan 1976; Hayward 1987; Reno 1995a). Rather, they have developed views of what the state and political representatives should do and of their failures. MacGaffey quotes the Bodo peasants of Haute Zaire as being:

> quite specific that they were avoiding the abuse and exploitation of the local administration – manifested in inordinate taxes and fines, false weighing practices, marketing difficulties and low prices for food and export crops –

when they turned to smuggling and artisanal gold mining in the 1980s. (MacGaffey 1994:174–5)

And, as one local official in Kono Province, Sierra Leone, wrote in a confidential memo in the 1970s, many illicit diamond miners believe 'that to live under laws imposes only burdens ... they believe that government is the cause of their misfortunes' (quoted in Reno 1995a:98).

One can safely say that, even when survival is uppermost in the minds of those engaged in the illegal second economy, views as regards the state's part in bringing about and failing to solve the economic crisis or to let them into the formal market are not far away. Nor are these views kept entirely to themselves; they are at least shared with their kin and personal networks – enough to assure the complainants that their critique is supported by others.

Dominant aims of economic survival must not be confused with the totality, or pragmatism with the exclusion of principles, or lack of explicit political organisation with the absence of a common cause. On the other hand, every action within the illegal second economy must not be made into an act of class warfare. Purely political and purely economic actions are rare where a state is so dominant an actor in the economy, so biased towards vested and elite interests and so inept and corrupt in its supervision. Few can escape the oppression of the state's demands, its barriers to entering legal business and the inadequacy of its provisions, and therefore few in the illegal second economy can be free of negative opinions about the state's impact. And few can resist the legal loopholes and illegal opportunities that its overstretched structure offers to facilitate evasion and thus survival and even prosperity. The illegal second economy may not be all about mounting resistance to the state, but, like so-called economic migration, it cannot be divorced from politics.

Sectors of the second economy

The schema of the second economy that I offer in this book makes a distinction between criminal, venal, unlawful, semi-legal and legal (see Table 6.1), with economic disengagement being confined to the first three, or the illegal, sectors. 'Criminal' refers to the production and distribution of goods and services that are illegal in and of themselves. For example, in North Kivu, Democratic Republic of Congo (Zaire), leopards, gorillas, chimpanzees and zebras are captured live for eventual sale to zoos or to provide valuable skins for the West (Vwakyanakazi 1991:52–3). Cars stolen in Zambia and Botswana (with or without the cooperation of the drivers in providing the keys, or allowing themselves to be 'abducted'!) are brought through customs with the help of bribes and sold in Democratic Republic of Congo (Zaire) (Rukarangira and Schoepf 1991:85–6). Oranges stolen by the plantation workers at night are sold in the town markets of Manica Province, Mozambique, to supplement their meagre wage (Chingono 1996:91). And, most tragically, there are the cases of the abduction of children for slave-like labour, as has happened in Mozambique (Chingono 1996:107–8).

'Unlawful' refers to the production and distribution of goods which, though legal in and of themselves, are traded in such a way as to evade taxes, licence fees and customs dues. It is estimated that 33 per cent of Shaba, Democratic Republic of Congo's (Zaire), maize requirements was smuggled from Zambia in 1985–6, exploiting the fact that the price of maize is lower in Zambia, due to subsidies; and 94 per cent of the 1988 bumper wheat harvest of Kano State (Nigeria) never reached the official mills but was apparently smuggled out through Benin (Davidson 1992:214). (Most of the smuggling is done openly by day, with the military on both sides of the border being paid off (Rukarangira and Schoepf 1991:78).) In Zimbabwe, the government estimates that it is losing between $Z250 million and $Z500 million worth of gold (16 per cent of the mining total) through illegal export, mainly from 80,000 illegal small-scale panners (*The Chronicle*, Bulawayo 1/1/97). In Uganda, the introduction of user fees has led to a mushrooming of drug shops and pharmacies where, despite their lack of the necessary licence, prescribable-only drugs are freely purchased by customers who have diagnosed their own complaints (Wallman 1996:147). Or, more simply, one can cite the hundred and one items retailed from people's homes or from market stalls and 'pitches', which pay no tax, although they do require varying degrees of bribes to the police, and where some or all of the goods are frequently obtained from smugglers or middlemen. Unlicensed and unrevealed trading and petty smuggling lie at the lower end of the scale of activities. At the upper end is large-scale smuggling of legal goods, gem and mineral dealing and currency dealing. Green argues that, in Uganda, following the destruction of the Indian trading network in 1972, 'magendo' took off and quickly created its own class structure, dominated by fewer than 500 wealthy individuals, who nevertheless controlled a trade he estimates to have been two-thirds of the country's gross domestic product (Green 1981:25–31). Kasfir, however, questions whether the evidence supports the claim that they organised themselves into powerful business hierarchies that integrated related economic sectors, and believes they may have remained fragmented (Kasfir 1983:95, 100).

Bestriding the large-scale/small-scale divide are 'mining enclaves', such as those in North Kivu, the Democratic Republic of Congo

(Zaire), and Kono, Sierra Leone (Vwakyanakazi 1991:52; Reno 1995a:127). Because of the value of metals such as gold and gemstones such as diamonds, areas rich in these deposits are normally parcelled out to licensed mining operators by the state. Even with private security 'armies' employed by the companies, the size of the concessions and the nature of the terrain make total supervision unrealistic. It is an opportunity, readily exploited by young men who live in remote semi-permanent villages in the forest, to dig for gold and diamonds. The illegality may be either the artisanal mining itself and/or that it is on land belonging to private/state companies. The competition is such that individuals would rarely survive on their own and so they tend to band together in teams, who, even then, may have to pay protection money to regional strongmen/local headmen and their armed gangs. Richards describes them in south-east Sierra Leone as not only spanning the two economies, but spanning national identities:

> The population of young diamond diggers on the border are especially ambiguous in their national loyalties ... Young people here [in the unlicensed forest workings] often belong to families divided by the border and before the [civil] war routinely maintained both Sierra Leonean and Liberian identity, finding supplies and entertainment at times easier to organise in Monrovia than in Kenema [the nearest regional centre in Sierra Leone]. (Richards 1995:159)

There are two categories of the second economy that I place outside economic disengagement. The 'semi-legal' category occurs where the unrecorded willingly meets the recorders, not so much to make full disclosure as to negotiate some kind of mutually acceptable *modus vivendi*. This usually entails second-economy operators gathering forces into a federation or union and agreeing with the state some form of revenue payment in return for unofficial acknowledgement of their right to ply their trade. In Ghana, unlicensed clothing manufacturers have, through their association, chosen to negotiate a tax settlement in exchange for freedom to trade without molestation (Edwards 1995), whilst, in Kenya, the Jua Kali manufacturers[2] have, through their associations, sought government assistance for shelters, loans, land ownership or simply freedom from 'slum clearance'. In return, they have offered, not payment of taxes, but a vital sector of the national economy, employing two million (King 1996). In view of the ambitions of those in the semi-legal sector to be fully incorporated within the formal economy, I do not regard this category as true disengagement.

---

[2] Jua Kali literally means 'hot sun', a reference to the fact that these unlicensed and unregistered micro-businesses were and are carried out in the open on unoccupied land.

Though this book has worked within a definition of the second economy as unrecorded, this does not necessarily mean it is illegal. Crafts, bartering and particularly subsistence farming are all legal unrecorded activities, at the level of the small-scale operator, as normally are hoarding and speculating at the larger end of the scale (though some countries set limits). Concerning subsistence farming, Kasfir is right to caution against careless assumptions that food cropping is necessarily subsistence farming. With growing urban demands for food and falling world prices for cash crops, there are good commercial grounds for switching, other than a return to subsistence as a form of disengagement. Although the majority of the produce of smallholders is for household consumption, probably very few produce purely for subsistence consumption. Maliyamkono and Bagachwa suggest that, for Tanzanian peasants, probably only 80–5 per cent of the maize and 50 per cent of the paddy is consumed at home (Maliyamkono and Bagachwa 1990:72). Yet what is marketable goes more often to the unofficial rather than the official markets, given the former's higher prices. Maliyamkono and Bagachawa (1990:76–7) go on to quote estimates of 66 per cent of the marketable maize and 80 per cent of the marketable rice going to the second-economy markets in 1986–7. It is clear, then, that a large proportion of food production and distribution goes unrecorded, as peasants circumvent 'the system' through their substitute set of exchange relations.

Can the state disengage from the state?

I have delayed referring to the illegal use of state position, or what I have called 'venal', since this raises fundamental issues concerning the whole concept of disengagement in the economic arena. For lesser state officials, their activity in the second economy amounts to little more than income generation or salary supplementation. Bearing in mind that wages, even when paid, are below subsistence levels, abuse of official position becomes a necessity. Indeed, it is such opportunities that provide the only incentive for taking or staying in these jobs. Extracting payments for government services that are officially free, such as the issuing of official licences, grants, approvals, documents and certificates; turning a blind eye to illicit activity for a fee; extortion under threat of prosecution; using contacts to obtain commodities in short supply and often at administered prices for resale; public theft – are all common methods.

The practice is vividly portrayed by one eyewitness account of the 900 km road journey of a yam trader from the north of Nigeria to Lagos in 1996 (Okonkwo 1996). The need for an 'escort' who was an expert in 'palm-greasing' to ride with the driver soon became apparent. At the local government office, 2,000 naira (N2,000) was paid for permission to transport the yams, N3,000 for a public hygiene certificate and N1,500 for the packing and loading fee. There followed a customs road-block (N3,000 to prove there were no smuggled goods); a police road-block (N4,500); a police checkpoint (N2,000); a customs post (N1,500); a roadblock manned by the Yiv Youth Organisation and the Yiv Farmers and Traders Association (N3,000, to save the tyres from being deflated!); traffic police (N2,000); customs (N2,000); a road repairer (N500, for pouring laterite filling into potholes!); a policeman (N1,000); a police patrolman (N1,500); a policeman (N500, for police protection along the road); a police inspector (N500); police and customs roadblock (N5,000); traffic police (N1,000); road safety marshals (N1,500); and that only got them halfway to Lagos, the remainder of the journey requiring another N5,000. In all, the N150,000 worth of yams cost N40,000 in bribes to transport.

With the state being such a vast network of agencies, the illicit activities of their officials is not, of course, coordinated. Indeed, officials are often competing with one another, or at least pulling in opposite directions, in their quest for personal gain. Nor is it to be thought that their actions are always proactive, for very often they are responding to those seeking to evade state regulations or to exploit state opportunities. Nevertheless, the dilemma for the disengagement construct is obvious: those who are responsible for state authority are also those who act directly to disengage themselves from state institutions. In other words, those who rule in the name of state authority are often active in disengagement and even instigate it. Apparently, the dominant as well as the dominated seek to escape from domination!

How is this inconsistency to be resolved? Once more, therefore, we are faced with straddling. A single individual can operate on both sides of the analytical divide, in this case, of the first and second economy. Disengagement is properly ascribed to actions, not persons. Individuals are not 'disengagers' as if this described the totality of their outlook. They evade domination as and when it is appropriate. And, when there is more to be gained by engaging and exploiting the dominated space, they pursue that course. Thus, a public official can operate now as a self-seeking individual breaking the law and now as an official upholding it. It should not surprise anybody that those closest to the state and most intimately aware of its intelligence (and blind spots) and rules (and loopholes) are those in the best position to evade it and those most tempted to market their knowledge.

The state, of course, is not a uniform but a hierarchical institution. Though the boundary line between the top and the bottom of the state personnel is obviously arbitrary, there is nevertheless a qualitative difference in their approach to the second economy. In the lower eche-lons of the civil service, they are far removed from rule-making and would scarcely recognise themselves as the dominant. In their own way, these lesser state officials are still participating in the illegal sec-ond economy so as to avoid the formal state constructed by their mas-ters, those that control the state. Certainly, they are compromised with the powers, which they see as no less predatory and exploitative than the families and friends they share their non-working lives with. Their disengagement, therefore, cannot be total and clear-cut. But is this not the nature of disengagement? The very attraction of the strategy for the weak is its pragmatism, flexibility and covert nature. To appear to be in collusion with the power you despise and seek to evade almost height-ens the rebellious achievement. (Mamdani (1996) makes a similar case for the Native Authorities of colonial rule, who maintained an auton-omy even while they acted as appointees of their rulers.) It is to abuse the delegated authority of the dominant, so as to strike at the domi-nant; it is to turn their very tools of domination against them.

When these officials do disengage, they are rejecting not so much the authority of the state as a total institution, but the authority of the pow-ers that control the state and who have failed them quite as much as they have failed the artisans, traders and peasants. Says Bratton:

> When officials engage in private accumulation and trade – even if only through relatives, intermediaries and employees – they are acknowledging that their behaviour is not governed by legal commands. The participation of state officials in the second economy amounts to a deconstruction of the formal architecture of the state in the face of a more compelling set of social imperatives. (Bratton 1994:247–8)

But it is not only lesser officials who are involved in the second econ-omy. For officials near the top and the political elite, the power- and wealth-generating potential of involvement in the illegal second econ-omy has attracted some of them to establish extensive and intricate illicit networks outside the institutional state boundaries – something lesser officials would find very much harder. The practices include large-scale smuggling, fraudulent export, speculation, embezzlement, sale of 'protection' to illegal operators, 'kickbacks' for government con-tracts and 'cuts' in the rackets run by regional strongmen who are exempted from prosecution (Kasfir 1983; Lemarchand 1988:161; MacGaffey 1994:183). From his study of Sierra Leone under Stevens and Momoh in the 1970s and 1980s and Zaire under Mobutu, Reno goes so far as to call their system a 'shadow state'. Here, the state elite works outside the institutions of the formal state, to secure control of resources and their associated wealth. By this, they maintain the patri-monial network that keeps them in power, even though the resources from the formal economy have evaporated as a result of creditor constraints. In the case of Sierra Leone, they targeted the most lucrative areas for exploitation, namely, gold and diamond mining. These were ceded to loyal regional strongmen or foreign intermediaries for rewards (Reno 1995a, b).

Such venal activity at the upper end constitutes the deliberate attempt by the state/political elite to invade the illegal second economy for its own political and materialistic ends. In my opinion, it is not disengaging from anything other than the state laws they themselves have made and should be excluded from disengagement. There is no higher authority for them to evade (unless it is one another!). The only resistance that this constitutes is resistance to restrictions on wealth-making; it is an enriching strategy, not a survival strategy. This resolution of the contradiction will not satisfy all and is perhaps a weakness in the concept.

Reno and others go so far as to argue that there would be no illegal second economy without the state officials, who at every level have invaded the illegal second economy for profit and/or political control. They assert that it is the product of state intervention. Thus, as formal state resources have declined, the consequence has been not so much for society to abandon a weak state that fails to provide benefits, but for a weak state to intervene in society's illegal second economy so as to sustain the resources it needs to hand out benefits to its clients. Whilst Reno's reminder of the interconnection of society and the state is welcome, it is an exaggeration to say that the relationship between state and society in the economic arena is 'distant from any notion of "disengagement"' (Reno 1995a:16). Not all economic disengagement involves the connivance of a public official – it may be the avoidance of economic powers like employers and landlords and local political 'barons'; nor is the activity of a government minister of transport to be equated with that of a minor official issuing driving licences, for the latter can very well evade the minister and the procedures and regulations of his ministry. The evidence is that the relationship between the two is complex and variable, as the next section will discuss.

The relationship between the state and the unrecorded economy

The relationship between the state and the unrecorded economy has been conceived in different ways, although the distinctions are, in part, the product of researchers focusing on specific sections of the unrecorded economy. These restricted studies have not necessarily argued for application to the whole of the second economy, nor are all concerned just with the illegal sector; nevertheless, their distinct emphases are helpful in building up a current understanding of its relationship to the state. Hyden (1980), in his research in Tanzania, was concerned with the activities of the peasantry. These he portrayed as 'uncaptured' by the state and indifferent to what the ruling classes had to offer. This did not entail total isolation, but did mean that, when they accepted state schools, dispensaries, water services, roads or even payment for cash crops, it was not out of necessity. Such relative luxuries, he argued, were seen as something that could be readily dropped if need be. In the case of cash crops, for instance, either they could switch to concentrating on the needs of their own household alone or they could turn to selling their produce to unofficial markets:

> this way they retain their autonomy and deny the rulers the opportunity to exercise power over them ... [P]easants by and large remain uncaptured by other social classes ... their dependence on the [world economic] system is marginal. They live in the boundary region of this system and there they have the unique prerogative of choosing to withdraw. They have a true exit option. (Hyden 1980:31–2)

The second economy is their guarantee of autonomy from the state. When they lift out the one foot that is in the market economy, they are free of the state's control over their productivity.

In Chazan's view, it is rare to find instances of completely isolated economic systems in contemporary Africa (Chazan 1988a). Nevertheless, with reservations, she echoes Hyden's thesis when she writes of processes of economic 'self-encapsulation', through which society becomes detached economically from the state. As examples of this trend, she cites 'the processes of ruralization' (the shift from public to private occupation and the move from town to village) and 'the resurgence of village industries'. Both, in her view, are quests for self-reliance in response to abject poverty, the chronic shortages in the formal economy and the failure of state provision. Chazan, therefore, argues for the intent of rural autonomy, even if the objective is not always realised.

If one can use a metaphor to summarise this conception of the relationship of the state to the second economy, one would describe it as two independent but cohabiting creatures; they might choose to drink from the same water-hole, but they can and do go their own separate ways when it suits. The question, however, is not to what extent individuals succeed in entering the second economy, but to what extent the second economy they enter is illegal and out of reach of the state, despite its intentions.

Many commentators have seriously questioned the degree of freedom from state restraints found in both the legal and illegal second economy. Both Kasfir and Herbst, for instance, argue that the ramifications of government decisions extend to both first and second economies (Kasfir 1983; Herbst 1990). In their view, much of the second economy relies on exploiting the distortions in the market economy brought about by the state's interventions – whether in keeping producer prices low, limiting import quotas, undervaluing the local currency and restricting production licences, or through inefficient management of nationalised industries or as a result of the bulky bureaucracy. In this view, there is parasitism, rather than two parallel economies, the second economy living off the scarcities and distortions of the state-controlled first economy. Consequently, as Hansen's (1992) historical study of Rhodesia and Tanzania concludes, the level of sales production among peasants, far from being, in their isolation, unresponsive and indifferent to government agricultural policies, does in fact respond to the vicissitudes of those policies. The peasants might appear uncaptured during periods of forceful government intervention and low prices, but that is not the whole story. Under positive encouragement, when 'favourable micro economic conditions for their productive activities were secured by the authorities' (Hansen 1992:83), peasants' sales production for the official market rose:

> Economic peasant participation was high in Tanzania 1924–38, 1961–70 and in Zimbabwe (Rhodesia) 1975–87 when government peasant policies were characterised by incentives, that is public measures which aim at creating an agricultural surplus by forcing positive social and economic conditions for the sector and otherwise letting the peasants themselves make their priorities concerning production and marketing. (Hansen 1992:82)

But there were low scores on the level of sales production among the peasants in Rhodesia in 1928–40 and in Tanzania in 1971–82 when government policies took the form of directives, that is, 'public measures which aim at creating a government surplus by intervention directly in the sector and decisions on behalf of the peasants, how production and/or marketing should be done' (Hansen 1992:82). This second conception of the relationship between the state and the second economy, therefore, sees a much closer relationship than Hyden's. It argues for a parasitic relationship, with the second economy, both legal and illegal, feeding off an unhealthy state, but becoming weak itself when the state is more robust. The two economies are integrated, rather than cohabiting.

A third view has portrayed a much more symbiotic relationship, that is, one where both parties openly acknowledge that they need one another and consequently negotiate (if they can't impose) working agreements. The state officials may be looking to control political challenges, to obtain essential services or to control lucrative areas of the economy outside formal institutional channels. Those in the second economy are seeking legalisation to gain for themselves the security of the first economy's contractual system and its credit/insurance benefits. De Soto's extensive survey of the second economy in Lima, Peru, covered three economic sectors, which surely have parallels in Africa. First, he described the informal 'housing estates' built by cooperative effort on invaded land, which sought and finally won legal status, including private land ownership. Secondly, he described the informal traders, both street vendors and those who have moved into market halls, which they had built without permission. These also fought long-running battles with the national and local authorities to secure acceptance. Like the organisers of the land invasions, they were able to use their political leverage of the collective vote and industrial action of their associations to secure at least tolerance, in exchange for the payment of excise and conformity to health controls. Thirdly, he examined the informal public transport operators. Desiring recognition of their routes and the right to extend these and to establish terminals, they also formed local committees and large federations to negotiate deals with the state. When the government was politically weak, they gained quite extraordinary tax concessions and exemptions from debts and even traffic fines. The more commonly prevailing mutual concessions, however, included a special kind of administrative recognition (somewhat short of full legal status), together with a right to participate in price control and industry regulating bodies, in return for controlled fares and/or no-strike pledges (De Soto 1989).

The federation of unlicensed clothing manufacturers, which negotiates tax settlements with the Ghanaian government in exchange for tolerance, has already been referred to (Edwards 1995). Clearly, there are groups within the second economy that, in order to survive, have had to act illegally – they could not afford to purchase land, or to put up shops, workshops and homes; nor could they afford the time and money to be legally registered or to run their business affairs according to the book. Their illegality was not antisocial in intent, but was designed to achieve the essentially legal objectives of building a house, providing a service or developing a business. These groups, however, have always desired the benefits of being in the formal/legal sector and, as their numbers have grown, they have used the political strength of unions and federations to 'knock on the door' of the state to be admitted as full members. Their disengagement, if that was what it was at the beginning, was temporary and has been followed by a policy of engagement. The ensuing negotiations have revealed that their continuance as illegal enterprises is more a problem of state acceptance than of business intransigence. The state's concessions have been granted reluctantly and with periodic reversals when the political pressure to concede waned. The state has also rarely granted full legal status, preferring very often the clientele's dependence to their taxes, and with an eye to the rumblings of the powerful formal business lobby. Clearly, this conception applies to the semi-legal second economy, which I have already excluded from economic disengagement.

Reno (1995a) also sees a symbiotic relationship, but his conception of its origin and driving motor is radically different. Whereas De Soto has seen this symbiotic relationship arising largely from the initiative of those in the second economy, Reno sees a large part of the initiative coming from the state itself. He tackles head-on the issue of the near-total participation by state officials, without whom, in his view, there would be no illegal second economy. He denies that it is the consequence of societal withdrawal from the state and asserts that it is, in fact, the consequence of state intervention in society, albeit society's illegal sector. And, as opposed to De Soto, who sees the illegal second economy as society excluded but trying to engage the state to draw on its benefits, Reno sees it as the state attempting to engage and draw on the lucrative illegal markets in society. As formal state resources have declined, it needs the opportunities of the illegal second economy to sustain its resources. There is some truth in his accusation that 'The symbiotic nature of state power outside institutional channels and informal markets is missed where observers see societal opposition in a context of state institutional failure' (Reno 1995a:16).

Rather than any one of the above accounts of the relationship between the first and second economies being true, I would argue that there are a diversity and complexity that ensure that all are to be found. Few would disagree that sexual services operate largely independent of state policy and state officials, even if not free of periodic harassment of their most visible activities. Yet smuggling and trading clearly exploit government-created distortions in the market and are parasitical. Whole trading areas can be wiped out by a change of government policy on pricing or import controls. The case, however, of unlicensed public transport operators is more than the seizing of an advantage created by inadequate state provision. Their scale and importance for urban inhabitants mean that urban politicians need them too; hence the total openness of this supposed 'illegal' activity.

The relationship between the two economies is not only various, but it is dynamic. Now an individual totally avoids the state; now there are weaknesses in the state's management of the market that entice him/her to re-emerge from isolation to seize the new advantages; now under threat of closure, the individual collaborates with public officials or procures 'lines' for trading networks initiated by officials; now an individual is surrounded by so many similar operators that he/she binds together with them in an open organisation that makes demands on the state, backed up by meaningful threats; and now a resurgence of state oppression leads the individual back to a more clandestine mode of operation.

Where, then, in this complex and dynamic second economy, does disengagement belong? Certainly, economic disengagement is not to be equated with the entire second economy. Legal unrecorded activity in the second economy by and large entails no intention to avoid the state. It is a case of unrecorded, rather than covert, activity. Semi-legal activity does indeed operate outside the law, but more out of necessity than choice, for its overall purpose is to be part of the first economy, although on its own terms. Its negotiations with the state, therefore, place it in the category of engagement. Venal activity at the upper end constitutes the deliberate attempt by the state/political elite to invade the illegal second economy for its own political and materialistic ends. It evidently is not disengaging from anything other than the state laws it has made.

The conclusion is that economic disengagement is to be found in the criminal, unlawful and small-scale venal economic activities. True, even these may have direct or indirect links to public officials, but they can be said to be primarily independent activities that avoid state procedures, regulation and taxation. Usually, there is also in their activity a clear rejection of state legitimacy.

How does illegal second-economy activity relate to the propositions?

At the end of Chapter 1, ten propositions were set forth as regards all forms of disengagement. Do those generalisations fit the account of the illegal second economy as it has been described above?

First, as regards the nature of disengagement, it was hypothesised that disengagement is a universal phenomenon, a multi-scale phenomenon and a responsive strategy.

The discussion of this chapter has shown that economic disengagement is indeed a universal phenomenon and not one restricted to the lower classes, as some earlier writers implied (Chabal 1992:81). Presidents and policemen, generals and privates, high-ranking bureaucrats and their spouses, big-time entrepreneurs and small-time retailers, landowners and peasants, the inhabitants of middle-class suburbs and of the townships – all are found having greater or lesser disengagement roles in the economic arena. Mukohya (1991), for instance, in her chapter on the illegal second economy in North Kivu, Democratic Republic of Congo (Zaire), refers to the illegal activities of large plantation owners and small farmers, large buyers/wholesalers and small traders, major and minor customs officials, company directors of export firms and retailers selling from their homes, young men gold mining in the forest with patronage from traditional headmen and wealthy gold buyers with patronage from politicians. Her estimate is that about 60 per cent of the towns' populations are involved in the illegal second economy, if only part-time. Beyond spanning the classes, it also spans gender, ethnic and age divides. The phenomenon of economic disengagement is now found throughout sub-Saharan Africa.

Economic disengagement is also an activity undertaken at every scale: by individuals, by extended family groups, as part of clan networks or in loosely bound federations and unions.

For most of those involved, the activity is clearly a responsive strategy. It may not be defensive in the sense of avoiding repression, but it does defend people from a state whose mismanagement of the first economy and neglect of state services threaten their livelihood and even survival. It is also, at the same time, opportunist disengagement, in that, were it not for the lax, 'pliable', or non-existent enforcement of legal restraints, those involved in illegal second-economy activity would never be able to conduct their business.

Secondly, concerning the pattern of this form of disengagement, it was hypothesised that disengagement depends on macro-scale and micro-scale factors.

Both are prominent in the illegal second economy. At the macro level, the availability of the strategy has been crucial to those holding public office and to those living near an international border and/or having relatives and clan contacts living across a border, as part of the trading network. Concerning cultural norms, it can be fairly said that what might be doubtful to many in prosperous countries is widely accepted and promoted in countries faced with a daily struggle to survive. Indeed, the very lawmakers and law enforcement agencies condone it, probably participate in it and, in extreme cases, encourage it. In other words, few have moral reservations about participation in this form of evasion of state control. Significantly, even the very terms for it are often amoral, such as 'getting by' and 'fending for ourselves'. At the micro level, there can be little doubt that the utility of the strategy is universally believed in sub-Saharan Africa. Linking the opportunities with those seeking them are personal networks. The more highly placed the connections reach, the greater the scale of the opportunities and degree of protection they provide.

Thirdly, concerning the significance of disengagement, it was hypothesised that it provides a measure of the nature of political authorities, threatens the power balance of political systems, delays democratic consolidation and usually provokes resistance by force.

The significance of the illegal second economy is controversial.

Given even roughly reliable figures for the size of the illegal second economy, some measure of regime penetration would be possible. But all the efforts to quantify second-economy activity have been insufficiently accurate (for methods and their critique, see Alessandrini and Dallago 1987:21–34; Maliyamkono and Bagachwa 1990:50–62; Turnham *et al.* 1990:10–48) and no systematic attempt has been made to separate the legal from the illegal. But, if quantifying the second economy is problematic, crude figures can be used alongside sociological and anthropological accounts to gain at least a 'fair impression'. Thus, looking at Table 6.2, it will not be a surprise to see that national estimates of a large second economy correspond with such local surveys and anecdotal accounts as have been published and that these, in turn, are states that are commonly regarded as weak in penetration. Economic engagement, therefore, is an indication of an authority's powers of law enforcement and of their penetration of the economy (both in general and in the marginal communities – socially and geographically – in particular).

It appears that economic disengagement has seriously unsettled the power balance of political systems. It has done this by opening the door to those outside the dominant classes, so that they can accumulate wealth and influence independent of the state. 'Proximity to the state and its power apparatus has lost some of its influence on social status. Power and authority have been detached, leading to increasing status incongruence' (Azarya and Chazan 1987:128). It is not clear how deeply resented it is by the formal business community. MacGaffey (1983, 1988a, 1991, 1994) has repeatedly argued that the illegal second economy has produced an African bourgeoisie. Whether these are treated as equals by those who have made their wealth legally has not been reported. But the fact that wealth made in the illegal second economy is often invested in the formal economy blurs the barriers. Perhaps

Table 6.2. Estimated scale of the second economy in selected countries

Country	Second economy as % of GDP (1980s)	Source
DRC (Zaire)	200	MacGaffey *et al.* (1991)
Uganda	66–100+	Green (1981)
CAR	75	Schissel (1989)
Tanzania	31	Maliyamkono and Bagachwa (1990)
Ghana	32	Maliyamkono (1990)

GDP, gross domestic product; DRC, Democratic Republic of Congo; CAR, Central African Republic.

wealth, however made, is the basis for status equality. Besides, as Azarya and Chazan point out, when personal networks, consisting often of largely kinship or wider lineage ties, predominate, class has far less significance.

Democracy has often been sold as the answer to material needs. For those struggling to survive by resort to the illegal second economy, therefore, the jury is still out. Will they come to see that economic performance is not directly linked to democratic institutions and that the latter deserve their support, whatever the state of the economy? Or will failure in economic growth undermine their support? What is certain is that consolidation will not take place without the masses regarding it as non-negotiable. Even should unshakeable support for the institutions be forthcoming, it is hard to see how democracy can be fully consolidated whilst the rule of law is so widely flouted. Here, then, is a vicious circle: no cessation of widespread flouting of state economic laws (and hence no democratic consolidation) prior to national economic prosperity and improved state service provision; and no economic prosperity based on government investment or improved services without tax and custom dues. It is not so much economic disengagement that undermines democratic consolidation as economic performance. When that turns upwards, the illegal second economy is likely to reduce to a point where it is no longer a barrier to the consolidation process.

Economic disengagement has tended to attract periodic but short-lived law-enforcement campaigns. Though these might reinforce faith in the legitimacy of the state and reassure citizens that the state is able and willing to tackle lawbreaking, they rarely do more than temporarily hinder the activity. Typically, when the growth of illegal second-economy activity has reached overwhelming proportions and/or the involvement of the coercive forces themselves, coercive measures are replaced by indifference or even negotiation. The campaign against economic 'sabotage' in Tanzania in April–June 1983 illustrates the point (Maliyamkono and Bagachwa 1990:ix–xix). Its intention, in Maliyamkono and Bagachwa's opinion (1990:ix), was 'to administer a sharp and salutary shock to the ailing economy' and to release consumer staples to the public. The prime minister said that the 'crackdown' was aimed at traffickers in foreign currency; smugglers of minerals, livestock, hoes and drugs; hoarders of scarce items; party, government and parastatal officials under investigation; and people with unlicensed arms (Maliyamkono and Bagachwa 1990:xii). Roadblocks, house searches, radio propaganda and the encouragement of denunciations led to 1,500 arrests, mainly of businessmen and civil servants (especially managers of regional trading corporations). In addition, large quantities of basic commodities were appropriated. It failed, however, to unearth the alleged 'conspiracy' to sabotage the government through the creation of shortages of goods.

Though not part of the propositions, my model of roles in the first and second economy (Table 6.1) has helped to organise a complex field into manageable discrete units that assist analysis. It is often the confusion between the categories that has led to inadequate and contradictory conclusions.

This chapter concludes the survey of disengagement in the arenas of territorial politics, institutional politics, constitutional politics, cultural politics and economic politics. Each has been examined for evidence of common disengagement strategies of autonomy, avoidance and deception, and indifference. Across the arenas and at the different levels of intensity, it has been shown that a major and persistent political undercurrent is at work in African societies. When domination is unacceptable and yet deemed to be beyond change by legal opposition or illegal force, withdrawal is to be anticipated. It is now time to attempt to weigh the significance of this in terms of the consequences for society and for the most salient authority in modern society, the state.

The Distribution
& Consequences
of Disengagement

*Any kind of organized revolt against the Party which
was bound to be a failure, struck her as stupid. The
clever thing was to break the rules and stay alive all
the same.* (Orwell, *Nineteen Eighty Four*).

Introduction

Thus far, disengagement has been explored separately in the arenas of
territorial politics, institutional politics, constitutional politics, cultural politics and economic politics, as indicated in my typology (see
Table 1.1). The worth of the typology in establishing analogous phenomena is revealed, in that in each arena individuals and groups have
been found attempting to detach themselves from the unacceptable
dominance of individual rulers and authoritarian systems. For all that
disengagement has been seen to be a process of variable breadth, scale
and significance, a similarity of withdrawal strategies in each arena has
been observed. But do the similarities go beyond strategy? What can be
said of disengagement as a whole? It is this question that this chapter
seeks to answer. Three issues in particular will be addressed. Is there a
pattern in the distribution of disengagement? Is there an historical
sequence to the development and consequences of disengagement? Is
there an overall effect on the prospects for democratic consolidation?

The distribution of disengagement

In proposition 2b (Chapter 1), I hypothesised that different disengagement phenomena were related, since they all arose from a common
rejection of domination. Phenomena, therefore, were expected to occur
concurrently as different expressions of the same rejectionism. This
section will look first at whether there is a geographical concurrence

(or what could be called zones of disengagement) and whether there is a social concurrence (or what could be called group disengagement). A theme throughout this book has been on the ubiquity of disengagement. No area, no social group, no historical period has been exempted from this particular response strategy to domination. Only the severest repression has stopped its outward manifestation and this, in turn, has only heightened the determination to disengage as soon as the next opportunity arises. Universality, however, does not exclude a certain degree of clustering in geographical, social and historical salience.

SPATIAL CLUSTERING

It has been noted throughout the book that those located in peripheral frontier locations have a special opportunity to pursue a strategy of withdrawal from central authorities. In these areas, penetration by such authorities may either be minimal by policy or hindered by inaccessibility. In addition, the proximity of a formal boundary to the authority's legal control offers the opportunity for disengagers readily to escape approaching military forces or to be supplied by supportive neighbouring authorities (possibly of the same ethnicity, if the boundaries were drawn insensitively). The nearby boundary also opens the door to the trading exploitation of cross-border variations in prices, taxes and availability of commodities. If the people of these border regions are themselves a minority, culturally distinct from their rulers (and historically such groups have often taken refuge in such areas), then cultural disengagement will also be a feature. This may be based on long-standing differences of language, custom and religion, which have arisen because of the separation, or where the separation attracts those of a counter culture (including the 'frontier mentality' characterised by extreme individualism and hostility to outside control). Alternatively, the cultural disengagement of the borderland may be based on the fact that disenchanted people make a fertile seed-bed for new ideological movements (Welch 1980: 24–5).

Secession, political migration, smuggling and cultural disengagement have all had a strong tendency to be concentrated in these peripheral areas. Only electoral discontinuance lacks prominence, this being largely due to the frequency of ethnically/regionally based political parties. Their presence is a reminder that the peoples of these areas see disengagement more as a means than an end. If engagement via political parties or rebel groups is thought to offer a genuine possibility of redressing the unjust oppression and neglect of the central authorities, then they may well be tried. Where such alternatives are not on offer or seem to be hopeless strategies (and, of course, the isolation that makes central domination difficult also reduces the likelihood of overthrowing that authority from that base), the well-trodden paths of disengagement will be followed. This is not to say that geographical marginality causes disengagement, but it does facilitate it.

The other concentration of disengagement is in the townships and slums of the cities. Once again, penetration by the authorities can be minimal as a matter of policy. There is a long history of disadvantaged urban areas becoming to some degree and for varying lengths of time no-go areas for the authorities. Concerning Nairobi, Kenya, in 1947–9, Throup writes:

> With only one policeman to every 1,000 inhabitants and no patronage net-work under the control of government nominees, the administration's authority ... was minimal [especially in] the 3 most overcrowded and badly constructed slums where well over half of Nairobi's Africans live. In these areas ... the 'street corner boys' of the 40 Group and the other semi-criminal gangs that made up the city's unemployed, ensured that during the long hours of darkness Nairobi's African locations were a 'no-go' area for the police. (Throup 1985:419)

Following the arrest of a political leader and the shooting by the police of strikers, the colonial administration warned that the government had virtually lost control over African Nairobi, which was firmly under the domination of the Kikuyu street gangs.

Another city which has seen repeated no-go areas is Brazzaville, Republic of Congo. In 1995 each political faction had strongholds in Brazzaville, controlled by its own militia. President Pascal Lisouba, leader of the Pan-African Union for Social Democracy (UPADS) had his militia, the 'Zulus', controlling Mfilou; Bernard Kolelas, leader of the Union for Democracy and the Republic (UDR) had his militia, the 'Ninjas', dominating the southern quarter of Bacongo; and Denis Sassou-Nguesso, former state president and leader of the Congolese Labour Party (PCT) concentrated his militia, the 'Cobras', in the areas of Talangai, Ouenze and Mpila.

Despite the pact of December 1995 disbanding militias and stipulating the collection of weapons distributed to them in the political/ethnic clashes of 1993, the situation remained largely unchanged until the outbreak of full-scale civil war in 1997. Thus from what appeared at first to be defensive areas from state control, the 'patches' became bargaining counters in the contestation for control of the centre and, finally, civil-war camps.

The poverty, unemployment and lack of policing in the townships also promote criminal and illegal economic activity and a rich variety of new religious movements. The lack of cultural homogeneity makes the mobilisation of opposition parties more difficult than in the rural peripheries, and very high rates of non-participation are recorded in elections. For instance, very low turnouts were recorded in the local elections in Libreville, Gabon, in 1996 (10–15 per cent); the parliamentary elections in Nouakchott, Mauritania, in 1996 (30 per cent); the municipal elections in Mozambique in 1998 (15 per cent); and the local elections in Bamako, Mali, in 1998 (20 per cent). In all the cases, the turnout was much lower than the national average.

SOCIAL CLUSTERING
Social marginalisation can be as important a factor in disengagement as physical marginalisation. Class has not been a prominent feature of this account: there is more to disengagement than the withdrawal of the poor. Haynes was struck by the number of state governors, university professors and top civil servants that have joined the syncretist Aladura churches in Nigeria: 'It is wrong to assume that only poor, disorientated, former peasants join the syncretistic churches. Rather, they attract followers from all walks of society, including the middle classes and the politico-economic elite' (Haynes 1996a:174, cf p182). Nor is the illegal second economy confined to the destitute; at the prosperous end of the illegal second economy sit those with influence and powerful contacts. Then, as regards political migration, the middle classes have been as quick to flee oppressive rulers as the peasants and, having more resources, have found transport and resettlement that much easier. Likewise, the ranks of the secessionists are filled not only with ethnically conscious peasants, but also with excluded intellectuals.

If class has not been prominent in group disengagement, gender has. Women are particularly active in the illegal second economy (MacGaffey *et al.* 1991), comprising, for instance, 60 per cent of traders in the 'flea markets' of Zimbabwe, according to a 1996 survey (reported in *The Financial Gazette*, Harare 23/1/97). They also appear to be the majority in many of the new religious movements (Haynes 1996a: 170–87). Their space for expressing their distaste for domination, however, is severely circumscribed by patriarchal systems. Decisions concerning political migration, secession and electoral discontinuance are very often in obedience to a husband or father. Even illegal second-economy activity may be chosen for them, or they have taken it up, not from choice, but because there was no choice – they are excluded from the formal economy. In the space that is left for them, it may be, as Staudt contends, that 'with both their marginality in conventional politics and the depoliticization of their issues ... many women withdraw or are alienated from contemporary politics, preferring instead to manage what is left of their own affairs autonomously' (Staudt 1987:207). A number of commentators go so far as to suggest that this quest for autonomy may even be leading to an increasing trend of divorce and avoidance of marriage among a large number of women (Chingono 1996; Hirschmann 1998). They prefer the freedom to manage their own affairs without the oppressive oversight (or violence) of men and within the greater security of female networks or multi-generational and sibling households. 'Translated into a massive trend particularly among working class and poorer [black South African] women, these individual practical decisions amount to a major strategic challenge to men's dominance and women's subordination' (Hirschmann 1998: 232, 234). There is therefore, as yet, no full picture of their own responses and therefore no true picture as to just how distinctive gender is in disengagement.

The social group that is increasingly drawing the attention of researchers for its distinct prominence in disengagement is youth, especially male youth (Goodwin-Gill and Cohn 1994; Furley 1995; Cruise O'Brien 1996; Richards 1996.). Youth in this context is defined as much politically as biologically – that is, as those school-leavers who have as yet to penetrate the power of office or even the status of waged employment and family life. This might include the majority of teenagers and twenty-year-olds. The marginalisation of male youth and their limited resources and leadership are similar to those of adult women, but without the same patriarchal restraints on movement, education and gender-linked employment opportunities. In Cruise O'Brien's view, the common material predicament of marginalised youth (he does not distinguish between the sexes) 'is that the young people have finished schooling, are without employment in the formal sector [and] are not in a position to set up an independent household' (Cruise O'Brien 1996: 57). Their very real fear is that their 'youth' will be prolonged indefinitely.

With national economies stagnant and population growth creating a very high proportion (40–50 per cent) of young people, it is no longer as straightforward as it was for their parents in the early days of independence to secure employment and to establish a family. The best they can hope for, in their effort to escape the dependence of junior status, may be to survive by activity in the legal or illegal second economy:

> Roughly 40,000 young people each year in towns come to working age in Senegal; of them, perhaps 5% find jobs in the formal or modern sector. The rest are either unemployed or are absorbed in the informal sector, in petty trade, hustling, getting by; with a significant residue in crime. A criminal life may look like a rational choice in this setting; more promising than political activity. (Cruise O'Brien 1996: 59)

There is no doubt that young males (and some young females) have been attracted to rebel groups, whether secessionist or not. Whole areas have lost their youth to secessionist recruitment, as in the Nuba mountains (African Rights 1995b: 68). The equal attraction to both types of insurgent suggests that the appeal of secessionism is not its particular constitutional solution. The issue for the young is not the political escape offered from the authority in the future (after the 'struggle is won'), but the escape from (ruler) indifference and unemployment upon becoming a rebel now. The rebel unit can offer the status of valued work, money, drugs and an alternative extended family, which makes them feel valued and provides shelter, keep, vision, an element of training/education and parenting (especially for the youngest and the orphans). (See interviews with teenage fighters in the Revolutionary United Front (RUF) and Sudan People's Liberation Army (SPLA) in African Rights (1995b:38, 69) and Richards (1996:90–5)). If this sounds somewhat idyllic, then an alternative view (Kaplan 1994) sees rebel groups, not as attracting abandoned youth, but as capturing or coercing young people and exploiting their dependency, naiveté, idealism, and plain unemployment and malnutrition.

For the same reason as other marginalised groups, young people have turned to religious movements with very different values and beliefs from those of the ruling class. The press in Zimbabwe have spoken of Pentecostal groups in particular as taking the nation 'by storm', with strong support from urban youth. 'Young professionals and youths are the biggest groups joining [the] mushrooming Pentecostal churches', attracted, allegedly, by the emotional worship and the absence of the legalism characteristic of the mainstream churches (*The Chronicle*, Bulawayo 12/1/97). Beyond that, Gifford notes that, within groups committed to self-help, mutual support, training and entrusting members with responsibility and leadership, young people can seek to escape the sense of valuelessness and alienation. He gives as an example Uganda, where he notes, pertinently, that Christian Pentecostalism 'need not be an opting out, it can be an opting in'. Where the Ugandan government has withdrawn, churches are 'increasingly tied up with the survival, jobs, health, schooling, prospects, travel, and the advancement of ordinary Ugandans' (Gifford, quoted in Cruise O'Brien 1996:64).

In the realm of formal politics, much has been made of the engagement role of college and university students in the democratisation movement in Africa since the late 1980s. Frequently, dissent broke out over the impact of government cut-backs in the universities. As the critique extended to government conduct in general, they were quickly joined by faculty, civil servants and unions. Bratton and van de Walle claim that students played the original or a leading role in the 1989–90 popular protests in Cameroon; Congo; Côte d'Ivoire; Gabon; Kenya; Niger; Mali; Mozambique; Senegal; Sierra Leone; Togo; Democratic Republic of Congo (Zaire); Zambia; and Zimbabwe (Bratton and van de Walle 1992: 422–3).

Nor was the engagement with the authorities confined to the youth of the universities.

In Senegal as in Mali, students in recent years have been to the fore in leading riots in the cause of democracy, helped by the more radical pupils from the secondary schools ... In Mali, students, together with the lycéens [secondary school pupils] and the unemployed, were involved in the demonstrations. (Cruise O'Brien 1996:64–5)

Cruise O'Brien goes on to quote from Thomas-Queh that in Liberia, when the opposition party called for a protest demonstration against the rice price increase, those quickest to respond were 'the market women, yenna boys, the unemployed, and school drop-outs – that vast majority of the population which really struggles to survive' (Cruise O'Brien 1996–69). But, just as high idealism and anti-authoritarianism are quick to mobilise youth, so the failure to live up to expectations and to produce rapid change of circumstances equally quickly dissipates enthusiasm. High levels of engagement among the young during the brief period of 1988–91, when the democratisation movement was at its height in Africa, seem to be being succeeded by discontinuance from formal politics among very many young people. The low registration and voter rates certainly include university students (Villalon 1994) and may be found to be particularly high among young people. Those in regions where regime change has brought little in the way of tangible benefits to them are likely to be suffering disillusionment; those in regions where old regimes have managed to hold on with only the smallest of concessions are likely to have lost belief in change being brought about through the electoral process.

A CULTURE OF DISENGAGEMENT

In proposition 2c (Chapter 1), I hypothesised that persistent hostile domination and networked histories would ensure that there would be particular concentrations of disengagement among particular people over an extended period of time (or cultures of disengagement). I expected that, given that these geopolitical and cultural/psychological elements are semi-permanent or, at the very least, are difficult and slow to change, long traditions of disengagement from the central authorities would have established themselves among the minorities of the peripheries. The conclusive evidence, however, has yet to be published and so this has to remain an unverified hypothesis. The closest I came to any evidence of a culture of disengagement was amongst the Bemba of northern Zambia. The Bemba were originally, of course, Luba followers of the Lunda until the seventeenth century, when they seceded because they felt neglected and humiliated (Vansina 1966:88–91). Whether this event in their history still had a strong impression on the people in the late nineteenth century only anthropologists can answer. In the twentieth century, their attachment to Watch Tower (and Lumpa) teachings has been a significant feature of society in northern Zambia for more than eighty years, or three generations. The same region, too, is noted for its cross-border smuggling of rice, maize, coffee and fish from Tanzania and cooking oil, sugar, salt, soap and car spare parts to Tanzania (Maliyamkono and Bagachwa 1990:xi, 102). Examining this story (and that of other cultures) with regard to disengagement must await another's research.

The failure to find disengagement persisting in regions over time may also reflect the ebb and flow between the dominant and the dominated. Power is not merely an instrument of an active agent set against a passive subject; rather, it entails a dynamic relationship. Authorities, as have been noted throughout the book, are rarely indifferent to the response of disengagement. If they cannot minimise it by their initial policies, they are likely to adopt different policies. These, in turn, may well evince different disengagement responses, but they may equally be met by non-disengagement responses. Increased force or surveillance, on the one hand, or more favourable terms of incorporation, on the other, may well entice those who have previously disengaged to reverse their strategy to engagement. Since the best interests of the dominated are prone to fluctuation, long-term strategies may well be the exception.

The consequences of disengagement

An attempt to summarise disengagement's progress over time and its impact on society is given in Figure 7.1. It shows the initial consequences of political migration, electoral discontinuance, cultural withdrawal, secessionism and illegal second-economy activity. Next, it traces through the medium term the consequences for rulers, international actors and the non-disengaging population, and the responses of these three groups. Finally, it indicates the long-term consequences which may range from system renewal and reform, to system instability and conflict, or even system collapse.

Before tracing these consequences in sequence, one general point should be made. It should be evident from the above study that, though normally a passive and non-confrontational form of response to domination, disengagement is no less effective for that. Perhaps it is best likened to the corrosion of metal, in that, though the process looks initially inconsequential, it can ultimately, if ignored or mistreated, undermine the most substantial political institutions. Much historical and political analysis has a 'crisis-centric' perspective (Adas 1986) – that is, social processes and development are viewed as leading up to

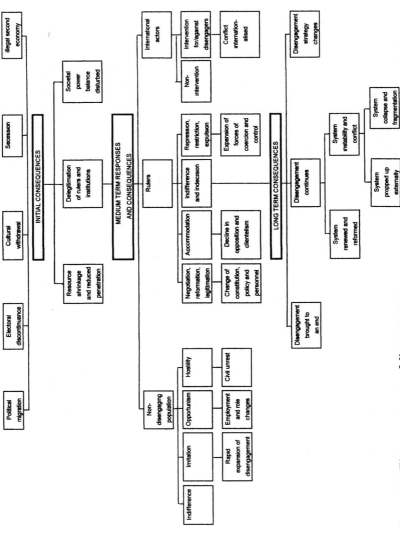

Figure 7.1 The consequences of disengagement

and being shaped by a major crisis. For opposition/resistance politics, this has meant a preoccupation with confrontational protests, such as riots, demonstrations, strikes, rebellions, coups and revolutions. These, however, need be no more effective in changing society and its rulers than disengagement and are, of course, rare compared with disengagement's typically everyday or, at least, regular nature.

Since detailed consequences of specific manifestations of disengagement have been described in each chapter, the aim of this section is to generalise and to underscore patterns previously noted in passing.

INITIAL CONSEQUENCES OF DISENGAGEMENT
FOR POLITICAL AUTHORITY

As a direct result of the withdrawal of support and resources, the capacity of the political authority is seriously impaired (see top left of Figure 7.1). Likewise, the leadership project to continually extend hegemony to the geographical and sectoral boundaries is undermined. Instead, formal penetration either shrinks or, in the case of secessionist conflict, is even abandoned. Normally this 'decay is not a single process or an absolute condition. Rather it consists of corrosion which occurs unevenly in different portions of the state' (Young 1984:81).

Formal agencies, like the security forces, and informal agencies, such as patronage and alliances with those operating outside the institutional system, may actually take a larger share of the shrinking resources. But others, like the bureaucracy, which is required to execute the authority's rules and implement its policies, are vulnerable to disengagement-induced resource loss. Economic disengagement targets almost exclusively the process structures of tax collection and control of the economy, reducing still further law-enforcement structures. Even though the illegal second economy is penetrated by colluding and participating officials, it must be regarded as highly successful in escaping the execution of an authority's rules when such large portions or even the majority of economic activity escapes either being recorded in the official statistics or contributing to the official coffers.

In the long term, loss of human resources physically, through migration, secession and the denial of a cultural and electoral contribution, may be even more significant than the loss of revenue. But human and financial resource restraint does not simply result in a loss of agents on the ground. Reduced capacity is measured in quality of service, as well as quantity, and in effectiveness as well as physical presence. Young notes that there is a 'decline of competence ... [that is] the growing inability of the state to relate material means to policy ends. State agencies become involuted mechanisms, solely preoccupied with their reproduction. Their formal activity becomes symbolic and ritualistic' (Young 1984:81). Even the legislature is not immune to resource loss.

Electoral discontinuance may not withhold finances, but it does reduce the authority's capacity indirectly. Whilst it is true that legislatures provide opportunities for representatives to penetrate the ruling elite, it is often overlooked that they also provide the elite with an opportunity to penetrate the representatives through co-optation and patronage. Through these representatives, it can then penetrate the client networks in the particular geographical areas and/or sections of the population that they represent, by the control of resources these representatives have to distribute. But, as support bases for politicians weaken, so the usefulness of clientelism declines. Where disengagement brings a decay of those components that promote the authority's system of meaning and legitimacy, there slips away the likelihood of securing the spontaneous moral consent of the ruled (to paraphrase Gramsci's definition of hegemony).[1] After that, power can only be achieved and maintained by coercion.

Besides the variation between agencies in the rates of decay caused by disengagement, there is also the variation within single agencies over time. In the short term, an agency can be excluded, for instance, on a semi-permanent basis, from a hostile secessionist region, a militia-controlled suburb or during the night-time hours in urban ghettos. The boundary throughout society between the penetration of the rulers' agencies and their exclusion/neutralisation should never be thought of as static. Hegemony is 'a process of continuous creation which, given its massive scale, is bound to be uneven in the degree of legitimacy it commands and to leave some room for antagonistic cultural expressions to develop' (Adamson, quoted in Lears 1985:571). The battle to penetrate society deeply enough to shape how individuals think and act and to secure their spontaneous support ebbs and flows. Disengagement sufficiently weakens the regime's capacity to ensure that victory is never entirely secured. It is part of that leakage of authority that keeps rulers weak, or at least weaker.

A second initial consequence of disengagement for political authority is the delegitimation of rulers and institutions (see top centre of Figure 7.1). Loss of legitimacy is an effect, as well as a cause, of disengagement. When less than 50 per cent of eligible voters cast their vote, the electoral system, and not just the individual government, is questioned. When law is so widely flouted as currently in illegal

---

[1] His full definition of hegemony is:

> The spontaneous consent given by the great masses of the population to the general direction imposed on social life by the dominant fundamental group; this consent is 'historically' caused by the prestige (and consequent confidence) which the dominant group enjoys because of its position and function in the world of production. (Gramsci 1971:12)

second-economy activity, then not just an individual law but the very rule of law is challenged. When key figures, elite groups or whole local populations flee the territory, then the very structure of that society is shown to be wanting.

Exclusivist and holistic groups are often accused of running communities as if they were a state within a state, but in actual fact they rarely keep any of the state organisational processes from fulfilling their legal requirements. For the most part, taxes are paid, as much as by anybody, and the police have access if they choose. Where the 'antisocial' charge of governments does stick is in the lack of cooperation and compliance with government ideological structures. What is resisted is the penetration of agencies that propagate elite values, such as the political party in a one-party state, the school system, military conscription, authority-controlled media and official religion. Likewise, the capacity of the authority to influence values and attitudes through the subtle and largely invisible micro-processes of professionals, who invariably are from the same elite as the rulers and share their values, is severely reduced in these inward-looking counter-cultures (see Foucault 1979).

Disengagement phenomena, however, do not always penetrate the whole range of the meaning of legitimacy. Beetham identifies three strands to the concept: conformity to rules, or legal validity; justifiability of rules in terms of shared beliefs; and receipt of the expressed consent of society (Beetham 1994). Disengagement in all its forms concerns the latter strand, for there is the withdrawal of consent to all or part of the structure of rule. It touches the second strand in that it almost universally insists that the rules made by the authority do not accord with the beliefs and norms of those withdrawing. But, over the first strand – namely, the legal validity of the authority – there are contrary attitudes. Most secessionism and some political migration and cultural withdrawal deny the elite's right to rule, arguing, for instance, that there was an illegal take-over, transference of power or constitutional change, made without the consent of the people. Other forms of disengagement, however, do not deny the authority's legal validity, but focus on its lack of performance legitimacy and on the need for reform. Nevertheless, a political authority where disengagement is widespread faces some degree of delegitimation. At the very least, it has lost the expressed consent of a significant minority.

Resource shrinkage and delegitimation affect political authority, but society is also unsettled by disengagement.

INITIAL CONSEQUENCES OF DISENGAGEMENT FOR SOCIETY

The diverse consequences for society can be summarised under the one heading of disturbance to the power balance (see top right of Figure

7.1). The change may either be that power becomes available outside the old system or that power is redistributed within the old system. The social and geographical movement associated with disengagement can create alternative foci of power, free of the previous restraints. For instance, political leaders of minority and/or oppressed groups have little opportunity of rising to pre-eminence in the political centre. However, in separatist regional situations, success is much more probable. And, in theocratic communities, small fish in the big sea of society can be big fish in their small ponds. Or, again, the first economy is often so tightly controlled by the dominant class as to close opportunities to the underclasses. But far fewer barriers to wealth creation and social mobility exist in the illegal second economy; strict and expensive regulations, time-consuming applications, draining taxes, profit-squeezing price controls and exploitative single markets that particularly cripple those with less capital (and fewer well-placed contacts) can be shrugged off. But disengagement can not only cause power to become available outside the old system: power can be redistributed within the old system. Thus, migration, being often skewed towards the young and one gender (according to circumstances), upsets the age–sex balance of sending communities and may affect the traditional social tasks attributed to various groups (Wallerstein 1965:153).

A striking example of a social barrier that is being eroded by disengagement is the restrictive gender boundary. Male-dominated domains and societies have tried to keep women in their homes as dutiful wives and mothers (Hansen 1989:158; Staudt 1987). But women entering the illegal second economy, autonomous communities or secessionist movements have frequently escaped these legal and social constraints on their employment and leadership opportunities and, in so doing, they have secured a living and status without having to depend on a spouse (who might be lost through death or divorce) and without being controlled by him. Disengagement weakens the legal and institutional basis of male control over women (MacGaffey 1988b:162; cf. Newbury and Schoepf 1989).

Large-scale internal migration disturbs societal power, in both the sending and the receiving communities – in the former, by creating political and economic vacancies and, in the latter, by intensifying political and economic rivalry. If political migration is outside the domain, this is often assumed to disturb the internal power balance of the sending society by irretrievably weakening the opposition 'voice' and thus strengthening the hand of the ruling regime. This popular view, however, makes certain assumptions that may be unjustified. First, it assumes that migration is uniform among regime opponents when their voice is unheard. However, migration has been found to be markedly reduced where would-be migrants saw labour militancy as offering the hope of a better redistribution of income at home in the future (Macdonald 1963–4). And this may well apply to those anticipating socio-economic improvements as a result of the democratisation of the 1990s. In other words, it may be that it is those unheard opponents who have no hope of being heard in the future who turned to political migration.

The second assumption is that the opposition of an individual to the regime stops upon emigration, that migration is synonymous with political discontinuance. In the past, slower modes of transportation and communication certainly drastically reduced effective contact. But, today, regime opponents of Nigeria, Equatorial Guinea, Sudan and the Congo Republic continue their campaigns and agitation from foreign bases with comparative ease. And, if they are residing only just across the border, then face-to-face contact and even military infiltration are relatively easy, as the Rwandan Hutus exiled in former Zaire found. My own view is that external political migration is not so disturbing to societal power as it once was. It is probably removing opposition 'voice' less thoroughly than ever before. Optimism in liberalising/democratising states may well be encouraging many who would previously have emigrated in despair to stay and continue their opposition within the country. And even those optimists who do flee out of consideration for their safety are likely to continue their campaigns abroad. As for the pessimists who leave the country, they may never have thought it worthwhile fighting their cause while in the land, so that it is not their emigration that silences them.

THE MEDIUM-TERM RESPONSES OF RULERS AND THEIR CONSEQUENCES

Disengagement does not set out directly to change the rulers and the rules of the prevailing system, and yet it has often been such a painful haemorrhage that rulers have rarely ignored it. Usually, they have taken steps to reduce or halt it by peaceful or coercive means (see middle centre of Figure 7.1). Peaceful responses may include persuasion, legitimation, negotiation or reformation. Persuasion entails the direct or indirect wooing of disengagers by marshalling the arguments for the benefits of engagement. Legitimation projects range from government propaganda through the media and/or the offer of multi-party elections to entice back voters; the adoption of token traditional customs to win over withdrawing communities, which are based on primordial ties; appeals to loyalty to a unified domain to reduce migration; and price/wage rises to draw farmers and government workers back into the first economy. These legitimation projects are not, of course, necessarily sincere.

Direct negotiation (and subsequent reform) has rarely characterised rulers' responses to disengagement. When faced with armed secessionists, for example, only a failure to impose on 'the rebels' a solution by force draws the authorities to the negotiating table. Thus, only after abandoning or stalling ineffective military options did the rulers of Sudan (1972 and 1998), Ethiopia (1993), Djibouti (1994) and Mali and Niger (1995) offer either recognition of legitimate grievances, constitutional changes, development packages or the co-optation of secessionist leaders on to the cabinet. For peace negotiators, as for conquerors, however, there has often been more to constitutional change than conciliation. For instance, General Gowon, following his success in the Biafran secessionist war, and Nimeiri, following the impasse in the southern Sudanese secessionist war, introduced smaller administrative divisions, not for more sensitive representation, but as a device for weakening regional opposition. The intention was that each unit would be too small to challenge the centre alone or to bargain effectively and that inter-regional rivalry could be exploited.

Non-violent disengagers have rarely had the same opportunity to enter into negotiation with the ruling elite. Either their numbers and/or their class status have worked against them being taken seriously in and of themselves. The few exceptions where reforms have been offered unilaterally have tended to occur in the economic field. For example, activity previously declared illegal has at times been decriminalised and brought into the first economy. This applied to the private mining and sale of gold and diamonds in Democratic Republic of Congo (Zaire) in 1983 (Rukarangira and Schoepf 1991: 84). These concessions, however, appeared to be a response to pressure more from international creditors than from the disengagers.

Not all peaceful strategies mark positive responses by rulers to disengagement. At the negative end of the spectrum are bare cessations of harsh laws and policies. There are many examples of colonial powers and capitalists reluctantly abandoning practices that provoked disengagement. Certainly, the French and Portuguese revised their harsh policies of forced labour and conscription with little enthusiasm after so many had migrated to the less harsh British colonies in the period 1890–1940.

As regards coercive responses, as already indicated, these tend to be the first resort of authorities, such is the seriousness with which disengagement is viewed. This does not only apply to armed secessionist contexts. Where practically possible, authorities usually go to considerable lengths to prevent political migration, from army patrols and barbed wire to hot pursuit. Individual and private electoral discontinuance is an invisible target and therefore one that force cannot easily be directed against. But, where autonomous communities and non-conformist groups openly broadcast their boycotts, pressure is assured. Their non-participation is seen as just one part of their non-conformity. Persecution, actual and threatened, is therefore usually much broader in its scope: it confronts the groups' denial of the authorities' right to rule. The conflict between the hegemonic project of the rulers and counter-culture is well illustrated in the way that Jehovah's Witnesses have been treated throughout Africa. For example, in the Zambian 1968 election campaign, forty-five Kingdom Halls were burned down, 469 Witnesses' houses were destroyed, some K50,000 of cash and property were looted and twelve Witnesses were killed (Roberts 1970: 250; Cross 1978:309). Subsequently, the freedom of Witnesses to hold meetings and preach from door to door was severely restricted. In Malawi, the persecution was so severe from 1967 that some 20,000 fled into Zambia and many hundreds were killed. The story of Banda's witch-hunt against them, in terms of compulsory redundancy, assault, arson and murder, is recounted by Hodges (1985). They were also violently persecuted in Uganda from 1973, harassed in Mozambique, and banned in both Tanzania (1968) and Kenya (1973). But the organisation is by no means unique in its experience. Strong campaigns have been conducted against syncretistic cults and pagan practices in countries like Guinea and periodically against the established religions of Christianity and Islam whenever their leadership was thought to offer a rival focus of support or of values at variance with the state, as in Amin's Uganda. The message of persecuting authorities is clear: disengagement will not be tolerated when it is perceived as a threat to absolute rule. As Mazrui said of the state, but which is true of all social power, it can be 'sometimes excessively authoritarian in order to disguise the fact that it is inadequately authoritative' (Mazrui 1983:293). If disengagement cannot be stamped out because it is too strong numerically, it is talked out or bought out, but it will not be ignored.

MEDIUM-TERM RESPONSES OF THE NON-DISENGAGING POPULATION

Disengagement may be the withdrawal of certain members of society from the political authorities, but these two are not the only parties involved. Within the polity, a third, and not disinterested, party is the non-disengaging population (see middle left of Figure 7.1). If disengagement is minor, contained, distant and unthreatening to their livelihood and safety or to the stability of the social fabric, then indifference is the most likely response. One might assume that this is universally true, particularly in relation to electoral discontinuance and passive autonomous communities. However, even these can have a personal and negative impact. Examples have already been given of those who felt that autonomous groups who did not participate in local elections or schooling threatened the development of the area and the lineage. Hostility is less surprising when directed towards small secessionist groups or participants in the illegal second economy, especially where these attract the unwelcome attention of, or even reprisals by, the military/police against the wider community. Nor should it be forgotten that people who are initially indifferent are always susceptible to propaganda that distorts their perception of minority groups and which may incite them to hostility or communal violence.

The very reverse can also be true, where the response is not antagonism but imitation. There can be little doubt that the illegal second economy has grown as fast as it has through the successful example of neighbours and acquaintances. Such networks also promote migration and the adoption of values counter to society as a whole. On the larger scale, there have been times when secession in one area of the country has had a knock-on effect in other areas, as in the case of Congo (Democratic Republic of Congo (Zaire)) immediately after independence and Ethiopia after Mengistu's downfall. Both states were in danger of unravelling, as more and more regions followed the secessionist, rather than negotiated, approach to disputes with the centre. Horowitz cites the demonstration effect from Côte d'Ivoire:

> The Ivory Coast was one of two African regimes to recognise Biafra. The Ivory Coast was in turn confronted with a resurgence of separatism among the Agni of the former Sanwi Kingdom who had earlier fought the Ivorian government. Threatening a Biafran type conflagration and citing Houphouet-Boigny's recognition of Biafra, the Sanwi movement turned again to armed warfare. Some months after this was suppressed, the Bete around Gagnoa, who had mooted an independent republic, went on the march. The Ivory Coast government had little difficulty putting these insurrections down. (Horowitz 1985:279)

Finally, the non-disengaging population may respond by exploiting the disorder often caused by widespread disengagement. Such opportunism may occur even at the social-group level, as illustrated by the Yoruba's seizure of employment vacancies left by fleeing Ibo in the north of Nigeria, following the outbreak of the secessionist war, and the Tutsis' seizure of housing and land left by the fleeing Hutus in Rwanda.

THE MEDIUM-TERM INTERNATIONAL RESPONSE

States at the individual and corporate level have consistently shown an interest in the strategic, diplomatic, economic and humanitarian aspects of disengagement (see middle right of Figure 7.1). Worldwide and continental groupings, such as the United Nations (UN) and the Organisation of African Unity (OAU), have fostered peacemaking and mediation, whilst superpowers, regional powers and former colonial powers have been more preoccupied with securing strategic and economic advantage from secessionist situations. Non-state organisations have also been active, both in encouraging and in discouraging disengagement, according to their political agenda. Non-governmental organisations (NGOs) have normally assumed a non-political posture, although even aid and development have a political edge when they are offered to secessionist-minded groups and 'rebel' migrants, as Hutus in Zaire in 1994–6 found. Religious organisations, however, have been much more willing to take sides where disengagers are of their own creed, or at least to agree on the common enemy. This, at least, has been the accusation of the Sudanese authorities as regards the activity of the Anglican Church in southern Sudan.

Rarely does disengagement reach the attention of the outside world but that it attracts comment and action, either in support of disengagers, seen as victims of the political authorities, or in support of the state, seen as threatened politically or economically by the withdrawal. This internationalising of the social conflict in the twentieth century has added a fourth dimension to disengagement.

THE LONG-TERM CONSEQUENCES OF DISENGAGEMENT

Should widespread disengagement continue over a length of time, despite efforts to restrain or crush it, the political system itself begins to show signs of instability (see bottom centre of Figure 7.1). In normal circumstances, when rulers fail to regenerate resources to provide the level of services expected by their society, the government, or even the regime, comes under severe opposition and falls, to be replaced by an alternative ruling group and/or system. In other words, demand-bearing groups within society rebound to fill positions, support government and rally round the successor. But with prolonged political disengagement, national political society is weakened absolutely and/or devolves to the periphery. Rulers can live with a certain level of authority leakage – they can apply emergency first aid to sudden haemorrhaging to staunch the flow (often increasing the forces of coercion) – but persistent large-scale disengagement (in one or several of its forms) can be a mortal wound, precipitating state collapse, where the basic functions of the state are no longer performed. This appeared to be the situation in Zaire under Mobutu:

> To say that Zaire has a government today would be a gross exaggeration. A small group of military and civilian associates of President Mobutu, all from the same ethnic group, control the city of Kinshasa by virtue of the loyalty of the 5,000-man Presidential Guard known as the DSP. This same group also controls the Central Bank which provides both the foreign and local currency needed to keep the DSP loyal. While the ruling group has

intelligence information about what is going on in the rest of Zaire, there is no real government authority outside of the capital city. (Cohen 1993, quoted in Weiss 1995:157)

Disengagement is not, of course, the only cause of this condition in states or other authorities. Resources to run the authority may dry up through external aid withdrawal, internal waste and corruption, market collapse or war. But a long history of widespread disengagement from the authority is an added danger hindering recovery.

It is common to equate state collapse (with the cessation of social and infrastructure provisions and universal territorial control) with regime collapse and the absence of a political community. Thus, Zartman describes state collapse as follows:

As the decision making center of government, the state is paralyzed and inoperative; laws are not made, order is not preserved, and societal cohesion is not enhanced. As a symbol of identity, it has lost its power of conferring a name on its people and a meaning on their social action. As a territory, it is no longer assured security and provisionment by a central sovereign organization. As the authoritative political institution, it has lost its legitimacy, which is therefore up for grabs, and so has lost its right to command and conduct public affairs. As a system of socio-economic organization, its functional balance of inputs and outputs is destroyed; it no longer receives support from nor exercises control over its people, and it no longer is even the target of demands because its people know that it is incapable of providing supplies. No longer functioning, with neither traditional nor charismatic nor institutional sources of legitimacy, it has lost the right to rule. (Zartman 1995:5)

In fact, regimes may survive despite state collapse and social disengagement for two reasons. The first is the phenomenon of juridical statehood (Jackson and Rosberg 1982–3) as supported by the postwar international community of states. Whatever the empirical statehood:

Post-independent governments were not required to exert authority throughout the territory under their jurisdiction because their legitimacy was guaranteed by international recognition following upon the wave of self-determination ... But, even though a state may be given the right of self-government, it may not necessarily possess the capacity to do so. (Kelley 1986: 2)

Take, for instance, the example of Chad. Chad was a state that had all but collapsed under the pressure of disengagement and other erosive forces. With civil war raging, the writ of central government by 1980 did not run throughout the land and large areas were under rebel control. That the regime survived and recovered, to a degree, control of the state was not simply due to the military power, shrewd diplomacy and potent nationalism of Habre and his victorious Forces Armées du Nord. It was because France and other donors would not let the juridical state and those legally accountable for its debts (the regime) go under. To that end, they paid civil servant salaries and balanced the national budget; French troops and French and American *matériel* deterred or quelled rebellions and Libyan incursions; and the OAU and the entire states system refused to allow the sovereignty and territorial integrity that they had recognised to break up or be tampered with (including Qadhafi's 1981 plan for the union of Chad and Libya) and so set an unacceptable precedent (Foltz 1995). With this level of practical and moral–legal support, the regime and the juridical state have, against the odds, survived. Referring to a similar situation in Mobutu's Zaire, Callaghy quotes Stinchcombe:

> A power is legitimate to the degree that, by virtue of the doctrines and norms by which it is justified, the power-holder can call upon sufficient other centres of power, as reserves in case of need, to make his power effective. (quoted in Callaghy 1980:481)

A second alternative to preserving the regime even when the empirical state hardly exists is for ruling elites to bypass formal government. Determined to hold on to power at all costs, ruling elites in Liberia, Democratic Republic of Congo (Zaire) and Sierra Leone in the 1980s and early 1990s (and quite possibly still) did not abandon the realm of the state so much as sidestep its faltering and enfeebled version, creating new positions for themselves in an alternative, non-formal 'state'. The old unstable system was, in effect, made redundant to state-elite requirements and left to its own devices, or to the pity of the international community of states and aid organisations. In its stead, a new parallel political structure was erected, where state business was conducted on the basis of informal and personal relationships and the marginalisation of rivals. Thus, civil state offices and the bureaucracy, which had been the source of rival clientelist networks, were severely reduced; customary state functions, with their associated perquisites, were contracted out to dependable foreigners with no local support base; and private military organisations were brought in which had no political ambitions of their own. Within this 'shadow state', authority depended on the power of wealth, networks of business contacts, and military capability. Given its ability to tap new private sources of finance through the sale of state commodities/resources, concessions and protection, the shadow state was ensured of survival whatever happened to its formal counterpart. Indeed, symptoms of formal state decay, such as hyperinflation, actually benefited it by increasing the opportunities for speculation and smuggling (Reno 1998).

This regime survival within a collapsing state may well suit the elite's desire to maintain its dominance and wealth, but it ill suits the general population. They must either pursue still further their disengagement from the ailing formal state and their project of constructing their own parallel organisations of protection or make their individual accommodations with the shadow state, or both.

> Personal connections with elite privilege may protect citizens against a state that does not protect them in an institutional sense. Rulers can then sell protection and favour. Zaire's 'new middle class' receives favoured access to diamond, timber and consumer goods trade through ties to the president especially as state institutions collapse. Outside the capital, private businessmen pay armed troops to protect them, those who do not pay are attacked. (Reno 1995a:19)

If the two holding devices for regimes fail, if the international community should grow weary of supporting non-viable states and regime leaders fail to maintain authority through new and unconventional means, then it may not just be the state that collapses but the regime. The point is well illustrated by Somalia. The immediate cause of state collapse was the civil war of 1988–92, undertaken to remove Siyad Barre from power, with its associated abandonment of Western development aid then and of Western government interest following the débâcle of Operation Restore Hope. But elements of disengagement were already present beforehand and have only escalated since, making the reconstruction of political authority at higher levels currently problematic, if not impossible. Somalia in its present condition has neither state nor regime, there being no single decision-making centre for the country which can make and enforce laws, protect and make social provision for the people or direct the economy and provide it with the necessary infrastructure. Instead, there exist over the area denominated Somalia (excluding Somaliland) five or six de facto micro-states, built on alliances of lineage groups and occupied by militias.

How helpful is the concept of disengagement in interpreting these events? The state, which was hijacked by one particular clan alliance, who creamed off development aid and state resources for is own benefit, has been soundly rejected by the Somali majority. Armed rebellion against the violent and oppressive domination of the Siyad Barre-ruled state was the solution of some (recalling the Somali proverb 'the medicine for fire is fire'). But by far the majority preferred to escape the domination of his and any other nationwide regime, through clan autonomy achieved by force. Consequently in the chaos that ensued in and after the civil war, the state split into half a dozen secessionist states (with or without a Mogadishu group constituting the rump juridical state). For hundreds of thousands of others, the solution was political migration within or outside the national boundaries. But, beyond secession and political migration, there has been cultural withdrawal. The independent state, whether in its 'democratic' form of 1960–9 or in its autocratic form of 1969–91, espoused nationalism and a shared culture as the basis for unity, whereas, to this day, all but a few intellectuals and urban dwellers regard genealogy as the source of unity. To construct a unified state, Siyad Barre spoke of the 'burial of clannism', but as one Somali analyst put it, 'the notion of politics outside clan affiliations has no roots in our minds' (quoted in Luling 1997:289). There was probably very little ever of engagement with the state outside the urban areas and it soon became apparent that there were very strong reasons for disengaging, not just because of the corruption and clan discrimination of Siyad Barre (Adam 1995), but also because such a large political unit could not meet the needs of the lineage groups of a few hundred to a thousand members who wandered the grazing lands of the region. They did not identify with an institution which was open-door, non-clan-based. Not only did they not identify with it, but it actually provoked disunity and conflict:

> Clans had always competed for resources such as land, grazing and water, but [with the construction of the independent state] ... control of all these resources and much more was vested in the state [and] competition between clans, which before had been only one aspect of their existence, became its permanent condition. The state was both the arena within which they fought and the prize for which they contended. (Luling 1997:290)

Yet the cultural disengagement that undermined the political construct of the state is still at work undermining the micro states of the militias. Based as they are on loose alliances of lineages within a clan family, they are inherently fragile and prone to repeated realignments as trust fails and self-interest reasserts itself. In other words, even that political unit is still too big and heterogeneous for Somalis to identify with. The ruling 'warlord' is therefore something of a misnomer: as one militia commander complained, 'If only I could make my militia do what they don't want to do!' (quoted in Luling 1997:298). The ability to mount a military attack should not be confused with the ability to govern, even over a relatively small area. With so many people armed and with many running 'businesses' that have a strong interest in not seeing a return to the rule of law, both militia leaders and local elders have little effective authority. In a situation where people rely on themselves and their small lineage unit for their everyday needs (and NGOs and private professionals for welfare) and eschew all political authority by cultural preference and bitter experience, government is not high on the agenda. It can only be a possibility in the long term (although others claim to see embryonic manifestations of government based on consociational mechanisms (Adam 1995:79–88). The situation is remarkable similar to that which prevailed in Chad in 1982:

> War weariness was a fact of life ... While most people were distrustful of what any group would do with power, they were likely to be at least as distrustful of opposition promises as they were of those of a government and they were hardly inclined to lead a public challenge to armed authority. Few Chadians felt they could trust anyone outside of their immediate group, and most defined that group in very restrictive terms. (Foltz 1995:18)

Such societies, which turn away from state government and fend for themselves on the local level, do not of necessity have to be characterised, as Zartman seems to think, by the rule of 'warlords and gang leaders' (Zartman 1995:8). The point about the so-called traditional stateless societies of Africa was not their inadequacy (in not having centralised control) but their conscious anti-dominance stance, often born of their experience of slave plundering by predatory states. Given that they were unable to resist the prevailing level of violence, is it any wonder that, between the fifteenth and nineteenth centuries, many precolonial groups chose to move from their forest/savannah boundary further into the forest to avoid state centrism and dominance (Amadiume 1995:42–5)? In the same way Somalis have turned their back on the state in the twentieth century. In neither case, it should be noted, does the absence of a state or of a regime mean the absence of ordered society, however hard this may come to Western political scientists (Simons 1998:61). Such a considered, rather than accidental, disengagement from the state may be harder to turn around by a determined effort for renewal than Zartman and his colleagues think (Zartman 1995). 'To fit into the international fold, [Somalis] are expected to (re)construct some sort of state, although the very requirements of state form – having a national capital, head of state, national treasury, etc. – invite contradiction.' The centralised control from Mogadishu is precisely why the northerners launched the civil war, whilst the conflict itself proved all too well that 'knowing genealogy *does* chart who can and cannot be trusted' (Simons 1998:70). If indeed such total disengagement from the state is not simply a passing response to a political crisis of corrupt government and physical violence, but rather an expression of deeply held preferences for non-centralised social systems, then repeated attempts by the states system to plug this gap in its world order (for it will not rest with the anomaly) are unlikely to meet with success.

Disengagement and democratic consolidation

The 1990s have seen the widespread reintroduction of democratic institutions. All but six sub-Saharan states have held parliamentary and/or presidential multi-party elections of a sort, though only five were holding them in the 1980s.[2] In the popular mind democracy has tended to embrace all the hostile attitudes to the former regime, rather than being a political form of considered advantages. It has been a response more of protest than of construction. Popular ideological conversion and institutional structures are likely to take time and to follow, rather than precede, practice. The practice may begin with the comparatively infrequent national and local elections, but democracy as a mass culture must penetrate the ethnic association, the trade union, the church, the club and the host of other voluntary organisations that form associational life. Access to decision-making through elected representation must cross social experience, so that it is no longer an alien or rare institution. Only when democracy is institutionalised to the point where it is regarded by the masses as non-negotiable can it be regarded as consolidated.

Disengagement is highly relevant to the whole democratic project. The institutions of democracy can be created by fiat, regardless of the disengagement of many, but the institutionalisation of democracy necessitates engagement. A culture of non-participation or active withdrawal cannot promote the consolidation of democracy. It may go so far as to cheer on any cry on the street that calls for the end of hostile rule and promises a new era, but it cannot normalise democratic politics. In an ideal world, it is to be hoped that the performance of democratic regimes will be sufficiently less hostile to its citizens for disengagement to be significantly reduced. However, democracy does not guarantee better economic growth and therefore make the illegal second economy irrelevant. Nor does it so guarantee ethnic fairness that migration and secession are unthinkable. In fact, first-past-the-post elections may institutionalise the domination of the majority group, even as the election itself may heighten ethnic tension through the use of ethnicity for mobilising political support (Newlan 1993:91). Perhaps more fundamentally, in the view of ethnic minorities, democracy has nothing to say about what the boundary of the state is, or how to decide otherwise. 'Slogans such as the self-determination of peoples and devices such as plebiscites ... simply beg the question of who is eligible to vote within which constituencies' (Schmitter 1994:66). Finally, democracy as a political philosophy might theoretically promote tolerance, but the initial introduction of multi-party elections does not ensure that the elected ruling group's values will not be imposed aggressively. Too

[2] The six states that had not held multi-party elections up until August 1998 are Eritrea; Rwanda; Somalia; Democratic Republic of Congo (Zaire); Nigeria; and Swaziland. Nigeria, of course, held one in 1993 but its outcome was annulled. The five states that held them throughout the 1980s were Senegal; Zimbabwe; Botswana; Mauritius; and The Gambia (which was subsequently under military rule in 1994–6).

often, therefore, significant disengagement continues under democracy and undermines attempts to consolidate it in an acceptable and predictable set of rules for political procedure. Hence the spectacle of democracies, in Schmitter's words, stumbling on in a 'lingering demise' (Schmitter 1994:58–9; cf. McAllister and White 1994), where not enough citizens have been captured by the democratic ideal to engage in promoting its success. A still worse scenario for democrats is that there will remain so many with inclinations to disengagement that the door will be left open for autocracy to return. In other words, if the regime is not perceived as bringing speedy improvements, then, with no prior loyalty to the rule of law, the 'sudden death' of democracy may be watched with the indifference of those who regard all central authorities as hostile to their well-being.

The reality of disengagement is a reminder of the need to qualify the enthusiasm for civil society amongst democracy-builders. As has been shown, there is no inevitability that organised social life outside the state either makes demands on the state, proceeds in a democratic fashion or even accepts the rule of law or the values of democracy. Associations forged in an atmosphere of fear, anger, indifference or despair regarding the state naturally have their back to the state. It will take more than the introduction of multi-party elections to convince all those that their interests are best served by turning towards the state, by representing their views and by challenging the abuses of office. It is with this difficulty in mind that Diamond, having argued strongly for the positive contribution of civil society towards democratic consolidation, makes the following caveat: 'Civil society must be autonomous from the state, but not alienated from it. It must be watchful but respectful of state authority' (Diamond 1994b:15).

Unfortunately, as he himself admits, the last thirty-five years of African authoritarianism have bred a cynicism, indiscipline and alienation from state authority that will be hard to eradicate. The legacy of disengagement will inevitably delay the construction of a civil society that develops and consolidates democracy in the way Diamond and others envisage. And, whilst states remain weak in the benefits they can offer or even in the implementation of law, there is little incentive to engage with it so as to seek resources and policy changes. Thus, ethnic and religious associations, acting as providers of services and benefits, are not diminishing under the new democracies. Not all have been convinced of the relevance of expressing to the state the interests and ideas of their members or of challenging its conduct.

Conclusion

Why raise your voice in contradiction and get yourself into trouble as long as you can always remove yourself entirely from any given environment should it become too unpleasant? (Hirschman, *Exit, Voice and Loyalty*)

A view of the dominated

So how are the dominated to be viewed? Disengagement is but one of many attempts to capture the outlook of the dominated in Africa. Though none of the concepts would claim exclusivity, there is an implied claim by their proponents that their own delineation captures the spirit of the response of most of the dominated. The thesis of this book is no exception. Early studies spoke of a 'culture of poverty' (e.g. Lewis 1970), but this entails a passivity and fatalism that, as has been argued, are a misreading of outward obedience and the lack of vocalised or physical hostility. Behind many a feigned compliance is a heart dreaming of, if not planning, revenge. It also implies a marginality and physical isolation that are rarely that clear-cut.

Another popular construct that has a long history is that of 'survival strategies' (e.g. Morrison and Gutkind 1982). Patterns of behaviour by the dominated are seen largely in terms of the efforts of the poor to maintain themselves. The chief problem with this is its characterisation of the dominated as victims who, at best, can only cope under domination and not escape from it. Further, it assumes that the dominant/dominated divide is based entirely on wealth, whereas, as has been shown, excluded groups may be defined by ethnicity and gender and may even be wealthy themselves.

The popularity of the 'class war' perspective (e.g. Fanon 1967) was a measure of the ascendancy of socialism in the social sciences. Mobilising Africa's lower classes, however, proved less straightforward than texts on peasant-led revolutions imagined, and to argue that any but a minority of patterns of behaviour can be explained in these terms would be an exaggeration. Rebellion, for all its romantic connotations to the Western intellectual, is known to those who are expected to carry it out to be hazardous in the extreme and to have a poor record of overturning the dominant/dominated relationship. Not surprisingly, as a tool for responding to the dominant, it is uncommon.

The same criticism must apply to those who see a return to primitive 'barbarism' as the hallmark of modern Africa. In other words, the dominated have no clear political purpose, but under environmental pressures resort to mindless violence against their neighbours (e.g. Kaplan 1994). Violence there might be, but it is rarely mindless; it is a direct response to political failure and its calculation that it will achieve results is only too correct. The violent conflicts that have occurred have not only involved a small minority of the population of Africa, but their causes lie as much in precolonial social stratification, colonial privileging, state marginalisation and external interference, as in interethnic hostility.

The 'everyday resistance' framework (e.g. Scott 1985) has much to commend it, with its emphasis on the defensive and deceptive, rather than the passive or the aggressive, and on the individualistic, rather than the corporate. Apart from the tendency to read political statements in every utterance and action of the disenfranchised, too much resistance to the dominant is done in the open, or at least is not cloaked in secrecy (as flight and autonomous communities), for this approach to satisfactorily capture the breadth of response.

A recent approach has sought to capture the nature of the struggle under the designation 'quiet encroachment', the idea being one of surreptitious offensive, by which public space, private land, city amenities and utilities and state provisions are slowly and quietly taken over by individuals, though defended collectively when threatened (Bayat 1997). At the level of landgrabs, street vendors and illegal water- and electricity-tapping, this certainly highlights both the initiative and the open evasion which were missing in some of the other representations. It is, however, very urban-centred, which makes it better suited to the more highly urbanised South American and Asian context than to Africa, and its emphasis on taking the offensive in seeking redress from the propertied and powerful neglects the multitudes who want no more than safety or to be left alone.

It is disengagement that contains the secretive and the open withdrawal, the urban and the rural resistance, the common preference for non-violence and yet active initiatives to escape and improve their condition. It portrays the African as too just to accept inequity sitting down, too wise to risk unequal confrontation, too industrious to be apathetic and too clever to be stopped from escaping in some way or other from unacceptable domination.

Disengagement defines power

Disengagement is a relational concept; it cannot be discussed outside domination. Just as a fretsaw defines not only the piece of wood cut out but the piece from which it was cut, so this book defines not only the nature of disengagement but the nature of power. Throughout the book, this has been referred to more in passing, but in this conclusion I would like to draw these together. This account confirms that the contemporary characterisation of power holds for this area of social investigation.

First, power is dispersed. There is no single, all-embracing, domination over all the arenas of society. Hegemony is not a project confined to nation-states. An array of ethnic, religious, regional, economic, military, patriarchal and criminal contenders are found coexisting with and competing with the state, predating the construction of the state and surviving as or after the state collapses. These multiple and cross-cutting powers are not formally designated power-holders, but they rest their power on tradition, charisma, wealth, status or violence.

Secondly, power is influence as well as coercion. Those disengaging not only evade those who seek to achieve their own will and to secure the cooperation of others through coercion (the use or threat of physical force, extortion, expropriation or confiscation). They also evade those whose weapon is influence (rational persuasion, respect, deference, bribery or corruption). The relationship between influence and coercion is perhaps the most important factor in defining political power in a particular context.

Thirdly, in the words of Knocke (1990:2), 'power is dynamic and potentially unstable'. What may be a compelling role/relationship in one situation may be insignificant or even reversed in another. Thus, the office-holder's superiority in the formal economy may be transformed to one of dependency in the informal, whilst the insignificant person in mainstream society may be a ruler in counter-society. Compliance may fluctuate not only in different contexts, but over time: force can weaken or become ineffective in certain areas due to financial restraints; and influence can be undermined or can fade if it is taken for granted and not sustained by communication or material benefits. As power fades, disengagement flourishes.

Fourthly, power is a limited commodity. Totalitarian power does not exist; the human spirit is too inventive and irrepressible to be totally conquered. Disengagement demonstrates just how limited power is; to impose one's will on others is harder than many aspirants to power suppose. Paradoxically, it is this very lack of power, manifest in the failure of the authority to deliver the services and protection expected of it that, in some cases, causes disengagement.

Fifthly, power, as has been so often observed, is regularly abused. Disengagement is the story of the search to escape power that has been used to oppress, terrorise, exploit, discriminate against and restrain, and power that has failed to use its resources to assist and care when called upon. The very scale of disengagement indicates the degree of dissatisfaction with, if not anger towards and fear of, powers.

The rejection of apathy

In this book, I believe I have established that the configuration termed disengagement identifies a true and distinct, bounded pattern of action. Against multiple and variable power that is unacceptable, the inhabitants of sub-Saharan Africa have devised a range of strategies so as to survive, avoid or at least mitigate its grip. For a strategy that offers a measure of relief with minimal risk and for minimal outlay of resources, disengagement has much to be said for it. True, it may only rarely offer the ideal of total escape from domination, but for many it is better than doing nothing, although it has often been mistaken for apathy. There have been those in every generation who have argued that those who hold aloof from participating in public life are 'useless' (Thucydides), mere 'colonists' in their own country, enjoying the benefits of society rules but contributing nothing to their improvement (Tocqueville), a 'political debauch, which is a neglect of all things that concerns the public welfare' (Neville). But disengagement is not apathy. Apathy is a lack of interest, whereas disengagement is lack of the prescribed activity because there is interest – an acute awareness that the powers that dominate have no solutions to their current needs. It is an act of the politically aware, not the politically 'unconscious'.

For every strategy of engagement within a political arena, there is (as my theoretical scheme in Figure 1.1 shows) a corresponding strategy of disengagement. And, as the dominated have discovered, there are political waves to be made by avoiding and escaping authority. Withdrawing from political activity, whether it is non-voting, non-rebellion, non-membership, non-conformity, non-payment of taxes, non-formal employment, though often overlooked, is a political act with political repercussions. Whether it transgresses a formal law or not, it is a refusal to be squeezed into a ruler's mould. It is an assertion by those individuals that they are not as easily controlled as was assumed by the dominant. It is the anonymous sabotage of the hegemonic project, learned by all children behind parents' backs and from the back row of the classroom, and translated on to the political stage of adults. In Ake's opinion, the disregard or brutalisation of the authorities has tended to make most Africans 'view the state and its development agents as hostile forces to be evaded, cheated or thwarted as opportunity permits ... [and for] many rural dwellers the state exists as a nuisance to be avoided in their daily struggle for survival ' (Ake 1991:36–7). Far from being a lame response, the evasion of power has 'proved to be the most devastating answer that Africa's poor could give to the irresponsibility of their rulers' (Lonsdale 1986:128). In sufficient numbers, it has forced political powers to reconsider and even to change their policies; such is the power of withdrawing from activity!

In summary

The pattern of action termed disengagement has been found in the five political arenas (territorial, institutional, constitutional, economic and cultural), warranting the analogy made between the wide-ranging social phenomena given in my typology in Table 1.1. In a word, there is a similarity in what those involved in these activities want and what they think they need to do to get it. I believe, too, that the breadth of the subject material that has had to be covered has justified the choice of the social power perspective. It has been made apparent that disengagement is not confined to being a response to either the state or the capitalist elite; nor is it focused only on issues concerning the political process or civic behaviour. Nothing less than perceiving disengagement as a reaction to social power would have encompassed the full breadth of the phenomena outlined above.

I began with ten propositions that sought to constitute a model of where, when and how disengagement will be found and what impact it will have on political systems (see the end of Chapter 1, pp. 15–17).

The weight of the evidence has shown that it is indeed a distinct response strategy to repressive and neglectful authority (1b). It is not confined to any single period of time, to any single social group or to any single region (1a). Occurring at the individual and the mass level (1c), it is a universal phenomenon.

The book confirms that both macro-scale factors (the availability of the strategy, the pattern of domination and cultural norms) and micro-scale factors (personal efficacy, assessment of utility, available resources and personal norms) are at work in shaping disengagement (2a). In practice, it seems they are often brought together by interpersonal networks of influence (Knocke 1990). The published research has not been available for these networks to have been thoroughly assessed in this book, but there are enough pointers to suggest that more detailed investigation will reveal that they are significant in both shaping the ideology, norms, outlook and interpretations that lie behind disengagement and in promoting and assisting practical agendas. Though people are commonly influenced and exercise influence at the level of their local personal network, at the higher level of the social group and the region the distinct social and geographical patterning predicted for disengagement is apparent. The book has drawn attention to the concurrence of many of the disengagement phenomena as people resort to different or simultaneous strategies to express their shared rejection of the domination they are under (2b). That the domination is often discriminatory rather than universal accounts for the clustering of the phenomena among marginalised groups, such as youth, women and minorities, and within marginalised areas, such as state peripheries (2c).

Although examples have been given of disengagement on a very small, unorganised scale, the more striking feature that has emerged is how widespread disengagement is. Clearly, very large numbers are currently involved. This in turn has had a demonstrable effect on governments and societies (as I have summarised in Figure 7.1). Unrestrained disengagement poses authorities with serious challenges to their legitimacy, penetration and control. Disengagement proves to be an erosive and destabilising force within political systems (3b). In such a condition of contested legitimacy and resort by the protagonists to non-democratic processes, it is impossible for democratic consolidation to take place (3c). The book has shown that the authorities' first response to the loss of authority and resources implied by disengagement is hostile (3d). Where initial coercion has been ineffective, reform, negotiation or further coercion follows. The success of these responses tells us as much about the strengths and weaknesses of the authorities as about those disengaging. This is why I contend that the nature and extent of disengagement at any given time provides a measure of the power of the individual political authority (3a).

At its centre, the study has sought to differentiate a bounded pattern of action or configuration from other similar but different patterns and to examine the internal structure and dynamics of this pattern. The aim, therefore, was not so much to bring forth fresh data as to make sense of previously published material, seeking to develop new explanatory generalisations about the essential characteristics and potential consequences of this distinct configuration. Inevitably, the emphasis of this book has been on qualitative rather than quantitative material. Narrative was vital to the argument, but not a vast collection of individual case studies that would do little more than convince in their fine detail how unique each event was in history. Since my aim was to establish analogies, not only between events bearing a single description, such as secession, but between events as distinct as political migration and the illegal second economy, the narratives have had to be contained and selective. They aimed to give sufficient detail to make a single concept convincing for apparently dissimilar events, but to exclude the rest. On the other hand, the greater the depth of historical analogy, the greater the sustainability of the concept. The historical dimension was also crucial since it demonstrated that the research question was one of explaining, not so much change over time, but persistence – the persistence of a phenomenon even throughout the social and cultural upheaval wrought by contact with the West. This raises the concept of disengagement to a level that is more profound than being the product of the exigencies of particular times, social conditions and types of regimes.

Unanswered questions

I believe the concept of disengagement has been validated and something of its nature and consequences defined. But large areas remain to be explored more thoroughly. It has been apparent throughout the book that there are no adequate accurate indicators with which the concept can be operationalised in the various political arenas. Political migration is not captured by involuntary, spontaneous flight from violence and persecution. Political discontinuance is not synonymous with those on the electoral rolls who did not vote. Secession is not to be attributed to everyone living within areas controlled by secessionist movements. Not every ethnic group association or independent religious movement was turning its back on the government, however abusive its delineation of their values and norms. Neither could statistics such as the 'non-agricultural and non-wage labour force', drawn from population censuses, or the 'non-agricultural and non-registered labour force', drawn from comparing population censuses with registration sources, adequately capture the informal market, let alone economic disengagement. Each time, the indicators come up against the problem of the clandestine nature of disengagement. Yet, as crime surveys have begun to penetrate the true levels of crime, exposing the inadequacy of police-recorded crime levels, so there is no need necessarily to assume that the task of quantifying disengagement is unfathomable.

Another limitation of this study is its failure to disaggregate 'unacceptable domination' so as to establish the relationship between types of domination and types of disengagement. It is still to be discovered what circumstances control the decision to choose one form of disengagement as opposed to another. Finally, there are still important gaps in our knowledge at both the local and continental levels. At the local level, subjects such as underground and secret communities, political nomadism and disaffiliation from political associations have only been mentioned in passing and need more detailed examination. At the continental level, there is a need to extend this study to provide an intercontinental comparison. Will the patterns described here really be repeated elsewhere, or will distinct continental patterns in terms of form or frequency be revealed?

The final result of any enquiry has to be a set of generalisations that will perfect the model most suitable for a particular situation, as well as the elaboration of rules about political behaviour that can help political scientists and historical sociologists researching different time periods or geographical regions with stimulating comparative notions. It is my hope that the definition offered of disengagement, the case made for the social power interpretative perspective and the specific propositions concerning the nature, pattern and significance of disengagement set out at the beginning of this book may contribute to this goal.

Country	1957-61	1962-66	1967-71	1972-76	1977-81	1982-86	1987-91	1992-96	1997-2001
Angola				?? LR 1976				91 PA 1992 91 PR 1992	
Benin	?? PA 1959 ?? PR 1960	92 LR 1964	**27 PR 1968** 73 RE 1968		81 PA 1979	93 PA 1984	86 PA 1989 ?? PR 1989 70 PA 1990 52 <u>PA</u> 1991 64 PR 1991	87 PR 1996	
Botswana		?? PA 1965	55 PA 1969	32 PA 1974	?? LR 1979 58 PA 1979	76 PA 1984			
Burkina Faso	?? PA 1959 ?? RE 1959 ?? PR 1960	98 PR 1965	?? PA 1970		?? RE 1977 **40 PA 1978** **43 PR 1978**		**25 <u>PR</u> 1991**	**35 PA 1992** 75 LR 1995	**44 PA 1997**
Burundi		?? PA 1965				95 PA 1982		97 PR 1993 91 PA 1993	
Cameroon	77 RE 1959 70 PA 1960 70 PR 1960	91 PA*1964 97 PA 1965	97 PR 1970 97 PA 1970	98 PA 1973 99 PR 1975	99 PA 1978 ?? PR 1980	99 PA 1983 98 PR 1984 93 PR 1986 90 PA 1986	99 LR 1987	72 <u>PR</u> 1992 61 PA 1992 ?? LR 1996	?? PA 1997

Elections (figures as % of registered voters and rounded up to nearest single unit)
LR local & regional   PR presidential   PA parliamentary/national assembly   RE referendum
≤50% turnout (in bold type)
* first election with universal suffrage   † recorded as being <20% in some places
?? no information available   – <u>multi-party elections reintroduced</u> (underlined)

Country	1957-61	1962-66	1967-71	1972-76	1977-81	1982-86	1987-91	1992-96	1997-2001
Cape Verde					75 PA 1980		65 LR 1991 77 PA 1991 ?? PR 1991	77 PA 1995 ?? LR 1996 45 **PR 1996**	**49 PA 1997**
Central African Republic	?? PA 1959	?? PR 1964 ?? PA*1964			?? PR 1981	?? PR 1986 91 RE 1986	50 PA 1987 ?? LR 1988	68 PR 1993	
Chad	?? PA 1959	87 PA 1962 ?? PR 1962 95 PA 1963	96 PA 1969	99 PA 1974			?? RE 1989 56 PA 1990 ?? RE 1990	71 RE 1996 68 PR 1996	**49 PA 1997**
Comoro Islands				?? PR 1976		?? PA 1982 ?? PR 1984	65 PA 1987 60 PR 1990	64 RE 1992 ?? PA 1992 ?? PA 1993 64 PR 1996 64 RE 1996 ?? PA 1996	
Congo Brazzaville	?? PA 1959	92 RE 1964 91 PA 1964			90 PA 1979 90 LR 1979	?? PR 1984	?? PA 1989	71 RE 1992 61 PR 1992 ?? PA 1992 ?? LR 1992 ?? PR 1995	
Côte d'Ivoire	?? PA 1959 ?? PR 1960	99 PA 1965	?? PR 1970 ?? PA 1970	99 PR 1975 99 PA 1975	82 PR 1980	99 PR 1985 50 PA 1985 ?? LR 1985	69 PR 1990 35 **PA 1990** 20† **LR 1991**	62 PR 1995 ?? RE 1996	
Djibouti					?? RE 1977 ?? PA 1977 ?? PR 1981		85 PR 1987	75 RE 1992 **49 PA 1992**	64 PA 1997

Country	1957-61	1962-66	1967-71	1972-76	1977-81	1982-86	1987-91	1992-96	1997-2001
Equatorial Guinea						?? RE 1982 ?? PA 1983		20 PA 1993 ?? LR 1995 86 PR 1996	
Eritrea								99 RE 1993	
Ethiopia		?? PA 1965	70 PA 1969	?? PA 1973	?? LR 1981		85 PA 1987	?? LR 1992 ?? PA 1994 ?? PR 1995	
Gabon	?? PA 1961 99 PR 1961	80 PA 1964	?? PR 1967 99 PA 1969 99 LR 1969	?? PR 1973 ?? PA 1973	?? PR 1979 83 LR 1979	95 PA 1985 99 PR 1986		63 RE 1995 ?? LR 1996 ?? PA 1996	
Gambia	?? PA*1960	?? PA 1962 ?? PA 1966		?? PA 1972 ?? PR 1972	82 PA 1977		80 PA 1987 ?? PR 1987 56 PA 1987 56 PR 1987	?? PA 1994 85 RE 1996 ?? PR 1996 73 PA 1996	
Ghana		97 RE 1964	63 PA 1969		?? LR 1978 **42 RE 1978** **38 PR 1979**		55 LR 1989	**49 PR 1992** **29 PA 1992** 77 PR 1996	
Guinea	99 PR 1961	99 PA 1963	?? PR 1968 99 PA 1968	99 PA 1974	96 PR 1980	?? LR 1986		78 PR 1993 62 PA 1995	

Elections (figures as % of registered voters and rounded up to nearest single unit)

LR local & regional   PR presidential   PA parliamentary/national assembly   RE referendum

≤50% turnout (in bold type)

* first election with universal suffrage   † recorded as being <20% in some places

?? no information available   – <u>multi-party elections reintroduced</u> (underlined)

Country	1957-61	1962-66	1967-71	1972-76	1977-81	1982-86	1987-91	1992-96	1997-2001
Guinea Bissau				?? LR 1976	?? PA 1977		96 PA 1989	?? PR 1994 81 PA 1994	
Kenya	?? PA 1961	?? PA*1963	47 PA 1969	?? PA 1974	75 PA 1979	48 PA 1983	?? PA 1988	68 PR 1992 68 PA 1992 68 LR 1992	?? PR 1997 ?? PA 1997
Lesotho								?? PA 1993	?? PA 1998
Liberia	?? PR 1959		?? PR 1967 ?? PR 1971	?? PR 1975	?? PA 1977	?? PR 1985 ?? PA 1986 ?? LR 1986			86 PR 1997
Madagascar	?? PR 1959	?? LR 1964 ?? PA 1965 99 LR 1966	70 LR 1969 95 PA 1970	?? PR 1972 ?? PA 1973 ?? PR 1975 ?? RE 1975	?? PA 1977 ?? LR 1977	?? PR 1982 ?? LR 1983 ?? PR 1983 74 PA 1983	81 PR 1989 70 PA 1989	65 RE 1992 80 PR 1993 ?? PA 1993 65 RE 1995 50 PR 1996	70 RE 1998 ?? PA 1998
Malawi	98 PA 1961	?? PA*1964			?? PR 1977 55 PA 1978	55 PA 1983	?? PA 1987	80 PA 1992 ?? RE 1993 ?? PR 1994 81 PA 1994	
Mali	?? PA 1959	89 PA 1964			97 PR 1979 97 PA 1979	99 PA 1982 99 PR 1985 ?? LR 1985	98 PA 1988 ?? LR 1988 ?? LR 1990	44 RE 1992 16 PR 1992 35 LR 1992 21 PA 1992	22 PA 1997 25 LR 1998

Country	1957-61	1962-66	1967-71	1972-76	1977-81	1982-86	1987-91	1992-96	1997-2001
Mauritania	99 PA 1959 90 PA 1959	94 PR 1962 99 PA 1963 92 PA 1965 96 PR 1966	99 PA 1968 95 PR 1971 94 PA 1971	94 PA 1975 ?? PR 1976		50 **LR 1986**	60 LR 1988 **26 LR 1989** 85 RE 1991	**46 PR 1992** **39 PA 1992** 70 LR 1994 ?? PA 1994 ?? LR 1996 ?? PA 1996	29 PR 1997
Mauritius	91 PA*1959	?? PA 1963		?? PA 1976		?? PA 1982 **45 LR 1982** ?? PA 1983 60 LR 1985	85 PA 1987 **41 PA 1988** 82 PA 1991		
Mozambique					?? LR 1977 ?? PA 1977	?? PA 1986		?? <u>PA</u> 1994 ?? <u>PR</u> 1994	**15 LR 1998**
Namibia					?? RE 1977		?? RE 1989	76 <u>PA</u> 1994	**34 LR 1998**
Niger	30 PA 1958 ?? PR 1960	99 PA 1965	98 PR 1970 97 PA 1970				95 PR 1990 95 PA 1990	57 RE 1992 ?? PA 1993 **38 PR 1993** **35 PA 1995** **35 RE 1996** 66 PR 1996 **39 PA 1996**	

Elections (figures as % of registered voters and rounded up to nearest single unit)

LR local & regional   PR presidential   PA parliamentary/national assembly   RE referendum

≤50% turnout (in bold type)

* first election with universal suffrage   † recorded as being <20% in some places

?? no information available   – <u>multi-party elections reintroduced</u> (underlined)

Country	1957-61	1962-66	1967-71	1972-76	1977-81	1982-86	1987-91	1992-96	1997-2001
Nigeria	?? PA 1960	?? PA 1964		?? LR 1976	?? PA 1977 35 PR 1979	39 PR 1983 54 LR 1983	20 LR 1990 ?? LR 1991	?? PA 1992 ?? LR 1996	
Rwanda			90 PR 1969		?? PR 1978	?? PR 1984	99 PR 1988 97 PA 1988		
São Tomé and Principe							?? PA 1991 60 PR 1991	50 LR 1992 80 PA 1994 ?? PR 1996	
Senegal	?? PA 1959	94 PA 1966	93 PA 1968	98 PR 1973 97 PA 1973 ?? LR 1976	63 PA 1978 63 PR 1978	58 PR 1983 58 PA 1983 43 LR 1984	59 PR 1988 59 PA 1988	40 PA 1993 51 PR 1993 50 LR 1996	?? PA 1998
Seychelles					?? PR 1979	59 PA 1983 ?? PR 1984		90 RE 1992 75 RE 1993 ?? PR 1993	82 PA 1998
Sierra Leone		?? PA*1962		?? PA 1973	?? PA 1977 ?? RE 1978	99 PA 1985 78 PA 1986		80 PR 1996 46 PA 1996	
Somalia		?? PA*1964			?? PA 1979	99 PA 1984			
Tanzania		73 PA 1965	72 PR 1970 67 PA 1970	82 PR 1975 82 PA 1975	86 PR 1980 ?? PA 1980	75 PR 1985	75 PR 1990 ?? PA 1990	?? PA 1995 77 PR 1995	
Togo	?? PR 1961 ?? PA 1961	89 PA 1963 91 RE 1963 72 PR 1963		99 RE 1972	99 PR 1980 99 PA 1980	79 PA 1985	?? PA 1990	74 RE 1992 36 PR 1993 ?? PA 1994	68 PR 1998
Uganda	85 PA 1959 78 PA 1961	?? PA*1962			?? PA 1980		?? PA 1989	73 PR 1996	

Country	1957-61	1962-66	1967-71	1972-76	1977-81	1982-86	1987-91	1992-96	1997-2001
Zaire (DRC)	80 PA 1960	?? PA 1965	99 PR 1970 99 PA 1970	?? PA 1975	?? LR 1977 ?? PA 1977		?? PA 1987 50 PA **1988**		
Zambia		90 PA*1962 95 PA 1964	82 PA 1968 ?? PR 1969 ?? LR 1970	43 PA 1973	65 PR 1978 65 PA 1978	63 PR 1984 66 PA 1984	56 PR 1988 ?? PA 1988 **46 <u>PR</u> 1991** **43 PA 1991**	**10 LR 1992** **40 PR 1996** **40 PA 1996**	
Zimbabwe					?? LR 1981	?? PA*1985	54 PA 1990 54 PR 1990	54 PA 1995 **31 PR 1996**	

Elections (figures as % of registered voters and rounded up to nearest single unit)

LR local & regional   PR presidential   PA parliamentary/national assembly   RE referendum

≤50% turnout (in bold type)

* first election with universal suffrage   † recorded as being <20% in some places

?? no information available   – <u>multi-party elections reintroduced</u> (underlined)

Sources: *Africa Research Bulletin, Political Series* 1964-98 and *Keesings Contemporary Archives* 1959-64

Bibliography

Abate, Y. (1979), 'Secessionism and Irredentism in Ethiopia,' in R. Hall (ed.), *Ethnic Autonomy*. New York: Pergamon.

Abrahams, R. (1987), 'Sungusungu: Village Vigilante Groups in Tanzania,' *African Affairs* 86, (343): 176–96.

Abucar, M. (1995), 'Mass Politics, Elections and African Social Structure: Botswana and Other African Countries,' *International Sociology* 10 (1): 5–22.

Adam, H. (1995), 'Somalia: a Terrible Beauty Being Born?' in W. Zartman (ed.), *Collapsed States*. Boulder: Lynne Rienner.

Adas, M. (1981), 'From Avoidance to Confrontation,' *Comparative Studies in Society and History* 23: 217–47.

Adas, M. (1986), 'From Footdragging to Flight: The Evasive History of Peasant Avoidance Protest in South and South-East Asia,' *Journal of Peasant Studies* 13 (3): 64–86.

African Rights (1995a), *Great Expectations: the Civil Roles of the Churches in Southern Sudan*. London: African Rights.

African Rights (1995b), *Facing Genocide: the Nuba of Sudan*. London: African Rights.

Agyeman-Duah, B. (1987), 'Ghana, 1982–86: the Politics of the PNDC,' *Journal of Modern African Studies* 25 (4): 613–42.

Ajayi, J. and Crowder, M. (eds) (1974), *History of West Africa*. London: Longman.

Ake, C. (1991), 'Rethinking African Democracy,' *Journal of Democracy* 2 (1): 32–44.

Alessandrini, S. and Dallago, B. (1987), *The Unofficial Economy*. Aldershot: Gower.

Almond, G. and Verba, S. (1963), *The Civic Culture: Political Attitudes and Democracy in Five Nations*. Princeton: Princeton University Press.

Alpers, E. (1984), 'To Seek a Better Life: the Implication of Migration from Mozambique to Tanganyika for Class Formation and Political Behaviour,' *Canadian Journal of African Studies* 18 (2): 367–88.

Amadiume, I. (1995), 'Gender, Political Systems and Social Movements: a West African Experience,' in M. Mamdani and E. Wamba-dia-Wamba (eds), *African Studies in Social Movements and Democracy*. Dakar: CODESRIA.

Apter, D. (1963), *Ghana in Transition*. New York: Athenium.

Asiwaju, A. (1976a), *Western Yorubaland Under European Rule 1889–1945*. London: Longman.

Asiwaju, A. (1976b), 'Migrations as Protest: the Example of the Ivory Coast and the Upper Volta Before 1945,' *Journal of African History* 17 (4): 577–94.

Assimeng, J. (1970), 'Sectarian Allegiance and Political Authority: the Watchtower Society in Zambia 1907–35,' *Journal of Modern African Studies* 8: 97–112.

Austen, R. (1986), 'Social Bandits and Other Heroic Criminals,' in D. Crummey (ed.), *Banditry, Rebellion and Social Protest in Africa*. London: James Currey.

Austin, D. (1964), *Politics in Ghana 1946–1960*. London: Oxford University Press.

Ayoade, A. (1988), 'States Without Citizens: an Emerging African Phenomenon,' in D. Rothchild and N. Chazan, (eds), *The Precarious Balance: State and Society in Africa*. Boulder: Westview Press.

Azarya, V. (1988), 'Reordering State–Society Relations: Incorporation and Disengagement,' in D. Rothchild and N. Chazan, (eds), *The Precarious Balance*. Boulder: Westview Press.

Azarya, V. (1994), 'Civil Society and Disengagement in Africa,' in J. Harbeson, D. Rothchild, and N. Chazan (eds), *Civil Society and the State in Africa*. Boulder: Lynne Rienner.

Azarya, V. (1996), *Nomads and the State in Africa: the Political Roots of Marginality*. Aldershot: Avebury.

Azarya, V. and Chazan, N. (1987), 'Disengagement from the State in Africa: Reflections on the Experience of Ghana and Guinea,' *Comparative Studies in Society and History* (1): 106–31.

Baeta, C. (1962), *Prophetism in Ghana: a Study of Some 'Spiritual' Churches*. London: SCM Press.

Baker, B. (1997a), 'Escape from Domination: the Concept of Disengagement in Third World Studies,' *Politics* 17(2):87–94.

Baker, B. (1997b), 'Beyond the Long Arm of the Law: The Pattern and Consequences of Disengagement in Africa', *Journal of Commonwealth and Comparative Studies* 35(3): 53–74.

Banfield, E. (1958), *The Moral Basis of a Backward Society*. Chicago: The Free Press.

Barkan, J. (1976), 'Comment: Further Reassessment of "Conventional Wisdom": Political Knowledge and Voting Behaviour in Rural Kenya,' *American Political Science Review* 70 (2): 452–5.

Barkan, J. (1992), 'The Rise and Fall of a Governance Realm in Kenya,' in G. Hyden and M. Bratton (eds), *Governance and Politics in Africa*. Boulder: Lynne Rienner.

Barkan, J. (1993), 'Kenya: Lessons from a Flawed Election.' *Journal of Democracy* 4 (3): 85–99.

Barkan, J. and Holmquist, F. (1989), 'Peasant–State Relations and the Social Base of Self-help in Kenya,' *World Politics* 41 (2): 359–80.

Barkan, J. and Okumu, J. (1978), '"Semi-Competitive" Elections, Clientelism, and Political Recruitment in a No-Party State: the Kenyan Experience,' in G. Hermet, R. Rose, and A. Rouquie (eds), *Elections Without Choice*. New York: John Wiley.

Barkan, J., McNulty, M. and Anyen, M. (1991), 'Hometown Voluntary Associations and the Emergence of Civil Society in Western Nigeria,' *Journal of Modern African Studies* 29 (3): 457–68.

Barrows, W. (1976), *Grassroots Politics in an African State*. New York: Africaner.

Barry, B. (1974), 'Exit, Voice and Loyalty,' *Journal of Political Science* 4: 79–107.

Bascom, J. (1995), 'The New Nomads: an Overview of Involuntary Migration in Africa,' in J. Baker and T. Aina (eds), *The Migration Experience in Africa*. Sweden: Nordiska Afrikainstitutet.

Baxter, P. (1994), 'The Creation and Constitution of Oromo Nationality,' in K. Fukui and J. Markakis, (eds), *Ethnicity and Conflict in the Horn of Africa*. London: James Currey.

Bayart, J. (1978), 'Clientelism, Elections and Systems of Inequality and Domination in Cameroun,' in G. Hermet, R. Rose, and A. Rouquie (eds), *Elections Without Choice*. New York: John Wiley.

Bayart, J. (1986), 'Civil Society in Africa,' in P. Chabal (ed.), *Political Domination in Africa: Reflections on the Limits of Power*. Cambridge: Cambridge University Press.

Bayart, J. (1989), *L'Etat en Afrique: la Politique du Ventre*. Paris: Fayard.

Bayat, A. (1997), 'Un-civil Society: the Politics of the Informal People,' *Third World Quarterley* 18 (1): 53–72.

Beach, D. (1980), *The Shona and Zimbabwe 900–1850*. London: Heinemann.

Beach, D. (1983), 'The Zimbabwe Plateau and its People,' in D. Birmingham and P. Martin (eds), *History of Central Africa*, vol. 1. London: Longman.

Beetham, D. (1994), 'Key Principles for a Democratic Audit', in D. Beetham (ed.), *Defining and Measuring Democracy*. London: Sage.

Bennett, G. and Rosberg, C. (1961), *The Kenyatta Election: Kenya 1960–61*. London: Oxford University Press.

Bienen, H. (1974), *Kenya, the Politics of Participation and Control*. Princeton: Princeton University Press.

Bienen, H. (1993), 'Leaders, Violence and the Absence of Change in Africa,' *Political Science Quarterly* 108 (2): 271–82.

Birmingham, D. and Martin, P. (eds) (1983), *History of Central Africa*, vol. 1 and 2. London: Longman.

Blaney, D. and Pasha, M. (1993), 'Civil Society and Democracy in the Third World: Ambiguities and Historical Possibilities,' *Studies in Comparative International Development* 28 (1): 3–24.

Boahen, A. (ed.), (1985), *General History of Africa*. London: Heinemann.

Bourmaud, D. (1988), *Histoire Politique du Kenya*. Paris.

Bozzoli, B. (1991), *Women of Phokeng*. London: James Currey.

Brady, H., Verba, S. and Schlozman, K. (1995), 'Beyond SES: a Resource Model of Political Participation,' *American Political Science Review* 89 (2): 271–95.

Bratton, M. (1989a), 'Beyond the State: Civil Society and Associational Life in Africa,' *World Politics* 41 (4): 407–30.

Bratton, M. (1989b), 'The Politics of Government–NGO Relations in Africa,' *World Development* 17 (4): 569–87.

Bratton, M. (1994), 'Peasant–State Relations in Post-colonial Africa: Patterns of Engagement and Disengagement,' in J. Migdal, A. Kohli, and V. Shue (eds), *State Power and Social Forces*. Cambridge: Cambridge University Press.

Bratton, M. and Liatto-Katundu, B. (1994), 'A Focus Group Assessment of Political Attitudes in Zambia,' *African Affairs* 93: 535–63.

Bratton, M. and van de Walle, N. (1992), 'Popular Protest and Political Reform in Africa,' *Comparative Politics* 24 (4): 419–32.

Bratton, M. and van de Walle, N. (1994), 'Neopatrimonial Transitions in Africa,' *World Politics* 46 (4): 453–74.

Buchanan, A. (1991), 'Toward a Theory of Secession,' *Ethics* 101 (2): 322–42.

Buchheit, L. (1978), *Secession: The Legitimacy of Self-Determination*. New Haven: Yale University Press.

Buijtenhuijs, R. (1985), 'Dini ya Msambwa: Rural Rebellion or Counter-society,' in W. van Binsbergen and M. Schoffeleers (eds), *Theoretical Explanations in African Religion*. London: Routledge and Kegan Paul.

Busia, K. (1968), *The Position of the Chief in the Modern Political System of Ashanti*. London: Frank Cass.

Callaghy, T. (1980), 'State–Subject Communication in Zaire: Domination and the Concept of Domain Concensus,' *Journal of Modern African Studies* 18 (3): 469–92.

Caplan, G. (1968), 'Barotseland: the Secessionist Challenge to Zambia,' *Journal of Modern African Studies* 6 (October): 343–60.

Caute, D. (1983), *Under the Skin: The Death of White Rhodesia*. (New Haven: Yale University Press).

Chabal, P. (ed.) (1986), *Political Domination in Africa: Reflections on the Limits of Power*. Cambridge: Cambridge University Press.

Chabal, P. (1992), *Power in Africa: an Essay in Political Interpretation*. New York: St. Martins.

Chabal, P. (1994), 'Democracy and Daily Life in Black Africa,' *International Affairs* 70 (1): 83–91.

Chazan, N. (1979), 'African Voters at the Polls: a Re-examination of the Role of Elections in African Politics,' *Journal of Commonwealth and Comparative Politics* 17 (2): 136–58.

Chazan, N. (1981–2), 'The New Politics of Participation in Tropical Africa,' *Comparative Politics* 14 (2): 169–90.

Chazan, N. (1982), 'Ethnicity and Politics in Ghana,' *Political Science Quarterly* 97 (3): 461–85.

Chazan, N. (1988a), 'Patterns of State Incorporation and Disengagement in Africa,' in D. Rothchild and N. Chazan (eds), *The Precarious Balance: State and Society in Africa*. Boulder: Westview Press.

Chazan, N. (1988b), 'Ghana: Problems of Governance and the Emergence of Civil Society,' in L. Diamond, J. Linz and S. Lipset (eds), *Democracy in Developing Countries: Africa*. Boulder: Lynne Rienner.

Chazan, N. (1992a), 'Liberalization, Governance, and Political Space in Ghana,' in G. Hyden and M. Bratton (eds), *Governance and Politics in Africa*. Boulder: Lynne Rienner.

Chazan, N. (1992b), 'Democratic Fragments: Africa's Quest for Democracy,' in S. Eisenstadt (ed.), *Democracy and Modernity: Studies in Human Society*, vol. 4. Brill: Leiden.

Chazan, N. (1994a), 'Engaging the State: Associational Life in Sub-Saharan Africa,' in J. Migdal, A. Kohli, and V. Shue (eds), *State Power and Social Forces*. Cambridge: Cambridge University Press.

Chazan, N. (1994b), 'Between Liberalism and Statism: African Political Cultures and Democracy,' in L. Diamond (ed.), *Political Culture and Democracy in Developing Countries*. Boulder: Lynne Rienner.

Chazan, N., Mortimer, R., Ravenhill, J. and Rothchild, D. (1992), *Politics and Society in Contemporary Africa*. 2nd edn. Boulder: Lynne Rienner.

Chikulo, B. (1993), 'End of an Era: An Analysis of the 1991 Zambian Presidential and Parliamentary Elections,' *Politikon* 20 (1): 87–104.

Chingono, M. (1996), *The State, Violence and Development: the Political Economy of War in Mozambique, 1975–92*. Aldershot: Avebury.

Citrin, J. (1974), 'Comment: the Political Relevance of Trust in Government,' *American Political Science Review* 68 (September): 973–88.

Clapham, C. (1986), 'Comparing African States,' *Political Studies* 34 (4): 647–61.

Clarence-Smith, W. (1979), *Slaves, Peasants and Capitalists in Southern Angola 1840–1926.* Cambridge: Cambridge University Press.

Cliffe, L. (ed.) (1967), *One Party Democracy: the 1965 Tanzania General Elections.* Nairobi: East African Publishing House.

Cliffe, L. (1989), 'Forging a Nation: the Eritrean Experience,' *Third World Quarterly* 11 (4): 131–47.

Cohen, R. (1980), 'Resistance and Hidden Forms of Consciousness Amongst African Workers,' *Review of African Political Economy* 19: 8–22.

Coissoro, N. (1966), *The Customary Laws of Succession in Central Africa.* Lisbon: Junta de Investigacoes do Ultramar, Centro de estudos politicos e sociais.

Coleman, J. (1988), 'Social Capital in the Creation of Human Capital,' *American Journal of Sociology* 94 (suppl.): s95–s120.

Collier, R. (1982), *Regimes in Tropical Africa 1945–75.* Berkeley: University of California Press.

Colson, E. (1970), 'African Society at the Time of the Scramble,' in L. Gann and P. Duignan (eds), *Colonialism in Africa.* Cambridge: Cambridge University Press.

Comaroff, J. (1985), *Body of Power, Spirit of Resistance: the Culture and History of a South Africa People.* Chicago: University of Chicago Press.

Constantin, F. (1995), 'Muslims and Politics,' in H. Hansen, and M. Twaddle (eds), *Religion and Politics in East Africa.* London: James Currey.

Cooper, F. (1980), *From Slaves to Squatters: Plantation Labor and Agriculture in Zanzibar and Coastal Kenya 1890–1925.* New Haven: Yale University Press.

Cordell, D. (1983), 'The Savanna Belt of North Central Africa', in D. Birmingham and P. Martin (eds), *History of Central Africa,* vol. 1. London: Longman.

Cordell, D. and Gregory, J. (1982), 'Labour Reservoirs and Population: French Colonial Strategies in Koudougo, Upper Volta 1914–39,' *Journal of African History* 23 (2): 205–24.

Coulon, C. (1985), 'Prophets of God or of History? Muslim Messianic Movements and Anti-colonialism in Senegal,' in W. van Binsbergen and M.Schoffeleers (eds), *Theoretical Explorations in African Religion.* London: KPI.

Crocker, C. (1974), 'Military Dependence: the Colonial Legacy in Africa,' *Journal of Modern African Studies* 12 (2): 265–86.

Crook, R. (1987), 'Legitimacy, Authority and the Transfer of Power in Ghana,' *Political Studies* 35 (4): 552–72.

Cross, S. (1970), 'A Prophet Not Without Honour: Jeremiah Gondwe,' in C. Allen and R. Johnson (eds), *African Perspectives.* Cambridge: Cambridge University Press.

Cross, S. (1978), 'Independent Churches and Independent States: Jehovah's Witnesses in Eastern and Central Africa,' in E. Fashole-Luke, R. Gray, and A. Hastings (eds), *Christianity in Independent Africa.* London: Rex Collings.

Crowder, M. (1968), *West Africa Under Colonial Rule.* London: Hutchinson.

Crowder, M. (1973), *Revolt in Bussa.* London: Faber.

Cruise O'Brien, D. (1988), 'Introduction,' in D. Cruise O'Brien and C. Coulon (eds), *Charisma and Brotherhood in African Islam.* Oxford: Clarendon Press.

Cruise O'Brien, D. (1995), 'Coping with the Christians: the Muslim Predicament in

Kenya,' in H. Hansen and M. Twaddle (eds), *Religion and Politics in East Africa*. London: James Currey.

Cruise O'Brien, D. (1996), 'A Lost Generation? Youth Identity and State Decay in West Africa,' in R. Werbner and T. Ranger (eds), *Postcolonial Identities in Africa*. London: Zed.

Cruise O'Brien, D., Dunn, J. and Rathbone, R. (1989), *Contemporary West African States*. Cambridge: Cambridge University Press.

Crummey, D. (ed.) (1986), *Banditry, Rebellion and Social Protest in Africa*. London: James Currey.

Curtin, P., Feierman, S., Thompson, L. and Vansina, J. (1978), *African History*. London: Longman.

Davidson, B. (1992), *The Black Man's Burden*. London: James Currey.

Davidson, B. (1994), *Modern Africa: a Social and Political History*, 3rd edn. London: Longman.

De Boeck, F. (1996), 'Postcolonialism, Power and Identity: Local and Global Perspectives from Zaire,' in R. Werbner and T. Ranger (eds), *Postcolonial Identities in Africa*. London: Zed.

Derman, W. (1973), *Serfs, Peasants and Socialists*. Berkeley: University of California.

Desai, R. and Eckstein, H. (1990), 'Insurgency: the Transformation of Peasant Rebellion,' *World Politics* 42: 441–65.

de St Jorre, J. (1972), *The Nigerian Civil War*. London: Hodder and Stoughton.

De Soto, H. (1989), *The Other Path: The Invisible Revolution in the Third World*. New York: Harper and Row.

Devisse, J. (1984), 'Africa in Inter-Continental Relations,' in D. T. Niane (ed.), *General History of Africa*, vol. 4. Paris: UNESCO, London: Heinemann.

Diamond, L. (ed.) (1994a), *Political Culture and Democracy in Developing Countries*. Boulder: Lynne Rienner.

Diamond, L. (1994b), 'Rethinking Civil Society: Towards Democratic Consolidation,' *Journal of Democracy* 5 (3): 206–24.

Diamond, L. (1997), 'Civil Society and Democratic Consolidation: Building a Culture of Democracy in a New South Africa,' in R. Siddiqui (ed.), *Subsaharan Africa in the 1990s: Challenges to Democracy and Development*. Westport: Praeger.

Diamond, L., Lintz, J. and Lipset, S. (eds) (1988), *Democracy in Developing Countries: Africa*. Boulder: Lynne Rienner.

Dillon-Malone, C. (1978), *The Korsten Basket Makers: a Study of the Masowe Apostles; an Indigenous Religious Movement*. Manchester: Manchester University Press.

Diouf, M. (1994), 'Senegal's Uncertain Democracy: the 1993 Elections,' *Africa Demos* 3 (3): 10–12.

Dirks, G. (1993), 'International Migration in the Nineties: Causes and Consequences,' *International Journal* 48 (2): 191–214.

Dogan, M. (ed.) (1988), *Comparing Pluralist Democracies: Strains on Legitimacy*. Boulder: Westview Press.

Doornbos, M. (1990), 'The African State in Academic Debate: Retrospect and Prospect,' *Journal of Modern African Studies* 28: 179–82.

Easton, D. (1965), *A Systems Analysis of Political Life*. New York: Wiley.

Easton, D. (1975), 'A Reassessment of the Concept of Political Support,' *British Journal of Political Science* 5: 443–4.

Edwards, S. (1995), 'Small-scale Tailors and Dressmakers in Ghana Create an Association which Engages and Shields against the Neo-liberal State,' paper presented to

'Transition in West Africa: Towards 2000 and Beyond,' Conference held at the University of Central Lancashire, September.

Ekeh, P. (1989), 'The Structure and Meaning of Federal Character in the Nigerian Constitution,' in P. Ekeh and E. Osaghae (eds), *Federal Character and Federalism in Nigeria*. Ibadan: Heinemann.

Ekeh, P. (1992), 'The Constitution of Civil Society in African History and Politics,' in B. Caron, A. Gboyega, and E. Osaghae, (eds), *Democratic Transition in Africa*. Ibadan: CREDU.

Eldredge, E. (1992), 'Sources of Conflict in Southern Africa c.1800–30: the 'Mfecane' Reconsidered,' *Journal of African History* 33: 1–35.

Ellis, S. (1995), 'Liberia 1989–1994: a Study of Ethnic and Spiritual Violence,' *African Affairs* 94 (375): 165–97.

Etzioni-Halevy, E. (1993), *The Elite Connection*. Cambridge: Polity Press.

Fanon, F. (1967), *The Wretched of the Earth*. Harmondsworth: Penguin.

Fashole-Luke, E., Gray, R., and Hastings, A. (eds) (1978), *Christianity in Independent Africa*. London: Rex Collings.

Fatton, R. (1989), 'Gender, Class and the State in Africa,' in J. Parpart and K. Staudt (eds), *Women and the State in Africa*. Boulder: Lynne Rienner.

Fatton, R, (1990), 'Liberal Democracy in Africa,' *Political Science Quarterly* 105 (3): 455–73.

Fernandez, J. (1964), 'African Religious Movements: Types and Dynamics,' *Journal of Modern African Studies* 2: 531–49.

Fields, K. (1985), *Revival and Rebellion in Colonial Central Africa*. Princeton: Princeton University Press.

Figes, O. (1996), *A People's Tragedy: The Russian Revolution 1891–1924*. Sydney: Random House.

Folbre, N. (1988), 'Patriarchal Social Formations in Zimbabwe,' in S. Stichter and J. Parpart (eds), *African Women in the Home and the Workforce*. Boulder: Westview Press.

Foltz, W. (1995), 'Reconstructing the State of Chad,' in W. Zartman (ed.), *Collapsed States*. Boulder: Lynne Rienner.

Foucault, M. (1979), *Discipline and Punish*. New York: Vintage Books.

Fox, R., De Craemir, W. and Ribeaucont, J. (1965–6), 'The Second Independence,' *Comparative Studies in Society and History* 8: 78–109.

Furley, O. (1995), 'Child Soldiers in Africa,' in O. Furley (ed.), *Conflict in Africa*. London: Tauris.

Gamson, W. (1975), *The Strategy of Social Protest*. Homewood: Dorsey Press.

Gann, L. and Duignan, P. (eds) (1970), *Colonialism in Africa*. Cambridge: Cambridge University Press.

Geertz, C. (1963), 'The Integrative Revolution: Primordial Sentiments and Civil Politics in the New States,' in C. Geertz (ed.), *Old Societies and New States*. Glencoe: Free Press.

Geisler, G. (1995), 'Troubled Sisterhood: Women and Politics in South Africa – Case Studies from Zambia, Zimbabwe and Botswana,' *African Affairs* 94 (377): 545–64.

Gertzel, C. (1970), *The Politics of Independent Kenya 1963–68*. Nairobi: East African Publishing House.

Gifford, P. (1991), 'Christian Fundamentalism and Development,' *Review of African Political Economy* 52: 9–20

Gilkes, P. (1994), 'The Effects of Secession on Ethiopia,' in C. Gurdon (ed.), *The Horn of Africa*. London: University College Press.

Gluxman, M. (1965), *Politics, Law and Ritual in Tribal Society*. Chicago: Aldine Publishing House.

Goodwin-Gill, G. and Cohn, I. (1994), *Child Soldiers: the Role of Children in Armed Conflicts*. Oxford: Clarendon Press.

Gramsci, A. (1971), *Selections from the Prison Notebooks of Antonio Gramsci*, translated and edited by Q. Hoare and G. Nowell-Smith. New York: International Publishers.

Green, R. (1981), '*Magendo* in the Political Economy of Uganda. Parallel System or Dominant Sub-Mode of Production?', Discussion Paper 64, Institute of Development Studies, University of Sussex.

Grobbelaar, J. (1992), '"Bittereinders" Dilemmas and Dynamics,' in G. Moss and I. Obery (eds), *South African Review 6: From 'Red Friday' to CODESA*. Johannesburg: Ravan Press.

Gurdon, C. (1994), 'Sudan's Political Future,' in C. Gurdon (ed.) *The Horn of Africa*. London: University College Press.

Halisi, C., O'Meara, P. and Winchester, N. (1991), 'South Africa: Potential for Revolutionary Change,' in J. Goldstone, T. Gurr and F. Moshiri (eds), *Revolutions of the Late Twentieth Century*. Boulder: Westview Press.

Hall, R. (ed.) (1979), *Ethnic Autonomy*. New York: Pergamon.

Hansen, H. and Twaddle, M. (eds) (1995), *Religion and Politics in East Africa*. London: James Currey.

Hansen, K. (1989), 'The Black Market and Women Traders in Lusaka, Zambia,' in J. Parpart and K. Staudt (eds), *Women and the State in Africa*. Boulder: Lynne Rienner.

Hansen, O. (1992), 'The African Peasant: Uncaptured or Participating? A Comparative Study,' *Forum for Development Studies* 1: 67–86.

Hanson, J. (1994), 'Islam, Migration and the Political Economy of Meaning: Fergo Nioro from the Senegal River Valley 1862–1890,' *Journal of African History* 35 (1): 37–58.

Harbeson, J., Rothchild, D. and Chazan, N. (eds) (1994), *Civil Society and the State in Africa*. Boulder: Lynne Rienner.

Harris, B. (1967), 'The Electoral System,' in L. Cliffe (ed.), *One Party Democracy* Nairobi: East African Publishing House.

Hart, K. (1973), 'Informal Income Opportunities and Urban Employment in Ghana,' *Journal of Modern African Studies* 11: 61–89.

Hart, V. (1978), *Distrust and Democracy: Political Distrust in Britain and America*. Cambridge: Cambridge University Press.

Hayes, B. and Bean, C. (1993), 'Gender and Political Interest: Some International Comparisons,' *Political Studies* 41 (4): 672–82.

Haynes, J. (1995a) 'Popular Religion and Politics in Sub-Sahara Africa,' *Third World Quarterly* 16 (1): 89–108.

Haynes, J. (1995b), 'The Revenge of Society? Religious Responses to Political Disequilibrium in Africa,' *Third World Quarterly* 16 (4): 728–37.

Haynes, J. (1996a), *Religion and Politics in Africa*. London: Zed.

Haynes, J. (1996b), 'Popular Christianity and Politics in Sub-Saharan Africa: an Overview,' paper presented for African Studies Association of the UK Biennial Conference, University of Bristol.

Hayward, F. (ed.) (1987), *Elections in Independent Africa*. Boulder: Westview Press.

Heald, S. (1998), *Controlling Anger: the Anthropology of Gisu Violence*. Oxford: James Currey.

Hechter, M. (1992), 'The Dynamics of Secession,' *Acta Sociologica* 35 (4): 267–83.

Hein, J. (1993), 'Refugees, Immigrants and the State,' *Annual Review of Sociology* (19): 43–59.

Heisler, B. and Heisler, M. (1986), 'Transnational Migration and the Modern Democratic State,' *Annals AAPSS* 485 (May): 253–75.

Herbst, J. (1990), 'Migration, the Politics of Protest and State Consolidation in Africa,' *African Affairs* 84 (235): 183–204.

Hermet, G., Rose, R. and Rouquie, A. (eds) (1978), *Elections Without Choice*. New York: John Wiley.

Hill, P. (1986), *Development Economics on Trial*. Cambridge: Cambridge University Press.

Hirschman, A. (1970), *Exit, Voice and Loyalty: Responses to Decline in Firms, Organisations and States*. London: Oxford University Press.

Hirschman, A. (1978–9), 'Exit, Voice and the State,' *World Politics* 31 (1): 94–110.

Hirschman, A. (1993), 'Exit, Voice and the Fate of the German Democratic Republic: an Essay in Conceptual History,' *World Politics* 45 (2): 173–95.

Hirschmann, D. (1991), 'Women and Political Participation in Africa: Broadening the Scope of Research,' *World Development* 19 (12): 1679–94.

Hirschmann, D. (1998), 'Civil Society in South Africa: Learning from Gender Themes,' *World Development* 26 (2): 227–38.

Hobsbawm, E. (1959), *Primitive Rebels*. Manchester: Manchester University Press.

Hobsbawm, E. (1969), *Bandits*. London: Weidenfeld and Nicolson.

Hobsbawm, E. (1973), 'Peasants and Politics,' *Journal of Peasant Studies* 1 (1).

Hodges, T. (1985), *Jehovah's Witnesses in Africa*, revised edn. London: Minority Rights Group.

Hooker, J. (1965), 'Witnesses and Watchtower in the Rhodesias and Nyasaland,' *Journal of African History* 6: 91–106.

Hornsby, C. and Throup, D. (1992), 'Elections and Political Change in Kenya,' *Journal of Commonwealth and Comparative Politics* 30 (2): 172–99.

Horowitz, D. (1985), *Ethnic Groups in Conflict*. Berkeley: University of California.

Horowitz, D. (1992), 'Irredentas and Secession: Adjacent Phenomena, Neglected Connections,' *International Journal of Comparative Sociology* 33: 118–30.

Horton, J. and Thompson, W. (1962), 'Powerlessness and Political Negativism,' *American Journal of Sociology* 67: 485–93.

Horton, R. (1971), 'Stateless Societies in the History of West Africa,' in J. Ajayi and M. Crowder (eds), *The History of West Africa*, vol. 1. London: Longman.

Hoskyns, C. (1969), *Case Studies in African Diplomacy: The Ethiopia–Somalia–Kenya Dispute 1960–1967*. Dar es Salaam: Oxford University Press.

Hyden, G. (1967), 'Selection and Election Processes in Bukoba and Karagwe Districts,' in L. Cliffe (ed.) *One Party Democracy*. Nairobi: East African Publishing House.

Hyden, G. (1980), *Beyond Ujamaa in Tanzania: Underdevelopment and an Uncaptured Peasantry*. Berkeley: University of California Press.

Hyden, G. (1990), 'Reciprocity and Governance in Africa,' in J. Wunsch and D. Olowu (eds), *The Failure of the Centralized State: Institutions and Self Governance in Africa*. Boulder: Westview Press.

Hyden, G. and Bratton, M. (eds) (1992), *Governance and Politics in Africa*. Boulder: Lynne Rienner.

Ihonvbere, J. (1994), 'The "Irrelevant" State, Ethnicity and the Quest for Nationhood in Africa,' *Ethnic and Racial Studies* 17 (1): 42–60.

Iliffe, J. (1967), 'The Organization of the Maji Maji Rebellion,' *Journal of African History* 8 (3): 495–512.

Iliffe, J. (1987), *The African Poor.* Cambridge: Cambridge University Press.

ILO (1972), *Employment, Incomes and Equality: a Strategy for Increasing Productive Employment in Kenya.* Geneva: ILO.

ILO (1989), *Training for Work in the Informal Sector.* Geneva: ILO.

Ingham, K. (1995), 'Obituary to the King of Toro,' *Guardian* 5/9/95.

Inglehart, R. (1988), 'The Renaissance of Political Culture,' *American Political Science Review* 82 (4): 1203–30.

Inkeles, A. (1969), 'Participant Citizenship in Six Developing Countries,' *American Political Science Review* 63 (4): 1120–41.

Isaacman, A. (1976), *The Tradition of Resistance in Mozambique: Anti-colonial Activity in the Zambesi Valley 1850–1921.* London: University of California Press.

Isaacman, A. (1977), 'Social Banditry in Zimbabwe (Rhodesia) and Mozambique 1894–1907,' *Journal of Southern African Studies* 9 (1): 1–30.

Isaacman, A. (1990), 'Peasants and Social Protest in Africa,' *African Studies Review* 33 (2): 1–120.

Isaacman, A. et.al. (1980), 'Cotton as the Motor of Poverty: Peasant Resistance to Forced Cotton Production in Mozambique, 1938–1961,' *The International Journal of African Historical Studies* 13: 581–615.

Ishemo, S. (1995), *Lower Zambezi Basin in Mozambique: a Study in Economy and Society 1850–1920.* Aldershot: Avebury.

Jackson, R. and Rosberg, C. (1982–3), 'Why Africa's Weak States Persist: the Empirical and Juridical in Statehood,' *World Politics* 35: 1–23.

Jackson, R. and Rosberg, C. (1984), 'Popular Legitimacy in African Multi-ethnic States,' *Journal of Modern African Studies* 22 (2): 177–98.

Jeffries, R. (1980), 'The Ghanaian Elections of 1979,' *African Affairs* 79 (316): 397–414.

Jeffries, R. and Thomas, C. (1993), 'The Ghanaian Elections of 1992,' *African Affairs* 92 (368): 331–48.

Jewsiewicki, B. (1980), 'Political Consciousness Among African Peasants in the Belgian Congo,' *Review of African Political Economy* 19: 23–32.

Jewsiewicki, B. (ed.) (1984), *Etat Indépendant du Congo, Congo Belge, République Démocratique du Congo, République du Zaire?* Ste-Foy, Quebec: SAFI Press.

Jochelson, K. (1995), 'Women Migrancy and Morality: a Problem of Perspective,' *Journal of Southern African Studies* 21 (2): 323–32.

Johnstone, P. (1990), *Operation World.* Bromley: OM Publishing.

Kaase, M. (1988), 'Political Alienation and Protest,' in M. Dogan (ed.), *Comparing Pluralist Democracies.* Boulder: Westview Press.

Kaballo, S. (1995), 'Human Rights and Democratization in Africa,' *Political Studies*, Special Issue: 189–208.

Kamrava, M. (1995), 'Political Culture and a New Definition of the Third World,' *Third World Quarterly* 16 (4): 691–701.

Kaplan, R. (1994), 'The Coming Anarchy: How Scarcity, Crime, Overpopulation, and Disease are Rapidly Destroying the Social Fabric of our Planet,' *Atlantic Monthly*, (February): 44–76.

Kasfir, N. (1974), 'Departicipation and Political Development in Black African Politics,' *Studies in Comparative International Development* 9 (3): 3–25.

Kasfir, N. (1976), *The Shrinking Political Arena: Participation and Ethnicity in African Politics, with a Case Study of Uganda*. Berkeley: University of California Press.

Kasfir, N. (1983), 'State, Magendo and Class Formation in Uganda,' *Journal of Commonwealth and Comparative Politics* 21 (3): 84–103.

Kelley, M. (1986), *A State in Disarray: Conditions of Chad's Survival*. Boulder: Westview Press.

Kibreab, G. (1985), *African Refugees: Reflections on the African Refugee Problem*. Trenton: Africa World Press.

Kimambo, I. (1969), *A Political History of the People of Tanzania* c 1500–1900. Nairobi: East African Publishing House.

King, K. (1996), *Jua Kali Kenya: Change and Development in an Informal Economy 1970–95*. London: James Currey.

Kinsman, M. (1983), 'Beasts of Burden: the Subordination of Southern Tswana Women, ca. 1800–1840,' *Journal of Southern African Studies* 10: 39–54.

Knocke, D. (1990), *Political Networks: the Structural Perspective*. Cambridge: Cambridge University Press.

Kohli, A., Migdal, J. and Shue, V. (1992), *State Power and Social Forces: Struggles and Accommodation*. New York: Cambridge University Press.

Kornberg, A. and Clarke, H. (1994), 'Beliefs about Democracy and Satisfaction with Democratic Government: the Canadian Case,' *Political Research Quarterly* 47 (3): 537–63.

Kuper, H. (ed.) (1965), *Urbanization and Migration in West Africa*. Berkeley: University of California Press.

Laakso, L. (1996), 'The Relationship Between the State and Civil Society in the Zimbabwean Elections 1995,' *Journal of Commonwealth and Comparative Politics* 34 (3): 218–34.

Laitin, D. (1978), 'Religion, Political Culture and the Weberian Tradition,' *World Politics* 30 (4): 586–601.

Lan, D. (1985), *Guns and Rain: Guerrillas and the Spirit Mediums in Zimbabwe*. London: James Currey.

Lancaster, C. (1993), 'Democratisation in the Sub-Saharan Africa,' *Survival* 35 (3): 38–50.

Lane, R. (1959), *Political Life: Why People Get Involved in Politics*. Glencoe: Free Press.

Lawless, R. and Monahan, L. (eds) (1987), *War and Refugees: The Western Sahara Conflict*. London: Pinter.

Lears, T. (1985), 'The Concept of Cultural Hegemony: Problems and Possibilities,' *American Historical Review* 90 (3): 567–83.

Legum, C. (ed.), (1960) *Africa Contemporary Record*. London: Rex Collings.

Lemarchand, R. (1988), 'The Changing Structure of Patronage Systems,' in D. Rothchild and N. Chazan (eds), *The Precarious Balance: State and Society in Africa*. Boulder: Westview Press.

Lemarchand, R. (1992a), 'Uncivil States and Civil Societies: How Illusion Became Reality,' *Journal of Modern African Studies* 30 (2): 177–91.

Lemarchand, R. (1992b), 'Africa's Troubled Transitions,' *Journal of Democracy* 3 (4): 98–109.

Lewis, O. (1970), *Anthropological Essays*. New York: Random House.

Lichbach, M. (1994), 'What Makes Rational Peasants Revolutionary? Dilemma, Paradox and Irony in Peasant Collective Action,' *World Politics* 46 (3): 383–418.

Lippert, A. (1987), 'The Saharawi Refugees: Origins and Organization, 1975–85,' in R. Lawless and L. Monahen (eds), *War and Refugees*. London: Pinter.

Lipset, S. (1981), *Political Man,*. expanded and updated edn. New York: Doubleday.

Lonsdale, J. (1978), 'The Emerging Pattern of Church and State Co-operation in Kenya,' in E. Fashole-Luke, R. Gray and A. Hastings (eds), *Christianity in Independent Africa.* London: Rex Collings.

Lonsdale, J. (1986), 'Political Accountability in African History,' in P. Chabal (ed.), *Political Domination.* Cambridge: Cambridge University Press.

Lonsdale, J. (1989), 'Africa's Past in Africa's Future,' *Canadian Journal of African Studies* 23 (1): 126–46.

Lonsdale, J. and Berman, B. (1979), 'Coping with the Contradictions: the Development of the Colonial State in Kenya 1895–1914,' *Journal of African History* 20 (4): 487–505.

Lovett, M. (1989), 'Gender Relations, Class Formation and the Colonial State,' in J. Parpart and K. Staudt (eds) *Women and the State in Africa.* Boulder: Lynne Rienner.

Low, D. (1971), *Buganda in Modern History.* Berkeley: University of California Press.

Lukes, S. (1974), *Power: A Radical View.* Basingstoke: Macmillan.

Luling, V. (1997), 'Come Back Somalia? Questioning a Collapsed State', *Third World Quarterly* 18(2).

Macdonald, J. (1963–4), 'Agricultural Organization, Migration and Labour Militancy in Rural Italy,' *Economic History Review, 2nd series* 16: 61–75.

MacGaffey, J. (1983), 'How to Survive and Become Rich Amidst Devastation: the Second Economy in Zaire,' *African Affairs* 82: 351–66.

MacGaffey, J. (1988a), 'Economic Disengagement and Class Formation in Zaire, ' in D. Rothchild and N. Chazan (eds), *The Precarious Balance.* Boulder: Westview Press.

MacGaffey, J. (1988b), 'Evading Male Control: Women in the Second Economy in Zaire,' in S. Stichter and J. Parpart (eds), *African Women in the Home and the Workforce.* Boulder: Westview Press.

MacGaffey, J. (1992), 'Initiatives from Below: Zaire's Other Path to Social and Economic Restructuring,' in G. Hyden and M. Brattton (eds), *Governance and Politics in Africa.* Boulder: Lynne Rienner.

MacGaffey, J. (1994), 'Civil Society in Zaire: Hidden Resistance and the Use of Personal Ties in Class Struggle,' in J. Harbeson, D. Rothchild and N. Chazan (eds), *Civil Society and the State in Africa.* Boulder: Lynne Rienner.

MacGaffey, J. *et al.* (eds) (1991), *The Real Economy of Zaire: The Contribution of Smuggling and Other Unofficial Activities to the National Wealth.* London: James Currey.

Mackenzie, W. and Robinson, K. (eds) (1960), *Five Elections in Africa.* London: Oxford University Press.

McAllister, I. and White, S. (1994), 'Political Participation in Postcommunist Russia: Voting, Activism and the Potential for Mass Protest,' *Political Studies* 42 (4): 593-607.

McGregor, J. (1994), 'People Without Fathers: Mozambicans in Swaziland 1883–1993,' *Journal of Southern African Studies* 20 (4): 545–67.

McNulty, M. and Lawrence, M. (1996), 'Hometown Associations: Balancing Local and Extralocal Interests in Nigerian Communities,' in P. Blunt and D. Warren (eds) *Indigenous Organizations and Development.* London: Intermediate Technology Publications.

Mainwaring, S., O'Donnell, G. and Valenzuela, J. (eds) (1992), *Issues in Democratic Consolidation: the New South American Democracies in Comparative Perspective.* Notre Dame: University of Notre Dame Press.

Maliyamkono, T. and Bagachwa, M. (1990), *The Second Economy in Tanzania.* London: James Currey.

Malwal, B. (1994), 'Sudan's Political and Economic Future: a Southern Perspective,' in C. Gurdon (ed.), *The Horn of Africa*. London: University College Press.

Mamdani, M. (1996), *Citizen and Subject: Contemporary Africa and the Legacy of Late Colonialism*. London: James Currey and Princeton: Princeton University Press.

Marshall, R. (1991), 'Power in the Name of Jesus,' *Review of African Political Economy* 52: 21–37.

Mathiason, J. and Powell, J. (1972), 'Participation and Efficacy: Aspects of Peasant Involvement in Political Mobilization,' *Comparative Politics* 4 (3): 303–29.

Mazrui, A. (1983), 'Political Engineering in Africa,' *International Social Science Journal* 25 (2): 291–308.

Mbilinyi, M. (1988), 'Runaway Wives in Colonial Tanganyika: Forced Labour and Forced Marriage in Rungwe District 1919–61,' *International Journal of Sociology of Law* 16: 1–29.

Merkl, P. (1988), 'Comparing Legitimacy and Values among Advanced Democratic Countries,' in M. Dogan (ed.), *Comparing Pluralist Democracies*. Boulder: Westview Press.

Migdal, J. (1974), *Peasants, Politics and Revolution: Pressures Towards Political and Social Change in the Third World*. Princeton: Princeton University Press.

Migdal, J. (1988), *Strong Societies and Weak States: State-Society Relations and State Capabilities in the Third World*. Princeton: Princeton University Press.

Migdal, J. (1994), 'The State in Society: an Approach to Struggles for Domination,' in J. Migdal, A. Kohli and V. Shue (eds), *Social Power and Social Forces*. Cambridge: Cambridge University Press.

Milbrath, L. and Goel, M. (1977), *Political Participation: How and Why Do People Get Involved in Politics?* 2nd edn. Lanham: University Press of America.

Miller, A. (1974), 'Political Issues and Trust in Government,' *American Political Science Review* 68 (September): 951–72.

Miller, D. (1989), 'The Limits of Dominance,' in D. Miller, M. Rowlands and C. Tilley (eds), *Domination and Resistance*. London: Unwin Hyman.

Miller, J. (1983), 'The Paradoxes of Impoverishment in the Atlantic Zone,' in D. Birmingham and P. Martin (eds), *History of Central Africa*, vol. 1, London: Longman.

Miller, N. (1970), 'The Rural African Party: Political Participation in Tanzania,' *American Political Science Review* 64 (2): 548–71.

Mitchell, T. (1991), 'The Limits of the State: Beyond Statist Approaches and Their Critics,' *American Political Science Review* 85 (1): 77–96.

Moore, B., Jr (1978), *Injustice; The Social Bases of Obedience and Revolt*. New York: Macmillan.

Morrison, M. and Gutkind, P. (eds) (1982), *Housing Urban Poor in Africa*. New York: Maxwell School of Citizenship and Public Affairs.

Moulakis, A. (1986), *Legitimacy; Legitimate*. New York: De Gruyter.

Mukohya, V. (1991), 'Import and Export in the Second Economy in North Kivu,' in J. MacGaffey *et al.*, *The Real Economy in Zaire*. London: James Currey.

Muller, E. and Jukam, T. (1977), 'On the Meaning of Political Support,' *American Political Science Review* 71 (December): 1561–95.

Muller, E. and Seligson, M. (1994), 'Civic Culture and Democracy,' *American Political Science Review* 88 (3): 635–52.

Muller, E. and Williams, C. (1980), 'Dynamics of Political Support-Alienation,' *Comparative Political Studies* 13 (April): 33–59.

Newbury, C. (1983), 'Colonialism, Ethnicity and Rural Protest,' *Comparative Politics* 5 (3): 253–80.

Newbury, C. (1984), 'Dead and Buried or Just Underground? The Privatization of the State in Zaire,' in B. Jewsiewicki (ed.), *Etat Indépendant du Congo*. Ste-Foy, Quebec: SAFI Press.

Newbury, C. and Schoepf, B. (1989), 'State, Peasantry and Agrarian Crisis in Zaire: Does Gender Make a Difference?' in J. Parpart and K. Staudt (eds), *Women and the State in Africa*. Boulder: Lynne Rienner.

Newitt, M. (1981), *Portugal in Africa: The Last Hundred Years*. London: C. Hurst.

Newlan, K. (1993), 'Ethnic Conflict and Refugees,' *Survival* 35 (1).

Niven, R. (1970), *The War of Nigerian Unity 1967–1970*. Ibadan: Evans Brothers.

Nkomo, J. (1984), *The Story of My Life*. London: Methuen.

Nwankwo, A. and Ifejika, S. (1969), *The Making of a Nation: Biafra*. London: C. Hurst.

O'Kane, R. (1993), 'Against Legitimacy,' *Political Studies* 41 (3): 471–87.

Okonkwo, C. (1996), 'Highway Robbery as Traders Run the Gauntlet of Sticky Fingers,' *The Chronicle*, Bulawayo, 23 November.

Omer-Cooper, J. (1966), *The Zulu Aftermath: a Nineteenth Century Revolution in Bantu Africa*. Harlow: Longman.

Omer-Cooper, J. (1969), 'Aspects of Political Change in the Nineteenth Century Mfecane,' in L. Thompson (ed.), *African Societies in South Africa*. London: Heinemann.

Oquaye, M. (1995), 'The Ghanaian Elections of 1992 – a Dissenting View,' *African Affairs* 94: 259–75.

Osaghae, E. (1995), 'The Study of Political Transition in Africa,' *Review of African Political Economy* 64 (22): 183–97.

Osirim, M. (1997), 'Barriers and Opportunities: the Role of Organizations in Nigerian Women's Quest for Empowerment,' in R. Siddiqui (ed.), *Subsaharan Africa in the 1990s: Challenges to Democracy and Development*. Westport: Praeger.

Ottaway, M. (1995), 'Democratization in Collapsed States,' in I. Zartman (ed.), *Collapsed States: Disintegration and Restoration of Legitimate Authority*. Boulder: Lynne Rienner.

Parry, G. (1972), 'The Idea of Political Participation,' in G. Parry (ed.), *Participation in Politics*. Manchester: Manchester University Press.

Peil, M. (1974), 'The Common Man's Reaction to Nigerian Urban Government,' *African Affairs* 74 (296): 300–13.

Peil, M. (1976), *Nigerian Politics, the People's View*. London: Cassell.

Pelissier, R. (1980), 'Autopsy of a Miracle,' *Africa Report* 25 (May–June): 10–14.

Pool, D. (1993), 'Eritrean Independence: the Legacy of the Derg and the Politics of Reconstruction,' *African Affairs* 92: 389–402.

Powell, G., Jr (1980), 'Voting Turnout in Thirty Democracies: Partisan, Legal and Socio-economic Influences,' in R. Rose (ed.), *Electoral Participation: a Comparative Analysis*. London: Sage.

Powell, G., Jr (1982), *Contemporary Democracies: Participation, Stability and Violence*. Cambridge: Harvard University Press.

Preiswerk, R. (1982), 'Self-Reliance in Unexpected Places,' *Genève-Afrique* 20 (2): 56–64.

Premdas, R. (1990), 'Secessionist Movements in Comparative Perspective,' in R. Premdas, S. Samarasinghe and A. Anderson (eds), *Secessionist Movements in Comparative Perspective*. London: Pinter.

Prunier, G. (1994), 'Somaliland: Birth of a New Country?' in C. Gurdon (ed.), *The Horn of Africa*. London: University College Press.

Putnam, D. (1993), *Making Democracy Work. Civic Traditions in Modern Italy*. Princeton: Princeton University Press.

Rado, E. (1986), 'Notes Towards a Political Economy of Ghana Today,' *African Affairs* 18 (1): 563–72.

Raftopoulos, B. (1992a), 'Democratic Struggle in Zimbabwe, Pt. 1,' *Review of African Political Economy* 54 (July): 111–15.

Raftopoulos, B. (1992b), 'Democratic Struggle in Zimbabwe, Pt. 2,' *Review of African Political Economy* 55 (November): 57–66.

Raghavan, N. (1990), 'The Southern Sudanese Secessionist Movement,' in R. Premdas, S. Samarasinghe and A. Anderson (eds), *Secessionist Movements*. London: Pinter.

Randall, V. (1987), *Women and Politics: an International Perspective*, 2nd edn. Basingstoke: Macmillan.

Ranger, T. (1975), 'The Mwana Lesa Movement of 1925,' in T. Ranger and J. Weller (eds), *Themes in the Christian History of Central Africa*. London: Heinemann.

Ranger, T. (1977), 'The People in African Resistance: a Review,' *Journal of Southern African Studies* 4 (1): 125–46.

Ranger, T. (1984), 'Religion and Rural Protest: Makoni District, Zimbabwe, 1900–1980,' in J. Bak and G. Benecke (eds), *Religion and Rural Revolt*. Manchester: Manchester University Press.

Ranger, T. (1985), *Peasant Consciousness and Guerrilla War in Zimbabwe*. Berkeley: University of California Press and Oxford: James Currey.

Ranger, T. (1986), 'Religious Movements and Politics in Sub-Saharan Africa,' *African Studies Review* 29 (2): 1–70.

Rashdeed, S. (1995), 'The Democratization Process and Popular Participation,' *Development and Change* 26 (2): 333–54.

Reno, W. (1995a), *Corruption and State Politics in Sierra Leone*. Cambridge: Cambridge University Press.

Reno, W. (1995b), 'Reinvention of an African Patrimonial State: Charles Taylor's Liberia,' *Third World Quarterly* 16 (1): 109–27.

Reno , W. (1998), 'Sierra Leone: Weak States and the New Sovereignty Game,' in L. Villalon and P. Huxtable (eds), *The African State at a Critical Juncture*. Boulder: Lynne Rienner.

Reyntjens, F. (1996), 'Rwanda: Genocide and Beyond,' *Journal of Refugee Studies* 9 (3): 240–51.

Richards, P. (1995), 'Rebellion in Liberia and Sierra Leone: a Crisis of Youth?,' in O. Furley (ed.), *Conflict in Africa*. London: Tauris.

Richards, P. (1996), *Fighting for the Rain Forest: War, Youth and Resources in Sierra Leone*. Oxford: James Currey and International African Institute.

Richmond, A. (1988), 'Sociological Theories of International Migration,' *Current Sociology* 36 (2): 7–26.

Richmond, A. (1993), 'Reactive Migration: Sociological Perspectives on Refugee Movements,' *Journal of Refugee Studies* 6 (1): 7–24.

Roberts, A. (1970), 'The Lumpa Church of Alice Lenshina,' in R. Rotberg and A. Mazrui (eds), *Protest and Power in Black Africa*. Oxford: Oxford University Press.

Roberts, R. and Klein, M. (1980), 'The Banamba Slave Exodus of 1905,' *Journal of African History* 21 (3): 375–94.

Roesch, O. (1992), 'Renamo and the Peasantry in Southern Mozambique,' *Canadian Journal of African Studies* 26 (3): 462–84.

Rose, R. (ed.) (1980), *Electoral Participation: A Comparative Analysis*. London: Sage.

Ross, M. and Thadani, V. (1980), 'Research Note: Participation, Sex and Social Class: Some Unexpected Results from an African City,' *Comparative Politics* 12 (3): 323.

Rotberg, R. (1965), *A Political History of Tropical Africa*. New York: Harcourt, Brace and World.

Rotberg, R. (1966), *The Rise of Nationalism in Central Africa: The Making of Malawi and Zambia 1873–1964*. Cambridge: Harvard University Press.

Rothchild, D. (1995), 'Rawlings and the Engineering of Legitimacy in Ghana,' in I. Zartman (ed.), *Collapsed States: the Disintegration and Restoration of Legitimate Authority*. Boulder: Lynne Rienner.

Rothchild, D. and Chazan, N. (eds) (1988), *The Precarious Balance: State and Society in Africa*. Boulder: Westview Press.

Rukarangira, N. and Schoepf, B. (1991), 'Unrecorded Trade in South East Shaba and Across Zaire's Borders,' in J. MacGaffey *et al.*, *The Real Economy of Zaire*. London: James Currey.

Rush, M. and Althoff, P. (1971), *An Introduction to Political Sociology*. London: Nelson.

Salih, M. (1994), 'The Ideology of the Dinka and the Sudan Peoples' Liberation Movement,' in K. Fukui and J. Markakis (eds), *Ethnicity and Conflict in the Horn of Africa*. London: James Currey.

Samoff, J. (1987), 'Single-Party Competitive Elections in Tanzania,' in F. Hayward (ed.) *Elections in Independent Africa*. Boulder: Westview Press.

Sandbrook, R. (1993), *The Politics of Africa's Economic Recovery*. Cambridge: Cambridge University Press.

Sangmpam, S. (1994), *Pseudocapitalism and the Overpoliticized State: in Search of a Theory of the Third World State: the Case of Zaire*. Aldershot: Avebury.

Sathyamurthy, T. (1986), *The Political Development of Uganda 1900–1986*. Aldershot: Gower.

Schatzberg, M. (1981), 'Ethnicity and Class at the Local Level: Bars and Bureaucrats in Lisala, Zaire,' *Comparative Politics* 13 (4): 461–78.

Schatzberg, M. (1993), 'Power, Legitimacy and "Democratisation" in Africa,' *Africa* 63 (4): 445–61.

Schissel, H. (1989), 'Africa's Underground Economy,' *Africa Report* January/February: 43–5.

Schmidt, E. (1992), *Peasants, Traders, and Wives: Shona Women in the History of Zimbabwe, 1870–1939*. Portsmouth: Heinemann and Oxford: James Currey.

Schmitter, P. (1994), 'Dangers and Dilemmas of Democracy,' *Journal of Democracy* 5 (2): 57–74.

Schultheis, M. (1989), 'Refugees in Africa: the Geopolitics of Forced Displacement,' *African Studies Review* 32 (1): 3–29.

Scott, J. (1985), *Weapons of the Weak: Everyday Forms of Peasant Resistance*. New Haven: Yale University Press.

Scott, J. (1987), 'Resistance without Protest and without Organization: Peasant Opposition to the Islamic Zakat and the Christian Tithe,' *Comparative Studies in Society and History* 29 (3): 417–52.

Seekings, J. (1992a), 'The Revival of People's Courts,' in G. Moss and I. Obery (eds), *South African Review 6: From 'Red Friday' to Codesa*. Johannesburg: Ravan Press.

Seekings, J. (1992b), 'Civic Organisations in South African Townships,' in G. Moss and

I. Obery (eds), *South African Review 6: From 'Red Friday' to Codesa*. Johannesburg: Ravan Press.

Shin, D. (1994), 'On the Third Wave of Democratization. a Synthesis and Evaluation of Recent Theory and Research,' *World Politics* 47 (October): 135–70.

Siddle, D. and Swindell, K. (1990), *Rural Change in Tropical Africa*. Oxford: Basil Blackwell.

Simons, A. (1998), ' Somalia: the Structure of Dissolution,' in L. Villalon and P. Huxtable (eds), *The African State at a Critical Juncture: Between Disintegration and Reconfiguration*. Boulder Lynne Rienner.

Skinner, E. (1965), 'Labor Migration Among the Mossi of the Upper Volta,' in H. Kuper (ed.), *Urbanization and Migration in West Africa*. Berkeley: University of California Press.

Skocpol, T. (ed.) (1984), *Vision and Method in Historical Sociology*. Cambridge: Cambridge University Press.

Smith, R. (1969), *Kingdoms of the Yoruba*. London: Methuen. 3rd Ed. (1988) London: James Currey.

Somerville, K. (1993), 'The Failure of Democratic Reform in Angola and Zaire,' *Survival* 35 (3): 51–77.

Sorensen, G. (1993), *Democracy and Democratization*. Boulder: Westview Press.

Staudt, K. (1987), 'Women's Politics, the State and Capitalist Transformation in Africa,' in I. Markovitz (ed.), *Studies in Power and Class in Africa*. New York: Oxford University Press.

Stepan, A. (1991), *Rethinking Military Politics: Brazil and the Southern Cone*. Princeton: Princeton University Press.

Stewart, C. (1986), 'Islam,' in A. Roberts (ed.), *Cambridge History of Africa*. Cambridge: Cambridge University Press.

Stichter, S. and Parpart, J. (eds) (1988), *Patriarchy and Class*. Boulder: Westview Press.

Stinchcombe, A. (1978), *Theoretical Methods in Social History*. New York: Academic Press.

Stokes, E. (1966), 'Barotseland: Survival of an African State,' in E. Stokes and R. Brown (eds), *The Zambesian Past*. Manchester: Manchester University Press.

Street, J. (1994), 'Review Article: Political Culture – from Civic Culture to Mass Culture,' *British Journal of Political Science* 24 (1): 95–114.

Suhrke, A. (1993), 'A Crisis Diminished: Refugees in the Developing World,' *International Journal* 48 (2): 215–39.

Sundkler, B. (1961), *Bantu Prophets*. London: Oxford University Press.

Suret-Canale, J. (1971), *French Colonialism in Tropical Africa 1900–1945*, English translation. London: C. Hurst.

Thomas, R. (1983), 'The 1916 Bongo Riots,' *Journal of African History* 24 (1): 57–75.

Thorn, W. (1986), 'Sub-Saharan Africa's Changing Military Capabilities,' in B. Arlinghaus and P. Baker (eds), *African Armies: Evolution and Capabilities*. Boulder: Westview Press.

Throup, D. (1985), 'The Origins of Mau Mau,' *African Affairs* 84: 399–434.

Tocqueville, A. (1968), *Democracy in America*. London: Fontana.

Tordoff, W. (1993), *Government and Politics in Africa*. 2nd edn. Basingstoke: Macmillan.

Trapido, S. (1978), 'Landlord and Tenant in a Colonial Economy: the Transvaal 1880–1910,' *Journal of Southern African Studies* 5 (1): 26–58.

Tripp, A. (1992), 'Local Organizations, Participation and the State in Urban Tanzania,' in G. Hyden and M. Bratton (eds), *Governance and Politics in Africa*. Boulder: Lynne Rienner.

Turnham, D. and Salome, B. (eds), (1990), *The Informal Sector Revisted*. Paris: OECD.
Turton, D. (1994), 'Mursi Political Identity and Warfare: The Survival of an Idea,' in K. Fukui and J. Markakis, (eds), *Ethnicity and Conflict in the Horn of Africa*. London: James Currey.
UNHCR (1993), *The State of the World's Refugees*. London: Penguin Books.
van Binsbergen, W. (1981), *Religious Change in Zambia. Exploratory Studies*. London: Kegan Paul International.
van Onselen, C. (1976), *Chibaro*. London: Pluto Press.
Vansina, J. (1966), *Kingdoms of the Savanna*. Madison: University of Wisconsin Press.
Vansina, J. (1983), ' The Peoples of the Forest,' in D. Birmingham and P. Martin (eds), *History of Central Africa*, vol. 1. London: Longman.
Vansina, J. (1984), 'Equatorial Africa and Angola: Migrations and the Emergence of the First States,' in D. T. Niane (ed.) *General History of Africa*, vol. 4. Paris: UNESCO, London: Heinemann.
Vansina, J. (1990), *Paths in the Rainforest: Towards a History of Political Tradition in Equatorial Africa*. Madison: University of Wisconsin Press and London: James Currey.
Verba, S. (1972), *Participation in America*. New York: Harper and Row.
Verba, S., Nie, N. and Kim, J. (1978), *Participation and Political Equality: a Seven Nation Comparison*. Cambridge: Cambridge University Press.
Villalon, L. (1994), 'The Senegalese Elections of 1993,' *African Affairs* 93 (371): 163–94.
Vinger, M. (1971), *The Scientific Study of Religion*. New York: Macmillan.
Vwakyanakazi, M. (1991), 'Import and Export in the Second Economy in North Kivu,' in J. MacGaffey, *et al. The Real Economy of Zaire*. London: James Currey.
Wallerstein, I. (1965), 'Migration in West Africa: the Political Perspective,' in H. Kuper (ed.), *Urbanization and Migration in West Africa*. Berkeley: University of California Press.
Wallman, S. (1996), *Kampala Women Getting By: Wellbeing in the Time of AIDs*. London: James Currey.
Warren, D. Adedokun, R. and Omolaoye, A. (1996), 'Indigenous Organizations and Development: the Case of Ara, Nigeria,' in P. Blunt and D. Warren (eds), *Indigenous Organizations and Development*. London: Intermediate Technology Publications.
Weatherford, M. (1992), 'Measuring Regime Legitimacy,' *American Political Science Review* 86 (1): 149–66.
Weil, P. (1971), 'Tradition and Opposition in Area Council Elections in the Gambia,' *Journal of Asian and African Studies* 6 (1): 106–117.
Weiner, M. (1995), *The Global Migration Crisis: Challenge to States and to Human Rights*. New York: Harper Collins.
Weiss, H. (1995), 'Zaire: Collapsed Society, Surviving State, Future Polity,' in I. Zartman, ed., *Collapsed States: The Disintegration and Restoration of Legitimate Authority*. Boulder: Lynne Rienner.
Welch, C. (1980), *Anatomy of Rebellion*. Albany: State University Press of New York.
White, G. (1993), *Riding the Tiger*. Basingstoke: Macmillan.
White, L. (1987), *Magomero: Portrait of an African Village*. Cambridge: Cambridge University Press.
White, L. (1988), 'Domestic Labor in a Colonial City: Prostitution in Nairobi, 1900–1952,' in S. Stichter and J. Parpart (eds), *Patriarchy and Class*. Boulder: Westview Press.

Widgren, J. (1990), 'International Migration and Regional Stability,' *International Affairs* 66 (4): 749–66.

Widner, J. (1994), 'The Rise of Civic Associations Among Farmers in Cote d'Ivoire,' in J. Harbeson, D. Rothchild and N. Chazan (eds), *Civil Society and the State in Africa*. Boulder: Lynne Rienner.

Widner, J. (1995), 'States and Statelessness in Late Twentieth Century Africa,' *Daedalus* 124 (3): 134–53.

Willame, J. (1972), *Patrimonialism and Political Change in the Congo*. Stanford: Stanford University Press.

Williams, C. (1982), *National Separatism*. Cardiff: University of Wales Press.

Williams, G. (1960), 'Egemonia in the Thought of Antonio Gramsci,' *Journal of the History of Ideas*, (October–December): 586–601.

Williams, P. and Falola, T. (1995), *Religious Impact on the Nation State: the Nigerian Predicament*. Aldershot: Avebury.

Wilson, B. (1975), *Magic and the Millennium*. St Albans: Paladin.

Wiseman, J. (1990), *Democracy in Black Africa: Survival and Revival*. New York: Paragon House.

Wood, J. (1981), 'Secession: a Comparative Analytic Framework,' *Canadian Journal of Political Science* 14 (1): 107–33.

Wunsch, J. and Olowu, D. (eds) (1990) *The Failure of the Centralised State: Institutions and Self-Governance in Africa*. Boulder: Westview Press.

Yinger, J. (1960), 'Contraculture and Subculture,' *American Sociological Review* 25 (5): 625–35.

Young, C. (1982), 'Patterns of Social Conflict: State, Class and Ethnicity,' *Daedalus* 16 (2): 71–98.

Young C. (1984), 'Zaire: Is There a State?,' in B. Jewsiewicki (ed.), *Etat Indépendant du Congo*. Ste-Foy, Quebec: SAFI Press.

Young, C. (1994a), 'In Search of Civil Society,' in J. Harbeson, D. Rothchild and N. Chazan (eds), *Civil Society and the State in Africa*. Boulder: Lynne Rienner.

Young, C. (1994b), 'Zaire: the Shattered Illusion of the Integral State,' *Journal of Modern African Studies* 32 (2): 247–63.

Young, C. and Turner, T. (1985), *The Rise and Decline of the Zairian State*. Madison: University of Wisconsin Press.

Zartman, I. (ed.) (1995), *Collapsed States: the Disintegration and Restoration of Legitimate Authority*. Boulder: Lynne Rienner.

Zolberg, A. (1968), 'The Structure of Political Conflict in the New States of Africa,' *American Political Science Review* 62 (1): 70–87.

Zolberg, A. (1992), 'The Specter of Anarchy: African States Verging on Dissolution,' *Dissent* 39 (Summer): 303–11.

Zolberg, A., Suhrke, A. and Aguayo, S. (1989), *Escape from Violence: Conflict and the Refugee Crisis in the Developing World*. New York: Oxford University Press.

Interviews

Feltoe, E. (1997), Deputy Director of The Catholic Commission for Peace and Justice, Zimbabwe; personal interview, 25.3.1997.

Kazembe, J. (1997), Director of Information, Policy Dialogue and

Public Relations, Southern African Regional Institute for Policy Studies, Harare; personal interview, 26.3.1997.

Manzvanzvike, T. (1997), Information Facilitator, Feminist Studies Centre, Harare; personal interview, 20.3.1997.

Nkiwane, S. (1997), Senior Lecturer, Politics Department, University of Harare; personal interview, 26.3 1997.

Wermter, O. (1997), Social Communications Secretary, Catholic Bishops Conference, Zimbabwe; personal interview, 24.3.1997.

Index